THE HISTORY OF THE SALVATION ARMY

THE HISTORY OF THE SALVATION ARMY

Volume IV
1886—1904

by

Arch R. Wiggins

Thomas Nelson & Sons Ltd
London Edinburgh Paris Melbourne Johannesburg
Toronto and New York

THOMAS NELSON AND SONS LTD

Parkside Works Edinburgh 9
36 Park Street London W1
117 Latrobe Street Melbourne C1

302-304 Barclays Bank Building
Commissioner and Kruis Streets
Johannesburg

Thomas Nelson and Sons (Canada) Ltd
91-93 Wellington Street West Toronto 1

Thomas Nelson and Sons
19 East 41st Street New York, N.Y. 17

Société Française d'Éditions Nelson
97 rue Monge Paris 5

First published 1964

Printed in Great Britain
by T. and A. Constable Ltd., Hopetoun Street
Printers to the University of Edinburgh

FOREWORD

THE passing of Colonel Robert Sandall, who so untiringly discovered the facts, effectively recorded the events and vividly described the characters covered by the first three volumes of *The History of The Salvation Army*, necessitated the appointment of a new Historian, and at my request the task involved in this position has been undertaken by another Salvation Army officer, Lieut.-Commissioner Arch R. Wiggins.

The break in the continuity of the authorship of the volumes embracing the history of so virile and swiftly-growing an international movement as The Salvation Army might well have had a detrimental effect upon the treatment of the story, but it will be agreed that the epoch-making period from July 1, 1886 to June 30, 1904 is commendably presented in this fourth volume.

At the best the remarkable happenings of these formative eighteen years can be but briefly described; nevertheless, what has been written bears striking witness to the guiding hand of the Lord during that period of the movement in which rapid extension was the order of the day. The present generation will surely find both inspiration and challenge within the covers of this revealing work.

WILFRED KITCHING,
General

CONTENTS

II Consolidating the Work Overseas

III World-Wide Campaigner

IV The Pen and the Press

V Organizing the Fighting Forces

LIST OF ILLUSTRATIONS

INTRODUCTION

THE history of the first forty years of The Salvation Army falls naturally into periods corresponding, in a general sense, to the stages of the development of its personalities. This fourth volume deals with the stage which may be described as that of a near approach to full growth, although in many important aspects the movement was still the subject of experiment, particularly in organization and leadership.

As events are recorded and described it will become apparent that some features, useful in the earlier days of this stage, had eventually to be abandoned, but none was without its value for the future. The demands made upon officers responsible for the direction of experimental systems of oversight had the inestimable effect of fostering in them ability to undertake still greater responsibility, and with marked success, when occasion arose. Especially was this evident in the development of the system for the training of officers, and in the organization of work in the evangelistic field, including that newly established among young people. While on the one hand this development had its salutory effect upon the Provincial Commanders, to whom was committed the direction of operations in large areas of the British Command, it produced excellent results in creating among their subordinates understanding and appreciation of the principles and procedure of Salvationism. To cope with the great and urgent demand for leaders occasioned by the many new openings throughout the country, and the almost sensational extension and maintenance of the work abroad, officers had to be hastily recruited and trained.

The International Congress of 1886 had emphasized the establishment of The Salvation Army as a world-wide movement and had given some prominence to what came to be called its Social Work, the development of which took place within the period here reviewed although, for convenient reference, this has already been traced through the years up to 1953 in Volume III. Such special treatment of the Social Work in no way indicates, however, that it is separate from, or in any way less part of, the Army than is any other aspect of its operations.

The period now under observation begins with the dispersal of the representatives to the first International Congress, and includes the continuous coverage of the world by The Salvation Army—the flag was planted in no fewer than twenty-six other countries—and the course of events throughout its service up to and including the still greater gathering of the third International Congress held in 1904.

William Booth, the erstwhile Methodist minister, is shown as being finally lost in the audacious globe-encircling General, although it should always be remembered that when he started to work in the East End of London, notwithstanding statements to the contrary,[1] he had no thought or intention of even establishing an organization, let alone one on military or international lines. He began, as he said, resolved to produce a plan for setting converts to work for the salvation of others, and the gradual evolution of this plan led to the formation of The Salvation Army as it is known today.

The dispatch of Commissioner George S. Railton to organize the Army's work in the United States of America in 1880 had meant that the duties which, in the main, had

[1] *The History of The Salvation Army*, vol i, Appendix D. William Booth's Call to the East End and His Plan of Work

fallen upon him as Secretary of the organization, passed entirely to the eldest son of the General and Mrs Booth, William Bramwell, who was thereupon, at the age of twenty-four, designated the first Chief of the Staff.[1]

One of the most noteworthy features of the Army's phenomenal progress was the unique relationship between father and son in its leadership, and about which Railton wrote in a small volume published within three months of William Booth's promotion to Glory in 1912:

> The comfort to the General, as he often testified, of the continual faithful service of this slave of a son was one of the most invaluable forces of his life. Whilst, on the one side, we may see in such self-renouncing abandonment a certificate to and evidence of the nature of the General's own life, we must read in it, at the same time, some part of the explanation of his boundless activities and influence. For the Chief... to have gone to and come away from his father's daily scenes of triumph without getting the slightest appetite himself for public displays, or yielding in the slightest degree to the craving after human support or encouragement, to turn him aside from the humdrum of duty, is one more proof of those gracious evidences of God's saving and keeping power with which the history of The Salvation Army abounds.

But, of course, the General and his Chief of the Staff, although exerting leadership indispensable to the formation and progress of the organization, would not have been able to pursue their objective without the men and women who gave willing and unquestioning obedience to their orders and maintained both interest and effort. The purposeful co-operation between leaders and led became even more evident when the initial glamour and attraction of the novelty of the methods employed began to wear off, and when the fruitfulness engendered by the first attacks had passed. And this volume of The Salvation Army's history

[1] *The History of The Salvation Army*, vol ii, p. 51

discloses how the remarkable co-partnership of father and son was developed in due proportion as the need for it increased. It tells also of the General's great soul-saving campaigns abroad, of the passing of his brilliant wife, of the irreparable loss to the Army of four of his children, and of the amazing courage of Salvationists in their "fight for the streets."

Throughout the story runs the clear-headed, stern, unswerving, selfless domination of every situation by William Booth and the evolution, under his direction, and in the providence of God, of The Salvation Army as a living embodiment of man's service to his fellow-man in the name and spirit of the Master of us all.

It must be strongly emphasized that while this volume is concerned with and faithfully records the fierce opposition, cruel persecution and, perhaps, understandable misunderstanding of The Salvation Army in the years between 1886 and 1904, which was then general in all parts of the world, official recognition, unstinted encouragement and warm-hearted co-operation have long since been afforded the movement by both Church and State ; and no-one is more friendly or generous today than that most important of all observers of the Salvationist's multifarious activities—the Man in the Street.

I THE WORLD FOR CHRIST

Chapter One

CHRIST FOR THE WORLD

THERE can be no doubt that the first International Congress gave a tremendous impetus to the Army's ever-widening influence. Representatives had come to the birth-place of the movement from the five continents and had caught a vision of the possibility of this seemingly irresistible Salvation force. They came, they saw, and now they were going forth to conquer the world for Christ; to take Christ to the world. Nothing should daunt them. They would "wrestle not against flesh and blood, but against principalities, against powers, against the rulers of the darkness of this world, against spiritual wickedness in high places." They had an indefatigable and courageous commander in their General; of that they were now definitely assured, for most of them had never before set eyes upon his patriarchal countenance, apart from the pictures some of them had seen of him in their *War Cry*, or heard the reverberating thunder of his denunciatory utterances. This was a man to follow to the death if need be, and follow they would, with fanatical zeal, when they returned to their native lands.

They had discovered that it was not always necessary to wait for an official landing party to be sent to open up warfare in a country; any man fully consecrated to God, with brains, initiative, courage, a fiery purpose, a will of iron and a heart of gold could be a John the Baptist. They considered that what had been accomplished by such men —or women, for that matter—all over the British Isles, in the United States of America, Australia, Canada, France, Switzerland, India and Ceylon, Sweden, South Africa and St Helena, and New Zealand, could be similarly accomplished in all other countries ; and so they went forward fearlessly " into all the world " at the divine command, determined to " preach the Gospel to every creature."

The following chapters tell the glorious story ; they tell of heroes and heroines who counted not their life dear, " choosing rather to suffer affliction with the people of God, than to enjoy the pleasures of sin for a season " ; they tell of golden deeds enacted both in victory and in occasional defeat, for now and again powerful governmental authority temporarily stemmed the flow of Salvationism ; they tell of the sometimes cold condemnation of those who should have been colleagues in the Christ-work, of kings who gave warm-hearted commendation and encouragement. Adventure in plenty and intrepidity in abundance filled the amazing years of new conquests and advance on all fronts between the first and second International Congress.

Chapter Two

GERMANY

The " Invasion of Germany " was effected from Zürich, Switzerland, by Staff-Captain Fritz Schaaff, a German who had been converted and become an officer in New York.[1] Having received orders from International Headquarters, he first tested the ground in Baden, but eventually opened fire in Stuttgart, Württemberg, in a former Methodist hall behind No 6 Eugenstrasse, on 14 November 1886. "Many ridiculous things" having been written since 1883 about the new movement, especially in some Protestant theological books and religious papers, it was thought best to commence operations without using the name "Salvation Army," and to let the work speak for itself. This proved to be the correct *modus operandi*, for the chief of police himself attended several of the meetings, about which he had no complaint to make. A few weeks later "Die Heilsarmee" became firmly established, but the work was very hard, "conversion" being a word rarely used in connection with any proclamation of the Gospel, and "instant conversion" a term utterly incomprehensible, even to those who professed to be Christians. *Der Heilsruf* (The Cry of Salvation) made its appearance in February 1887 as a monthly newspaper, but the name was afterward changed to *Der Kriegsruf* (The War Cry) in keeping with the name of the official organ in London. Three years later it became a weekly periodical.

A reporter writing in the *Neues Tagblatte* concerning an evening meeting conducted by these early-day German Salvationists had this to say:

> The way the Salvation Army people try to convert others is really against all manners and customs, and if they could only keep before themselves the example of our Lord and Master, who did not call His disciples "saved," they would not go to such extravagancies. One could only think what a pity if this sect should gain ground in our country, for it does not represent a quiet and sober, and serious Christianity, but encourages self-righteousness and spiritual pride.

[1] *The History of The Salvation Army*, vol ii, p. 342

One Sunday night the meeting was attended by a few noisy young people who shouted during the prayer period, and this was witnessed by a newspaper reporter who wrote an outrageous article for his paper "making out of an insect an elephant." Reprinted in other papers this article was responsible for bringing larger crowds to the meetings; indeed, hundreds could not get into the hall. These happenings eventually brought along the chief of police, the inspector and some detectives, who attended a Sunday night gathering in private clothes, while two uniformed policemen patrolled outside the building. On that occasion, and to their surprise, many of those who had wrecked the meeting had their names taken, but no action was taken against them. The police chief was apprehensive and issued an ordinance forbidding meetings to commence after 5 p.m. on weekdays and after noon on Sundays; so the Salvationists turned their attention to the public-houses, where they were, on the whole, respectfully received. As the hall was located in an aristocratic neighbourhood, the owner felt himself obliged to give the Salvationists notice to quit. A new hall was almost immediately found in a working-class district.

Staff-Captain Schaaff, who had set up his headquarters at 68 Olgastrasse, appealed to the State Director of Police for a cancellation of the ordinance of the local chief of police, which was really an infringement of the religious liberty of the country guaranteed by the Constitution to all Germans in all Germany, but the appeal was rejected in a letter which read:

> Your peculiarities cause one part of the people to be amused and another part disgusted. They cause excessive demonstrations against you. Therefore the police does quite right, in the interest of order, to stop your holding meetings at times when those who would disturb can attend.

Policemen were posted at the hall door to see that the ordinance was carried out, and a detective in plain clothes attended every gathering, large or small. Admission was granted only to those who had in advance given their name, address and profession to and had obtained a card of admittance from the corps officers. These cards were collected by two policemen at the door, a fresh ticket being required for each meeting. This practice was upheld in Stuttgart for fifteen years, but nevertheless the soul-saving work continued. On his first visit to Stuttgart corps Commissioner Railton "had the pleasure of addressing an audience consisting of the Director of Police, an official of the Ministry of the Interior, a detective, two men, two women, and two lads!" Although in this city of 126,000 inhabitants accommodation was provided for fewer than 26,000 people in the score or so places of worship, *Der Methodistan Herold* could write in its issue of 23 April 1887:

The Salvation Army would have done better either to give up the idea of commencing a campaign in Germany, or, at any rate, to have commenced in some other place, and to have operated more according to German usage.

German usage, among other things Protestant, was to hold no service whatever after five o'clock on Sunday afternoons. A second corps was soon at work in Esslingen, an important manufacturing town a short distance from Stuttgart, and opposition from the secular and religious press became less offensive, although an officer was fined for selling a copy of *Der Kriegsruf* to a policeman in the street. A side-line on the enthusiasm of the German pioneers is contained in the concluding sentence of Railton's report on his visit:

The last re-inforcement, little Pauline Schaaff, was just three weeks' old when her mother went out to lead the meeting the police said should not be held.

Worms-on-the-Rhine, made famous by its association with Martin Luther, was the third city in South Germany to be invaded within eight months ; and then followed Murrhardt where, as in the other openings, the pastors were afraid of those who wanted to do for Christ what they themselves were not prepared to do.

Toward the end of 1887 Major (later Lieut.-Colonel) Robert Perry, who with his wife had pioneered Salvation Army work in Denmark in May of that year, was sent to Kiel, in Schleswig-Holstein, to see an elderly Methodist, Gottlieb Strohmeier, who, having attended the Army's meetings in Switzerland and Denmark, wanted it to commence operations in North Germany. Being unable to find a suitable hall, Strohmeier bought a piece of land and built one himself, but while painting the roof he fell to the ground and was killed. The hall was the first Army property to be built in the country.

When Railton called to inspect this hall in the February of the following year, he was informed by the police that he had been expelled from Germany as an undesirable alien. Nevertheless, within a few days he was conducting the first Salvation Army meeting to be held in Berlin. Some 600 people were present, among them Members of Parliament, professors and professional men who mingled with students, working men and very unsympathetic leading Social Democrats. Railton described this Sunday afternoon as a wonderful opportunity.

Captain Carl Treite [1] opened the newly-erected hall in Kiel on 4 May 1888. Although he had been for seven years a local officer in a London corps, he had maintained his German nationality, and so was the best available Salvationist to commence the work in Northern Germany. As far back

[1] Lieut.-Colonel Treite became leader of The Salvation Army in Germany during the First World War

as 1881 he had offered his services to William Booth for opening Salvation Army operations in his native country, but evidently the General thought the time was not then ripe. Many soldiers were enrolled at Kiel before Treite was appointed a year later to Stettin, to re-open the hall which the police had closed. Here 700 seekers were registered in nine months.

When Railton again visited Stuttgart, in February 1889, he found seven officers "raised in spite of all difficulties out of the three little congregations I saw there in 1888," thirty or forty converts, many in full uniform, and increased congregations in "as promising a corps as anybody need wish for." This did not mean that all opposition had died, for a man bearing the same name as a convert in the village of Gross Assbach had the following announcement published in the local gazette, an announcement which Railton thought worth world-wide circulation :

> To avoid any possibility of mistake, I declare that the souls saved by The Salvation Army are not to be found in my family and amongst my relatives, but that under the firm of Gottlieb Angerbauer, Shoemaker, they may be found and known.
>
> Gross Assbach, 15 February, 1889,
> Jacob Angerbauer.

In March 1890 Commissioner Railton, having expressed his desire for a field appointment on the Continent, was given command of the Army's work in Germany, and the headquarters was later transferred to Berlin, first to 214 Friedrichstrasse. In 1895 it was moved again to 1 Blücherplatz. As his expulsion order was still valid, Railton had to live in the free city of Hamburg until permission for residence in Germany was granted him.

In the same year that Railton took command Jakob Junker, a forty-year-old wealthy Rhineland industrialist, who had taken part in his meeting in Berlin as an orderly—he also paid the rent of the hall—left the great concrete works and collieries of which he had control and entered the Clapton training garrison. He had been attracted to the Army by what he had read in *Der Kriegsruf* concerning the activities of Salvationists in the Fatherland. Soon after his commissioning, Junker was appointed the first Divisional Officer in Germany, with responsibility for establishing the Army in the East. He quickly rose to greater rank and position, but in 1901, when a Lieut.-Colonel and Chief Secretary, he was promoted to Glory soon after conducting a young officer's funeral. Junker was Germany's most outstanding Salvationist. With his private money he purchased five sites and built on each of them a hall and officers' quarters, four in Eastern Prussia and one in West Germany. He was also the founder of the Grundstücksgesellschaft der Heilsarmee (Property Company of The Salvation Army). The large sum of money he left to the Army in his will helped in the main to purchase the National Headquarters in Dresdener Strasse, which was partly destroyed in the Second World War and is now in the East Berlin Sector.

Opposition to the " foreign heretics " was rife almost everywhere throughout these early years. Sneezing-powder and stink-bombs were thrown into the Army's halls, alarm clocks were brought into the meetings and set off, gas-lights were extinguished, the doors of halls and officers' quarters were barricaded or broken, door-keepers were struck and wounded, and bricks were hurled through windows. On one occasion a horse was driven to the penitent-form ; on another, young people tied themselves to the seats. Bottles of beer were used in the streets to attack Salvationists, children spat on them, their uniform and bonnets were torn and their hair plucked from their heads.

In 1891 William Booth conducted meetings in Hamburg,

Kiel, Stettin and Berlin. His first meeting in the capital, on 23 February, was attended by a crowd of more than 1,000 persons, hundreds of others being turned away. Five years later Berlin was the venue for the first German Congress, which commenced with a council of war with the officers and lasted more than four days. Commissioner Thomas McKie was then the Territorial Commander and the Foreign Secretary, Commissioner Booth-Tucker, represented International Headquarters. The first corps in Saxony—Leipzig—was opened in 1896.[1] In October 1897 the General, *en route* to Germany, wrote in his regular *War Cry* feature, "Reflections," that a German naval officer, in conversation with a member of his entourage, had stated that "from being regarded as a kind of parody on religion, the intelligent portion of the nation now look upon The Salvation Army as the practical friend of the people." There were then 59 corps, 192 officers and cadets, and 1,931 soldiers and recruits. Among William Booth's 112 converts during his four days' visit to Berlin was an eighty-four-year-old baroness. The Social Work was launched in the same year by the opening in Berlin-Steglitz of a rescue home for women [2] which served as the Territorial Headquarters from 1947 until 1960.

In 1901, when Commissioner Oliphant commenced his seven years of leadership, Germany gave its first officer to missionary service, Adjutant (later Major) Catherine Giebler, who was to serve in both India and Indonesia for more than twenty-five years before she entered retirement.

Among books criticizing the Army during these years were *Was ist die Heilsarmee?* (J. Pestalozzi, 1886), *Die Heilsarmee nach Geschichte* (Th. Hardeland, 1898) and *Die*

[1] The Russians closed down all Salvation Army operations in the Eastern Zone after the Second World War

[2] *The History of The Salvation Army*, vol iii, p. 200

Heilsarmee und ihr Wesen (Professor D. Theodor Kolde, 1899). The Army also published a number of books including *Der beste Weg* (Carl Hilty, 1902), *Die Heilsarmee und der Trunksuchtsgesetzentwurf* (The Salvation Army and the Draft Law against Alcoholism, Jakob Junker, 1891), *Offizierinnen der Heilsarmee* (Women officers of The Salvation Army, Jakob Junker, 1891), *Die Lehren der Heilsarmee* (The Doctrines of The Salvation Army, 1900), *General Booth und die Heilsarmee* (General Booth and The Salvation Army, Wilhelm Muller, 1904) and *Salutismus* (Salvationism, W. Elwin Oliphant, 1904).

Chapter Three

ITALY

Mr and Mrs Gordon, [1] long resident in Rome, had their own mission hall at 10 Via Gioberti, and were eager to give up themselves and all they had to the service of The Salvation Army. Staff-Captain James Binks (Giacomo) Vint, a most versatile officer who could sing, play the violin and piano, compose music and write shorthand, in addition to speaking several languages, including Italian, and who for more than two years had been working in his spare time among the organ-grinders of the Italian Colony in London at Saffron Hill, Clerkenwell, and had established a corps there,[2] was asked to go to Rome to report on the prospects. He arrived in January 1887, and on his first day in the city participated

[1] Later Mr Gordon was given the honorary rank of Major

[2] *The History of The Salvation Army*, vol ii, p. 342

in a family meeting held in the Gordon home where two young men knelt at a sofa, which was thereby transformed into a penitent-form, to give their hearts to God. They became the first Salvationists in Italy.

On Thursday, 10 February, the General conducted a farewell meeting in Regent Hall, London, where some eighty cadets received their commissions as officers, and the newly promoted Major and Mrs Vint were dedicated to open officially the work in Italy with the assistance of Mrs Vint's sister, Lieutenant Fanny Hack, who was only eighteen years of age. Three days later, in the Great Western Hall, Paddington, of which corps Captain Eva Booth was the commanding officer, the General presented colours to the expedition. "The advance on Rome," as the *War Cry* described the event, took place on the following Sunday, 20 February, a great carnival day. Twenty-five persons attended the first meeting and sixteen of them "stood up for pardon."

Mr R. C. Morgan, of *The Christian*,[1] paid an unexpected visit to a gathering a few weeks later and made an appeal to sinners. Two of the first converts testified for the first time in the first open-air meeting. The International *War Cry* of 26 February gratefully acknowledges the receipt of a gold ring from a friend and a silver watch from a brother which, presumably, would have been sold and the money devoted to the Italian Expedition. It was not long before Commissioner Railton was in Rome to inspect the work, and in June he could report :

> Rome was an astonishment so great that I hesitate to write about it. In spite of what I saw with my own eyes, it seems almost too good to believe that in that city The Salvation Army has more liberty, a better congregation, and a better prospect than in many a place in England, and yet so it is.

[1] *The History of The Salvation Army*, vol i, p. 251 ; vol ii, p. 3

But Railton spoke too soon, for in September opposition and persecution were manifested in the attempted assassination of a cadet. A gang of "gentlemen roughs," armed with thick sticks and knives, had broken the windows of the hall and later the leader levelled two fearful blows with his heavy stick at the cadet who was acting as door-keeper. These blows—either of which might have caused him serious injury—he evaded, but another member of the gang suddenly made a knife-thrust at the cadet's stomach. Fortunately he sprang back in time and the wound was less serious than it otherwise would have been, albeit his uniform was sadly ripped. One day a man bent on murder called at the Major's quarters carrying a stick with metal running through it and a heavy knob of lead at the top. On another occasion Mrs Vint found a man hidden under her bed. He also had gone to the house to kill.[1]

Major Vint was "run in" more than once for selling the *Grido di Guerra* (The War Cry) on the streets, but was let out after an admonishment. The name of the paper was the difficulty, but as many as 300 copies were disposed of in one afternoon in a very short time, students purchasing them surreptitiously as they walked to and from the monasteries. The officers were often on the verge of starvation and had to go out early in the morning to sell *War Crys* in order to get sufficient money to buy a few rolls for breakfast. Many tradespeople were forbidden to serve the Salvationists and two young women confessed to having been bribed to put poison in the food they purchased. On the other hand, at Christmastime, when nothing but a small quantity of flour was left in the pantry—this was put in a cloth and boiled, only to turn out to be as hard as a bullet !—a waiter from a hotel brought to the door a large tray containing a hot meal sufficient for each of the five members of the

[1] P. 53 (Belgium)

household. A card on the tray was addressed "For Major Vint," but he never learned the name of his kindly benefactor, although the waiter called back for the tray and the crockery. The Major had an idea that the meal had come from the American Ambassador, whose son he had helped in India some time before.

Serious difficulties, including lack of financial support, eventually resulted in the Army's withdrawal from Italy, but at the end of 1890 a marvellous work, described in the *War Cry* as a "gale of grace," was commenced in the Waldensian Valleys in North Italy, where Fritz Malan (later Lieut.-Colonel) held meetings in his native village, conversions taking place every day. Operations were re-established in the country after two years when Major (later Commissioner) and Mrs Hugh E. Whatmore were appointed to the command of the territory. The work in Italy was attached to the French Territory in 1903.

Chapter Four

HOLLAND

A young Dutch wood-carver, studying in Paris, became interested in the newly-established "Armée du Salut," and made himself known to the *Salutistes* as a member of the Emmanuel Mission of the Evangelical Free Church in Amsterdam. This had been brought into being as the result of a 100 days' campaign conducted in 1881 by the American evangelist, Philip Phillips. To his younger and nineteen-year-old friend Gerrit J. Govaars, a member of the mission and a government school-teacher, the wood-carver forwarded copies of *En Avant*, and an article on uniform-wearing made so strong an appeal to him that he asked his friend in Paris to obtain for him a pair of brass S's, which his mother sewed on the lapels of his coat. Thus, about the end of 1885 Amsterdam saw a " Salvationist " for the first time ; one who had never heard of the Articles of War, let alone signed them, and who had never been sworn-in as a soldier under the Army flag. Govaars had contracted to give so many years to teaching, but upon discovering him to be even remotely associated with The Salvation Army, about which doubtless they had read, the responsible authorities of more than 400 schools refused to employ him.

Govaars stemmed from Roman Catholic stock, his father having been turned out of his home when he broke with the Church. It was from his father that Gerrit, then a boy of eleven years of age, first heard of The Salvation Army, which was being scurrilously attacked in a weekly paper, and of which attack Govaars, senior, strongly disapproved. That disapproval made the son a champion of the organization long before he had set eyes on a Salvationist.

The French Headquarters reported to London that a Dutch mission-worker was attending the meetings in Paris, and this was later remembered when Commissioner Railton —during a period of semi-inaction—wished to visit Holland in the hope of finding someone to assist him to translate an English song-book into Dutch for use in South Africa. By this time the wood-carver had returned to Amsterdam. A telegram sent to him from Paris asking that Railton should be met and fixed up with a billet, greatly disturbed him. His parents, who were very strict church people, had no desire to be associated with the much-criticized Salvation Army, and consequently the young fellow sought out his friend Govaars, whose widowed mother suggested that the

Commissioner should stay with them. So it was that Govaars met a Salvationist for the first time and learned for what purpose he was visiting Holland. As Railton could not speak Dutch and Govaars could not speak English, they had to converse in French. This was early in February 1886.

Unable to discover friends willing to help him with the translation of the song-book, Railton returned despondently to England ten days later, taking with him the unemployed school-teacher. Govaars was to spend two or three weeks in London assisting Railton with the Dutch song-book, but the two or three weeks lingered into three months, during which the "Hallelujah Dutchman," as he came to be called, accompanied the General on several of his campaigns and participated in the first International Congress gatherings. He was then permitted to wear uniform and was made a Lieutenant by the General himself.

About this time Captain Joseph Kelly Tyler, of Wrexham, who in his youth had served on a ship plying between Harwich and the Hook of Holland, being anxious for the salvation of two Dutch lady school-teachers who were holidaying in Wales, and who were attending his meetings, felt led to offer himself for service in their country. It was therefore arranged for Lieutenant Govaars to teach him the Dutch language.

Before Govaars left Amsterdam for England, however, Mr C. F. Schoch, branch president of the Emmanuel Mission, together with Mrs Schoch and the pastor of their church had visited London—this was in 1884—to study the Army's methods. Schoch was so impressed that he and Mrs Schoch again went to London in the following year, when they visited the General and Mrs Booth in their home. Schoch wanted to become a Salvationist right away, but the General advised him to wait until the Army opened up work in Holland. The upshot of these visits was that Railton was invited by the Schochs to " come and see if any good thing can come out of Amsterdam," being convinced that the Army was needed in their country. Thus it came about that Railton celebrated in Holland The Salvation Army's Coming of Age, addressing meetings in the Emmanuel Mission Hall on Sunday, 4 July 1886. The governing committee of the mission offered it to the Army whenever it was ready to take over. The mission had three halls and also an orchestra to accompany the congregational singing.

Another visitor to the International Congress was a Mr J. Van Petegem who, describing himself as a preacher of the Gospel, wrote to the General from Veendam in the September stating that he had decided to establish a Salvation Army in the Netherlands, seeing that the " English Salvation Army " had not accepted his propositions to give himself with all that he was and had to its work. He had, he said, erected a " wooden tent " and had thirty persons in his army who would wear uniform, but with " R. L."[1] instead of " S. S." on the collar. " We have no General," he continued. " I don't think I may give myself this title, and I believe one General is sufficient for the whole world." He asked for a Dutch-speaking officer to be sent, or for the General himself to come, to open his work in Holland. "We will help him with all, for the glory of God, to prove that we serve our King, though we are not under the same command. . . . Trusting you are pleased we have started in Holland a Salvation Army." William Booth was *not* pleased and Bramwell caused a reply to be sent to Mr Van Petegem that :

we should very much prefer that you do not adopt the name and style of The Salvation Army, and that while we appreciate your desire to work on our lines, we have found it very much better that only those who are authorized officers should operate in any

[1] Reddingsleger (Salvation Army)

way under our name. We shall, in all probability, before many months have expired, be sending officers to Holland, and it would be a pity to come into collision with you.

On 6 March 1887 Captain and Mrs Tyler—a very frail woman—and Lieutenant Govaars, made their farewells from Newtown, Montgomery, and went to open the work in Holland. On their last Sunday at the corps, Commissioner Railton had been unexpectedly present. It was not, however, until exactly two months had passed that the newly-promoted Staff-Captain Tyler, with his wife and Govaars—who, with Mr Schoch, had been temporarily assisting in Germany, where the work had commenced a few months previously—arrived to open the first corps in Amsterdam. The Army had taken over the lease of the Emmanuel Mission Hall and bought the furnishings, Mr Schoch personally making a grant of the full amount required. International Headquarters had generously given Tyler a £5 note with which he was to meet all his expenses, including travelling.

Although 3,000 handbills had been distributed announcing the opening, Railton reports that only a limited number of friends had been expected at the meeting convened for seven o'clock on the morning of Sunday, 8 May, to pray for God's blessing on the day's campaign; nevertheless, no fewer than 200 curious persons, mainly men, entered the "Volkzaal" in Gerard Donstraat, over the door of which the Army crest had been placed. The knee-drill [1] was at once resolved into a salvation meeting, which ended with four "respectable" seekers kneeling at the penitent-form, then a novelty in Holland. One thousand of the South African song-books were sold within a few days, the hall was overcrowded for every meeting with a most respectful congregation, although the sudden inrush of a mass of people into the hall after the start of the Sunday night

[1] Early morning prayer-meeting

gathering caused a temporary pandemonium, and " a fine row of sixteen penitents, mostly men," was the crowning victory. Mr and Mrs Schoch and Pastor Bromet, the translator of Sankey's hymns, who opened the meeting, had seats on the platform. At half-past ten at night when the final meeting concluded, the officers found " two lines of fine-looking fellows in their brass helmets . . . stretched across the streets patiently keeping all right." Railton says that he had never found a people so prepared for Het Ledger des Heils (The Salvation Army), nor a truer band of friends ready to rally round it without delay. Among the few voices that were raised adversely was that of the German preacher, Otto Funcke. He had seen Salvationists in the Exeter Hall, London, and knew that they were " only a vile troop of comedians who whistle and dance and sing in the most abominable manner."

It is interesting to note that Staff-Captain Tyler spoke in " not so very bad Dutch," according to the reporter of *Het Nieuws van den Dag*. Lieutenant Govaars accompanied the singing on his violin, Mrs Railton spoke in English, " failing a little on the ' holy fire ' expected." Her words were translated by Mrs Schoch who, in giving her own testimony, stated that " neither riches nor honour had made her happy." Three weeks later " Stafkapitein " Tyler reported that " 100 souls have sought salvation. 400 are reported within eleven weeks, and of these more than 100 have become soldiers." The old-fashioned tea-making, or hallelujah feast, was introduced into Holland, where it was yet another novelty. There were occasional disturbances in the hall, and some violence in the streets, but the police were always sympathetic and helpful. Because the Salvationists wore red guernseys the authorities at first thought them to be associated with the rabid Socialism of those days, but two or three hundred ridiculing extremists used to escort

Major Tyler home night after night, singing an uncomplimentary song which introduced his name. On his first Christmas Day in Holland he was struck violently in the face.

A large hall, the "Frascati," was engaged in another part of the city for a public explanation of the Army's measures and principles by Commissioner Frank Smith, of International Headquarters. A flag, on which was sewn a small Dutch emblem, was presented and the first corps was officially instituted. Among the converts was a publican who had shut up his business, much to the chagrin of the brewers. Another man, prior to his conversion, had given Tyler and Govaars a guilder to buy a glass of beer as an expression of his appreciation of the way they had conducted a meeting.

On 1 October Captain (later Lieut.-Commissioner) Wiebe Palstra, who was converted in and entered the Army from Hull, England, and Cadet J. C. Hilligenberg opened the corps at Haarlem.

Before the end of 1887 Mr Schoch who, upon his father's death, had become a "Cadet du Roi" (Cadet of the King) at the King of Holland's personal suggestion, and later had been commissioned an artillery officer, had not only been accepted as a Salvationist, as had his wife, but had been given the rank of Adjutant after a course of training in England. He eventually held the rank of Lieut.-Colonel. A second hall was opened in the same year in Amsterdam, cadets were being trained, and a new hall was being built at Utrecht by a generous lady friend.

Among the group of officers whose picture appeared on the front page of the International *War Cry* for 11 February 1888 was Lieutenant Salomonson, a Jewess by birth, who could not become a Salvationist, she said, unless the Army "believed in music and flowers." Susa de Jong, formerly a servant in the Schoch family, was a Captain.

Major Tyler was succeeded in April 1888 by Major (later Commissioner) Henry C. Hodder, and on the occasion of the first anniversary, conducted by Commissioner T. Henry Howard, it was announced that eleven corps had been opened and were being worked by 35 officers, with 11 cadets in training; the circulation of *Strijdkreet* (The War Cry) was 14,000 copies per week; 3,000 seekers had knelt at the penitent-form and more than 1,000 soldiers had been sworn-in.

During the command of Commissioner W. Elwin Oliphant, who had married Célestine Schoch in 1888, the Queen Regent—a substantial donor to the Army's funds—received him in friendly audience one morning and commanded him to attend a levée the same night. Of the seven children of Lieut.-Colonel and Mrs Schoch three others were to become the wives of Commandant Herbert Booth (Cornelie), Colonel Roussel (Henriette), and Lieut.-Colonel Fritz Malan (Wilhelmine) respectively.

Eight booklets, each containing an address by Mrs General Booth, were published during 1889; later these eight addresses were collected into one volume. *In Darkest England and the Way out* was translated into Dutch in 1890, and in 1896 Commissioner Oliphant's *War Memories from the Netherlands* was produced.

Commissioner and Mrs Booth-Clibborn succeeded Commissioner and Mrs Oliphant in the command of Holland, with Belgium as a province, in 1896.

Chapter Five

DENMARK

A pioneer detachment was sent from London to Copenhagen in April 1887 under the leadership of Major (later

Lieut.-Colonel) and Mrs Robert Perry, and a capitally-situated hall in Zinnsgade was leased. The *War Cry* describes "our attack upon Denmark" on 8 May as "a march forward in the dark, such as we have rarely undertaken," but "the Major met with a reception such as one could only have expected from the very warmest friends." For the first meeting the hall, seating 500, was crowded to excess, and a number of persons ventured to the penitent-form. Within a few weeks, however, there were 150 more of them, most becoming uniformed soldiers, and within a few months a second corps, St Kongensgade, was opened. This later became known to everyone as the "Little David" corps, presumably because of its comparison with the "Goliath" at Zinnsgade. The police were kind and treated the Salvationists as an allied force.

The General paid his first visit to Copenhagen during the first weekend in November and conducted a packed-out meeting in the large Methodist Church on the Saturday night. The Sunday morning gathering, the building being "as full as it could possibly be squeezed," with more than a thousand turned away, was one of the best he had ever held, according to "One who was there." Thousands could not get in at night and an unruly element caused a disturbance. Monday night's meeting had never had its equal in Scandinavia. Nowhere in the world, declared the General, as he looked upon the splendid body of troops which had been won during the first six months, had the Army had such a successful career as in Denmark.

When William Booth visited Odense, the birthplace of Hans Andersen, on 31 December 1888, a good soul who had no idea of the hustle and bustle of such an event, wrote to say that her home was open to entertain the "Pastor," as she called him, and that if he would spend the night there she would fetch him from the nearest railway station in her cart! A military captain and his wife were among the converts at Odense.[1] While much friendliness prevailed and invitations were received from friends anxious for the Army to commence its work in their district, inevitable opposition was encountered here and there. The police in some places were negligent in their duties, although by demand of the burgomasters Major Perry paid about £14 per week for police protection. One gentleman advertised in a Copenhagen newspaper that he had opened an office for the reception of witnesses and evidence that the "Frelsens Hær" teachings were false. By February 1889, eight corps had been opened. At Køge the parish priest wrote a two-column article in a local newspaper accusing the General of having said that God wiped away tears with five-pound notes, and that the Army dared to say that salvation did not, of necessity, mean being dipped. And the editor severely took to task the lad-Captain in charge of this new corps for waving his arms so much when speaking. He was reminded that "religion is not gymnastics." On the other hand, Christian ministers and friends welcomed the admittedly peculiar movement and even spoke of it as "the last cry of God's father-heart to a perishing world." Money was scarce in those days and Major Perry had to borrow from a friendly tailor the necessary kroner for a railway ticket before he could send a lass to her new corps. Open-air meetings were not permitted and the *Krigsråbet* (The War Cry) could not be sold in the streets.

Failing health compelled Major Perry to relinquish the Command and Major (later Commissioner) and "Majorina" Richard Wilson took over in the summer of 1889. Almost the last thing Perry did in Denmark was to accept as a cadet

[1] It is interesting to note that upon his return to London the General addressed a letter in the *War Cry*, "To the Officers and Soldiers of the Danish *Division*"

a young Bachelor of Philosophy, Jens Anders Hansen Povlsen, who was eventually to become the Territorial Commander of his native land. On New Year's Day 1890, an onslaught on the Copenhagen Salvationists was made by roughs, one comrade being nearly blinded by a dastardly knife-attack from behind. By this time twenty corps had been opened, seven in four months, twenty-one cadets were in training as officers and the weekly circulation of *Krigsråbet* had reached the 4,000 mark. The first General Congress was held in July of that year and was conducted by Major Oliphant, who had " seldom met a people who were readier to receive divine impressions." An innovation during the Congress was a meeting held on one of the ferry-boats plying between the many islands that are to be found in the Great and Little Belts.

Eighty-six officers had been commissioned by August, and buildings were easily secured ; even publicans came forward to offer their dancing saloons without payment. A new training home at Helgesensgade had been opened by Major Oliphant, the circulation of *Krigsråbet* had run to 8,500 copies, 31 corps had been opened and 1,000 soldiers were in uniform.

The burgomasters were very much in control of the towns and cities of Denmark and not all of them were sympathetic to the Army. When Captain Else Hansen was making her farewells to the Rudkøbing corps, the burgomaster, wishing to annoy the Salvationists, instructed her to close her public meeting at 9 p.m. She did so, but invited her soldiers and some other Christian friends to stay on a little longer for a private farewell. The burgomaster came in person to see that his orders were carried out, but when he knew of the private gathering he was furious and commanded the Captain to send her friends away. She refused and he dragged her from the platform through the streets to the prison, followed by a rapidly-growing crowd who stoned the building crying: "Out with the Captain and in with the burgomaster!" Frightened of the consequences of his action, the man of authority eventually released his prisoner—at two o'clock in the morning—to the exultant cheers of the crowd which had remained in the street throughout the night.

This young Captain, Else Hansen, and her fiancé, Adjutant Bojsen, Divisional Officer for Jutland, were refused marriage by the Head of the Ecclesiastical Department of the Danish Government unless they were attired in other than Salvation Army uniform, and the Bishop of Själland issued a fiat that no priest under his jurisdiction should marry them in their uniform. The difficulty was overcome by the purchase of a king's brief, a special permit by which they might legally be married in guernsey and norfolk jacket. Lutheran intolerance forbade singing, speaking or praying at a graveside, and so both the baby-girl of Major and Mrs Perry and later the son of Major and Mrs Wilson, were buried in silence.

Learning from the leader of the Indre Mission in Slagelse that members of "Frelsens Haer" were heretics, the burgomaster forced police protection at a cost of nearly two pounds per week on the two lasses in charge of the corps. "Protection" meant that if a policeman saw a man even smile in the hall he would fine him five shillings and fivepence on the spot. Naturally this imposition frightened people away, and brought the lasses to a starvation diet of black bread and tea. Major Wilson was able to get this police-money reduced to five shillings and sixpence per week. On occasions a policeman would insist upon smoking in the hall and be put out by the officer. At Nyborg, Fünen, the officer was sent an account for the services of the police who had arrived to quell a disturbance in the street after the hall had been closed. The officer refused to pay, but one day, when she was in her quarters counting some money with which to pay her *War Cry* dues, a police officer entered and, seeing the money, grabbed it all and departed.

This State protection and patronage became most embarrassing and expensive to the territory as a whole. When a new corps was opened half a dozen gendarmes would be appointed to preserve order; when a festive gathering was announced two or three officers of the law would suitably represent it. When a corps officer was desirous of collecting a few subscriptions for the benefit of the starving people he had discovered in some wretched slum, a policeman would politely accompany him to the residences to be visited. This was all very good and kind, but when the head of the police sent in a weekly bill calculated upon a liberal scale of allowance per hour per officer, it was difficult to settle such an account. It was useless to protest. The assurance that the police were not needed was conclusive evidence to their head that they ought to attend on the Salvationists, and the disposition to complain about the charges was considered as a sign of unreasonableness.

Next on the list of civic persecutions came the demand that officers should pay income tax on their extremely uncertain salary. The officer at Nykøbing, Själland, had her personal property attached for this iniquitous tax—a pair of old boots and her box. Grenaa, an out-of-the-way fishing place in the north-east island of Jutland, was remarkable for being almost the only place where Salvationists were ill-treated by men other than policemen. Here our girl-officers were both kicked and beaten.

One of the difficulties of attendance at meetings was that almost everyone worked on Sundays; not one shop in ten closed, factories were run, and even so-called "religious" people attended to business for part of the day. Junior work was hampered. The chief of police in Odense, giving his reason for not allowing anyone under eighteen to enter the hall, said: "They have no sense. You cannot get them saved."

By January 1891 the first brass band, known as the Danish Staff Band, was "doing famously" after three weeks, although "the Danish people," says the *War Cry* reporter, "have the credit of being unmusical."

In this same month the General paid another visit to Denmark,[1] a countess and "an important official about the King's person" vying with each other to entertain him, and Cabinet ministers, attachés of the Court, Members of Parliament, judges, professors, clergymen and representatives of the highest circles of the city being present to hear him in the Oddfellows Palace in Copenhagen on a Wednesday and Thursday night. The Circus Pantheon in Odense was crowded for his lecture on the Darkest England Scheme on the following afternoon, one of the leading police authorities—presumably the not-too-accommodating Chief of Police—being included in the audience, which gave wonderful attention.

After nearly three years in command of the territory Colonel Wilson and his wife made their farewells and left for Norway. They were succeeded by Colonel Charles Sowton; this was in 1892. In the following year the King contributed to a fund to aid the poor of Copenhagen.

Chapter Six

CENTRAL AMERICA AND THE WEST INDIES

JAMAICA

Within ten days of receiving instructions from the Chief of the Staff (Mr Bramwell Booth) to proceed to open the

[1] p. 152

Army's work in the West Indies, Colonel Abram Davey,[1] his wife—who was expecting her tenth child—their five young children, and a blind Salvationist, Mark Sanders, an accomplished song-writer of both words and music, had sailed from Liverpool for New York. This was on 15 November 1887. Following about two weeks spent in the United States of America in collecting funds for the expedition, the little party arrived in Kingston on 15 December to be welcomed by people who had been in communication for some time with the General. First among them was Mrs (" Mother ") Foster, whose daughter was an officer in England. She had started a small mission which she wanted to hand over to The Salvation Army as a corps. Then Brother W. Raglan Phillips, a young English land surveyor, who had spent nearly twenty years in the West Indies, and who was a member of a Salvationist family in the English Midlands, had formed the nucleus of a corps at Bluefields, a mountain village in the western part of the island. The Colonel had been sent to consolidate the work at Bluefields, where quarters and a hall had been provided, but on the advice of others he decided to make a start in the capital. Phillips later moved into Kingston to assist with the editing of the *War Cry*, the first issue of which was published on 2 January 1888. Within a month it had the largest sale of any religious paper on the island and was the only one illustrated.

The first meeting conducted by Colonel Davey was one of thanksgiving held in the quarters outside of which a great crowd had assembled. No 5 Duke Street was to become both headquarters and home for the pioneers. On the evening of the next day the Colonel visited the room which had been used for evangelistic purposes by Mrs

[1] *The History of The Salvation Army*, vol ii, facing p. 53. The *War Cry* of 26 Nov. 1887 refers to the Colonel as *Superintendent* Davey

Foster for the past three years, but found the street blocked by some thousands of people. The veranda of the house was made into a temporary platform, and the great congregation listened with closest attention to the Colonel, who won their sympathy from the outset. Eleven seekers came forward.

The secular press was friendly on the whole, but the *Daily Budget* assured Colonel Davey that what reports he may have heard concerning the extreme wickedness of the inhabitants of the island were entirely unfounded ; it also was fearful lest Salvation Army teaching should prove to be " revivalism " such as " would drive people to frenzy, and cause them to neglect their industry, their social duties, their homes and families, and give themselves up to excesses that would level them to the condition of the brutes." The Mayor of Kingston, however, was evidently of like mind to the editor of *Gall's News-Letter*, quite prepared to believe that The Salvation Army was an uproarious and mischievous community, for he refused the use of the town hall for a meeting ; but Mr James Gall had promised his clergyman-father in England that he would not place any obstacle in its way, even though he did not see clear to help the Army. So it was that Colonel Davey held his first Sunday afternoon meeting on the lawn of the Myrtle Bank Hotel lent by Mr Gall himself. The converted captain and crew of a Norwegian vessel were present among the four or five thousand people who attended, and who were favourably impressed. Three persons stepped forward at the close to declare their desire to begin a new life. The Norwegians had participated in a little street skirmishing on the previous evening, when seven people were brought " to the feet of Jesus."

On the following evening many of the local magistrates, city councillors, storekeepers, foreign consuls and members of various denominations—some of whom took part—listened to an address on " The Rise and Progress of The Salvation Army " given by the Colonel in the Theatre Royal, the place being " packed from pit to dome, as it probably never had been before." The President of Calabar College took the chair. A property was secured in Church Street for a Salvation Army Temple which, with alterations and extensions, would hold 1,500 people ; the upstairs portion of the front premises was to be a headquarters and a women's training home. Things moved very quickly and the Temple was opened on 27 March, when 2,000 packed the building. Special gatherings were held for the blind and Mark Sanders started a Braille class.[1]

Despite the *Daily Budget's* protestation of the island's comparative goodness, Colonel Davey had not been many weeks in Jamaica before he discovered that thousands never attended a place of worship, that government statistics testified to the fact that 75 per cent of the babies in the island were illegitimate, that there was " a marvellous lack of love amongst the majority of the black people we have met," that they did not particularly care for their children, that many had no conscience, that modesty and shame were scarce commodities, that the blackest of lies could be told without a blush, that petty pilfering abounded on every hand, that idol worship was prevalent, that witchcraft held many in bondage, and that very many called evil good and laughed at virtue ; all this Colonel Davey attributed to the reactions to slavery which had been abolished but fifty years before. He described the rum for which Jamaica is celebrated as " liquid damnation," but averred that while even children drank rum, drunkenness was not *the* sin of Jamaica. Tobacco grew wild and one could buy a thousand cigars for fifteen shillings, or a yard of dried and twisted

[1] *The History of The Salvation Army*, vol iii p. 284

tobacco for threepence, which accounted for little boys of eight smoking in the streets. But within seven months of the Army's arrival in Jamaica hundreds of men and women gave up both rum and tobacco for love of Christ.

All this information was incorporated in an article entitled "Jamaica, past and present," which appeared in *All the World* in July 1888 under Colonel Davey's name. While the Colonel chivalrously took full responsibility for this article it is believed that he was not the actual author. James Gall read it, criticized it mercilessly in his *News-Letter*, and, according to the *Evening Express* of 1 October, thereby incensed the rough, hooligan elements among those who were unfavourably disposed toward the Army. The previously orderly indoor meetings in the Temple were now regularly disturbed, then stones were thrown at those taking part on the platform, the roughs smashed up the seats and piled them into the centre of the hall in order to set fire to them and burn down the building. Fortunately, a posse of police arrived in the nick of time and ultimately—they were at first unable to cope with the situation—cleared the hall, but the hostile crowd found ammunition from piles of stones, old bricks, and even lumps of cement torn up from the street. They smashed every window and then threw stones on the roof, continuing their havoc until after midnight on one occasion, 28 September. The little group of Salvationists, including the Davey children, were marooned in the building for three days and nights. Stones actually fell on the face of the Colonel's infant daughter Katie, rendering her unconscious. When Gall saw what he had started he tried to modify matters, and meetings were again held in the repaired hall, but things were strained. "Income dwindled to vanishing point, and the circulation of the *War Cry* dropped from 6,100 to 1,500 copies," wrote Commissioner William Booth Davey, son of the Colonel, in after years. "Our private goods, including my violin, were sold to raise money for food and to meet expenses. Baby Evangeline, the youngest member of the family, sickened and died." Let it be said that the *Evening Express* and the *Jamaica Post*, while differing from Colonel Davey's statement, very strongly condemned James Gall and the violent attack made by the unruly mobs on the Temple, the Colonel and his family.

Before each enrolment of soldiers the Colonel had to conduct many weddings, as converts not previously aware of anything undesirable about their former relationship wished henceforth to conform to Christian standards.

The difficulties which arose in 1888 resulted in the recall to London of Colonel Davey. Staff-Captain William Darracott was then sent out, but the reactions were such that he stayed for only a short time, and for four years the country was left without a European leader; then, in 1892, Major (later Colonel) James Cooke was appointed to the command of Jamaica and arrived there in May with Mrs Cooke and four other officers, including Raglan Phillips, now an Adjutant, who, when the country lost its leader, had declared his intention of "being the Army." Continuing to devote all his spare time to the cause, he had gained several thousands of converts. Phillips had eventually found it impossible to carry the dual responsibility of his government appointment and of the Army, and wrote to the General asking him to send another Territorial Commander. When no response was forthcoming he took the journey to London to make his appeal in person.[1] "He wore," says Commissioner Henry Bullard, who interviewed him, "a very shabby, long ministerial black coat, with several rows of red braid across the front, and a cap, round the band of which were the words, hand-painted: *The Salvation*

[1] *A Missionary's Memories*, p. 54

Army." The General also saw him, and promised that if he would give up his government position, and become an officer, he would send a Territorial Commander back with him to Jamaica. At first reluctant, he finally agreed, and was provided with a regulation uniform and given the rank of Adjutant and the position of A.D.C. to the Territorial Commander. "Although somewhat of a 'stormy petrel,' Phillips' contribution to the Army in those early days was considerable. His psychological handling of a West Indian crowd was fascinating to watch," writes Colonel Walter Shaw, who served for some years in the territory. Phillips was an officer for twelve years and then became a Baptist minister. Major Cooke found it difficult to shape up the irregular forces comprising Raglan Phillips' army of 123 Jamaican officers and 8,000 soldiers into a consistent body of Salvationists, but eventually was able to build up several corps during his term of office. A unique feature of Salvation Army work in Jamaica at that time was that no corps paid rent for its hall, this being freely loaned. Major Cooke was succeeded by Major (later Brigadier) Immanuel Rolfe, whose son Victor was to become a Lieut.-Commissioner.

BRITISH GUIANA

As far back as the summer of 1888 British Guiana was "desperately calling for the Army." Many godless people, having seen Salvationists at work in different countries, were saying, "We could not but surrender ourselves were you to cross our shores"; but it was not until 10 April 1895 that Adjutant and Mrs Widgery were dispatched to open up the work in the colony. This was the direct outcome of a personal appeal to the Chief of the Staff by a coloured Salvationist-steward who travelled between London and

Georgetown on a steamboat. Souls were being saved and soldiers raised through an unofficial agency known as "Marshall's Army," which had been working on Salvation Army lines for some nine years. It appears that a young man named Marshall had visited Jamaica, become a Salvationist there and then returned to British Guiana, where his witness had resulted in many converts.

A man saved in a Methodist chapel on the island of Grenada, read an old copy of the *War Cry* until he became a Salvationist in spirit. His going to Demerara, in British Guiana, setting up a tiny cobbler's shop, working all day, and testifying every night in the open air, caused him to send to England for a guernsey and cap and write asking the General to send officers to the only British possession in the South American continent.

The pioneer officers arrived in Georgetown on Wednesday, 24 April, were well received, held their first open-air meeting on the same afternoon, and had an attendance of 500 interested people. Within a few weeks this figure had grown to 1,000 whenever the officers took their stand, and more than 100 seekers, mostly men, were recorded, many becoming Salvationists. Among those who knelt at the Mercy Seat were a schoolmaster, a school-mistress, an infidel, a chemist, and a hospital matron. When the Adjutant held a meeting in a Congregational church on the west coast more than 200 people sought salvation. First "The Hand of Justice Society's" hall was acquired, and later "The Rose of Sharon" hall was taken over for week-night meetings, the Sunday gatherings being held in the historic town-hall. By August the Adjutant had divided his corps into four brigades and was holding two meetings every night except Friday. The town-hall became far too small for the crowds that came to the meetings, and as many as six were being held at the same time. By October the soldiers' roll in Georgetown numbered more than 400. At the end of 1896 Georgetown could boast of 40 local officers, and there were 10 officers in the country and 8 corps and outposts. Commissioner Edward Higgins, father of General Edward J. Higgins (elected in 1929), visited the central corps some months after its official opening and swore-in 160 men and women as soldiers.

In June 1897 Mrs Widgery and Corps Sergeant-Major Dowridge were arrested for conducting open-air work at Den Amstel, and were sentenced to a month's imprisonment with hard labour as they would not pay a fine. Public opinion, however, was so strongly in favour of the Army that the fines were paid by a friend in the course of a few days. Demonstrations of protest were held upon Mrs Widgery's release and the police authorities began to give Salvationists facilities that they did not previously enjoy.

When the Widgerys farewelled on 19 December 1897, there were 5 corps, 12 outposts and a shelter for coolies with accommodation for 200 men. The soldiership was 600 and included Europeans, East Indians, Creoles, Chinese and coloured folk. The Widgerys were followed by Adjutant and Mrs Walter Shaw.

While on leave in 1895, Alexander Alexander, a Scottish Highlander and manager of a sugar plantation in Demerara, heard William Booth speak. He also read of the remarkable work Frederick Tucker was doing in India,[1] and was fired to undertake similar work for the Indians in British Guiana. Some years before, when on leave, he had come into contact with the Army in his native Kemnay, and had eventually become a cadet, but illness had terminated his officership. Back in Georgetown by the following year he flung up his job, and launched out on this new venture entirely on his own account, dressing as an Indian fakir, and walking bare-

[1] *The History of The Salvation Army*, vol ii, p. 272

footed as he proclaimed the Gospel. Soon he had opened a cheap shelter for destitute jobbers in Georgetown, which in due course he offered to the Army with his service. William Booth, recognizing his worth, accepted both and gave him the rank of Captain. On 1901 he was married to Mary Howell in the town-hall, both of them being dressed as Indians. When they left Demerara in 1926 Major Alexander was one of the best-known men in the colony, he having accomplished a magnificent work, for which Bramwell Booth awarded him the Order of the Founder.[1] "For 30 years," ran the official citation, "he laboured with outstanding devotion and enterprise in seeking the safety and salvation of East Indians settled in British Guiana."

ST LUCIA

A lonely coaling-station of the West Indies, St Lucia was opened by a young sergeant of the Royal Artillery whose interest in The Salvation Army was aroused by his reading of the *War Cry*. He was already converted, but felt that the Army's warlike tactics were akin to his own ideas. He wrote to Headquarters for a book of procedure, a concertina and a song-book, with which he started to make a Salvation Army on his own account, holding open-air meetings among the natives of the sugar plantations and having the assistance of a negro fruit-seller, a Mrs Grant, who had become his first convert.

With his own money he hired a little hall, which he christened "The Barracks," and disposed of two dozen *War Crys* weekly. The sergeant was known as the "Captain" and Mrs Grant as the "Corps Sergeant-Major." A small corps was thus established, although its "Commanding Officer" could claim no association with the Army save

[1] Instituted in 1917

that of his enthusiasm in the work of saving souls. He had, however, read the Articles of War in the *Field Officer*, which had been sent him, and these he signed. The " Captain " made a number of converts among the black folk before he was recalled to the Old Country.

Two years later, Lance-Corporal King, of the Royal Engineers, and a Naval and Military leaguer, found himself in St Lucia. He was surprised to contact The Salvation Army in the person of Mrs Grant, who had, she informed him, also signed the Articles of War, which her " Captain " had sent her after he went away to become a Salvation Army officer. She had them fastened to the wall of her living-room, which was arranged as for a meeting. She had carried on the work after her " Captain " had gone, and King now took up the shepherding of this little flock. No dates of these happenings can be obtained, but the story appeared in *All the World* for 1896. Officers were sent to the island in September 1902, in the persons of Staff-Captain and Mrs Morris. It was a honeymoon appointment. At that time a large garrison of British soldiers was stationed in St Lucia, but when it was withdrawn the corps continued to flourish.

BARBADOS

On their way to Jamaica in 1892 Major and Mrs Cooke touched the Island of Barbados, " Little England," as it was called, and took the opportunity to conduct three meetings, but not until 30 April 1898 did Staff-Captain Widgery arrive in Barbados with his wife to commence operations officially.

The Widgerys were not entirely new to the island for they had paid several brief visits during the Staff-Captain's command of British Guiana, and had taken part in meetings which paved the way for the opening of the work. They began in the Y.M.C.A. Hall, lent for a few nights free of charge, and were assisted by a handful of faithful followers who had been converted while on a visit to Demerara. Within a week they were prosecuted by the police for "holding an open-air meeting to the annoyance of the public." The Staff-Captain was found guilty and committed to Glendairy Gaol. By July, however, 150 conversions had taken place, the first corps had been opened and the first flag unfurled, and within nine months some 1,000 people had knelt at the penitent-form. In the first six months one of the largest halls in Bridgetown was rented for the Sunday gatherings, until the landlord, wanting to raise the rent, drove out the Salvationists. The fruit of this first nine months was 310 soldiers, 386 recruits, 156 junior soldiers, and 5 candidates for officership. A hurricane fell upon the area and gave the Army an opportunity to show its willingness to help in time of national distress.

At the beginning of January 1900 it was announced that a new territory was to be created with headquarters in Bridgetown to include the whole of the West Indies and British, Dutch and French Guiana, and Brigadier Gale was appointed to be the first Territorial Officer. The territory comprised 126 corps and outposts, 128 officers and cadets, 2 social institutions and a Naval and Military home.[1]

This headquarters was transferred in 1902 to Kingston, Jamaica, as was the training home. During the autumn of 1902 smallpox caused great distress in the island, no fewer than 1,072 cases being reported up to 10 October, and of them 40 had died. Staff-Captain Walter Shaw, the Divisional Officer, made a free distribution of food, many of the islanders being thrown into a destitute condition owing to

[1] *The History of The Salvation Army*, vol iii, p. 290

the strict quarantine restrictions. At this time a revival broke out in some of the corps, particularly at Speightstown, where more than 200 professed conversion ; many of them became Salvationists.

TRINIDAD

"Ensign and Mrs Grasspool [of British Guiana] and Captain Luther Atkins have claimed Trinidad for God," so runs a report in *All the World* for February 1902. By then some twenty converts had been secured in Port of Spain, to which the captain had been appointed on 7 August 1901. Trinidad was the stronghold of Roman Catholicism in the West Indies ; nevertheless, another corps was soon opened, and a sailor's home was established in the capital.

CHAPTER SEVEN

NORWAY AND ICELAND

A group of zealous Christians (The Christian Alliance) having appealed to the Army's only woman-Commissioner, Hanna Ouchterlony (" The Scandinavian Army Mother "), then Territorial Commander in Sweden, to start work in Norway, the General visited Christiania, or Oslo as it is now called, to give a lecture on " The Salvation Army, its aims and methods," and thereby dispersed much misconception. A Christian business man, P. Th. Halvorsen, built a hall at 9 Grønland in readiness for the coming Army. " Wanted a man for Norway," said a paragraph in the *War Cry* for 31 December 1887, " which we contemplate taking possession of shortly. We are the people that can straighten out the European difficulty," and on 22 January 1888 Staff-Captain Albert Orsborn, the new district officer, carrying a future General [1] on his arm, Mrs Orsborn, and two or three other officers, arrived from England during a raging snowstorm to join the invaders of Norway's capital. It was Sunday evening and they were directed straight to the hall, which was crowded, a large number of people also standing outside in the snow. On the platform were Commissioners Ouchterlony—under whose direction the pioneers were to work—and Railton—the last-named seemed to be everywhere present in those days—and a little handful of men and women, including an officer from Sweden and a Norwegian woman who had become a Salvationist in South Africa. They had already conducted a morning meeting which had resulted in some score of persons coming forward "to seek a fighting salvation;" an afternoon open-air and indoor meeting in which other seekers were registered; and the evening gathering. Now they were commencing the prayer-battle, which ended with forty-three seekers. Meetings were held every morning and night of every day following, so eager and interested were the crowds in the salvation message. A larger building was secured for the Wednesday night gathering and more than 1,000 were present. The first four days resulted in more than 100 people seeking mercy.

A report from Staff-Captain Orsborn in the *War Cry* for 3 March states that Commissioner Ouchterlony and he had visited a lady who until recently had been in attendance on Her Majesty the Queen of Norway and Sweden,[2] and she had proposed that the Army should take up rescue work

[1] Albert William Thomas Orsborn, International Leader from 1946 to 1954

[2] The two countries were then united under one sovereign

among the young women of the city. "That work begins today," says the Staff-Captain, but the first rescue home was not opened until 1896.

The original hall in Grønland being too small to accommodate the large congregations, the Methodist minister lent his church, holding 800, to the Salvationists on the evening of Sunday, 5 February, when an overflow meeting was also held in the Army building. On 4 April Christiania II corps was opened with about seventy recruits in a large hired barracks accommodating 1,200 people ; but already Orsborn had opened fire in Arendal, where within six months 300 had sought salvation, and at Konigsberg. Grønland had 600 soldiers and recruits within six months, some of whom were transferred to Christiania III on Sunday, 15 July 1888, 246 being present at the early morning knee-drill. A ship's captain, who had sought salvation with all his crew and who had become interested in Colonel Davey's work in Jamaica [1] heard in England of what was happening in his native Norway, cast in his lot with the Army, got into full uniform and subscribed handsomely to a new building fund. The first Norwegian Salvationists to become officers were Bertha Hansen (now Lieut.-Colonel) and Carl Breien (later Colonel). Colonel Henry A. Tandberg, famous throughout Norway as a song-writer, became an officer in the following year.

Krigsropet (The War Cry) was issued after four months' warfare and a new Territorial Headquarters, including a large hall for the No 1 corps, was opened by the General in the centre of the capital at 22 Pilestredet, exactly eleven months to the day following the "invasion." The Norwegian public received "Frelsesarmeen" (The Salvation Army) with more goodwill and toleration than had been the case in Sweden ; nevertheless, as in almost every country,

[1] p. 28

Salvationists had to endure prejudice, disapproval, opposition and the accusation that its doctrines were erroneous. "The attitude of educated people acted upon the lower elements of the public as an incentive to annoyances," says Colonel Tandberg in his voluminous history of fifty years of Salvation Army warfare in Norway. A "skeleton army" was formed only to meet a sudden end in its leader's conversion; but the newspapers generally were opposed to the invading force. Open-air meetings were at first hampered by disobliging police officials, who also caused Salvation Army officers to suffer imprisonment for holding indoor meetings after 9 p.m. An appeal to the Storting (Parliament) in 1895 resulted in a declaration of freedom to preach the Gospel without let or hindrance.

A controversial pamphlet entitled "Up to war with The Salvation Army," containing all the old fables about "General Booth's nice salary," and so forth, was produced by some enterprising persons who did a roaring trade with it, rousing the people to war with the Army on creeds and ceremonies. The excitement was intense, ministers of religion holding councils among themselves and lecturing Salvationists upon the proprieties of religious worship. Orsborn made no reply, but carried on with his soul-saving. Prayer meetings were interrupted by stalwart "choristers" singing hymns, the leader often being the editor of the offensive pamphlet. The police, however, were most helpful at this time, many of them, according to a sergeant, being Salvationists at heart, and the head policemaster a regular *War Cry* customer. A night in the cells for five of the obstructionists and a fine of £10 imposed upon the leader quietened things down.

A law having been passed on 21 April 1888 that no-one of foreign nationality was allowed to own property in Norway without the King's consent, Staff-Captain Orsborn made a written application and received royal permission for the Army to own land and to build ; "another mighty victory," as he described it, because only a few days before a meeting to express indignation with the Army and to urge its removal from the capital had been called in Christiania. The King's consent turned the tide of opposition, to the utter chagrin of the Army's persecutors.

At Horten, where marines were stationed and an arsenal situated, the "church clergyman" announced that he would lecture against the Army. He had an audience of five, while the hallelujah barracks was crowded, as it had been every night from the opening, with more than 500 persons. The penny booklet, "All about the Army," had given the folks all the information they needed.

The Orsborns left for England after nine months of pioneering and by this time three corps had been established in Christiania and five others were in operation in the provinces ; the last being Hønefoss, away among the woodmen of the mountains. There were some 300 soldiers and 30 officers, and a training home had been established. Major (later Commissioner) Charles Sowton was appointed to succeed Staff-Captain Orsborn, Norway being then separated from the Swedish command. Colonel Richard Wilson followed Sowton, who was in turn followed by Commissioner Ouchterlony for a second term. A few weeks prior to Commissioner William Ridsdel's taking command in May 1900, a life-saving ship for service among the fishermen and other isolated folk on the northern coasts of Norway was launched.

A so-called "Holiness Crisis" arose in 1891-2, when a considerable number of officers and soldiers left the Army, they holding extremist views and being unable to subscribe to the Army's more sober teaching of this doctrine ; but the Army emerged from the difficulty more stabilized and strengthened. In 1893 work among young people was organized.

ICELAND

Iceland's pioneer officers left Denmark on 24 April 1895, under the leadership of Adjutant Christian Eriksen, a former miller. He was accompanied by Captain Davidsson—a native of Iceland who had first seen the Army in Canada, but had become converted on the island of St Helena, and had returned to Canada, entering the training home from Winnipeg—and Lieutenant Lange, an erstwhile university student.

Information about the Army's world-wide work having already reached Iceland, the party was given a most friendly reception from the magistrate downward and soon got to work. The opening meeting was held on 12 May in the Good Templars' Hall in Reykjavik, many being unable to obtain admission. A number of fishermen speedily became Salvationists, and a monthly four-page sheet, *Heropid*, first issued in the October of the following year, proclaimed the news of salvation, Captain Davidsson being its first editor. Finance was a problem, for the officers received their salary in kind; indeed, almost all business was transacted in this way. The people, too, were very poor. Captain Davidsson took orders for photographs and Lieutenant Lange painted in order to help raise funds.

The main hotel in Reykjavik—which had only 5,000 inhabitants—was bought for use as the Army's barracks, and a school was acquired for the use of the children. As elsewhere, however, a "skeleton army" soon came into being and it became most difficult for Salvationists either to march or to sing in the streets. In 1896 a corps was opened at Isafjord and two years later a home for sailors was established.

Chapter Eight

MAURITIUS

Of a detachment of 420 men of the North Staffordshire Regiment sent to Mauritius at the end of 1888, five were Salvationists who had been converted at Pietermaritzburg, South Africa. So soon as they landed they started a soldiers' mission under Salvation Army rules, and conducted several meetings during the week in the military schoolroom with the commanding officer's permission, there being no Nonconformist Church on the island. One brother was responsible for *War Cry* distribution and another for hospital visitation. No leader was appointed, the men accepting the conducting of the meetings in turn, but Corporal Harry Brookes was the unofficial secretary. The governor of Mauritius Gaol in 1892 was at one time doorkeeper at 272 Whitechapel Road, The Christian Mission's headquarters.

Mauritius is not mentioned again until in *All the World* for June 1897, the story is told of a Naval and Military leaguer attached to the Black Watch who started Salvation Army meetings especially for children in a borrowed schoolroom in Port Louis, the capital. Children attended by the score, but later the room became filled with adults, numbers of whom found the Saviour. A flag and a drum were sent from International Headquarters, a corps was constituted and local officers appointed. When this leaguer, whose name is not known, was transferred to India, a leaguer serving in the York and Lancs Regiment carried on the work, but when he, too, left the island, Salvation Army activities would have come to a standstill, as none of the converts was mature enough to be the leader, had not a diminutive young teacher in an Anglican mission, who loved the Army's teaching of holiness, come to the rescue. With the permission of his bishop he gave an eye to the running of the corps and, with the aid of the *Handbook of Doctrine*, a copy of the Articles of War, and a Salvation Army song-book, conducted holiness meetings on Salvation Army lines. This young Mauritian priest of Indian extraction eventually travelled to England and became a Cowley Father and so, apparently, the work lapsed until, in 1902, a petty officer of the Royal Navy arrived in Mauritius. He, with some devoted leaguers belonging to H.M.S. *Highflyer*, re-started meetings in Port Louis in a lodge-room belonging to the Good Templars and, as usual, was able to record converts.

More than 40 years later Father Rangasami told Lieut.-Colonel Thomas Lewis, who was returning on the *City of Hong Kong* to missionary service in Africa, that when he returned to Mauritius every church on the island contained members who had been converted through the ministrations of these enthusiastic Salvationist-servicemen. The record of their efforts could be read in the police files, wherein it was stated that largely because so many people had become converted in the open-air meetings they conducted in a notoriously wicked district, it had been found possible to close its special police station.

Chapter Nine

FINLAND

First news of the forthcoming attack on Finland, "The Land of a Thousand Lakes," appeared in the London *War Cry* for 27 April 1889: "Three cadets—a man and two women—have arrived from Helsingfors, the chief city of

Finland, and are now in training ; we shall attack as soon as possible." The young man, Baron Constantin A. L. Boije, a member of one of the noblest families in Finland—then an autonomous grand duchy within the Russian Empire—having been sent by his government to inspect the night refuges for the poor in different countries, had seen the Army at work in Stockholm, Berlin and London. Already influenced by revival meetings conducted by Lord Radstock—a British peer—in Helsingfors, Boije had formed the converts into what had become known as the Free Church ; but when he saw the Army at work he was greatly impressed, and, returning to his native land, tried to run the Free Church on Salvation Army lines. This, however, did not suit the majority of the congregation, and so he began another mission in a small room with a group of enthusiastic evangelists which included Mrs Louise af Forselles, wife of a military colonel and sister of Princess (later Brigadier) Ouchtomsky, who had contacted the Army in Switzerland.

Mrs af Forselles, after attending meetings conducted by William Booth in London, had written to him suggesting that The Salvation Army should take over their mission and that Constantin Boije, Hedvig Eleonora von Haartman and Alva Forsius should be trained as officers in England. This was agreed to, and Boije's wife remained at home with her five young daughters to supervise the mission while her husband was in London. Miss von Haartman, one of the twenty-four children of the noble Director of the Governing Body of Finnish Physicians, had been a teacher of languages in a girls' school before coming into contact with and eventually participating in the Free Church meetings held by Baron Boije. She had received much spiritual light through the reading of Salvation Army literature. The women were trained at the Upper Norwood garrison and the man assisted at Hammersmith corps. Hedwig von Haartman was once stoned in England, her bonnet and uniform being damaged beyond repair.

Operations began in Finland on 8 November 1889, the whole staff of officers consisting of only Captain and Mrs Boije and Lieutenants von Haartman and Forsius. The inauguration took place in Broholm's Riding School, Helsingfors, and attracted great interest from the impressive general in his gold-trimmed uniform to the lowly workman, from the fashionable lady to the poor shop assistant. Also present was one of the outstanding figures of Finland's public and intellectual life, Professor Zacharias Topelius. Within a few weeks, however, Bishop G. Johansson had published a book attacking the organization, and predicting that it would try to push itself into Russia and cause misunderstanding between the two peoples. Soon after its commencement the Army submitted its statutes to the Imperial Senate for approval. They were rejected and Salvationists were now beset with all manner of difficulties. They were forbidden to open their halls, to advertise, to take up collections, to sell their papers, to wear uniform—they were brought before the police authorities and their insignia removed—and finally, to continue their operations.

Captain Boije had been a personal friend of the Governor-General, General von Heyden, since military academy days and, being well acquainted with the Russian authorities' fear of all international movements, stressed the importance of the work being put on a national basis. This proposal was laid before William Booth, who, contrary to his usual attitude in such circumstances, gave his consent in the hope that the national Army would join the international Army at a later date. But the majority of Finland's Salvationists did not subscribe to Boije's idea. They desired to profit from the international link and requested that it should be maintained, whereupon Boije withdrew and at the beginning of May 1890, Lieutenant von Haartman took over the responsibility for the work provisionally, she being definitely appointed leader in the September with the rank of Adjutant. This was a tremendous task for a young woman not too strong physically. Of an academical turn of mind—she could converse fluently in French, German, Swedish and English—and somewhat reserved, the Adjutant was more accustomed to obey than to command; nevertheless, she possessed an indomitable spirit and soon had things moving.

The Army's work attracted the attention of the Russian Government and, having fears regarding the future, von Haartman sent the Governor-General a copy of William Booth's *In Darkest England and the Way out*, and then sought an interview with him. The Governor-General was greatly impressed by the Adjutant's calm, modest dignity, her common sense and her message, and gave his consent for the continuation of the activities of the Salvationists. Captain (later Lieut.-Colonel) George Bramhall arrived from England soon after the opening to help the little group of officers with music and book-keeping. Souls became converted despite the opposition. Within four months the names of 80 soldiers and recruits had been placed on the roll, and the average Sunday night congregation numbered 900. The first meeting in Finnish was conducted on 23 May by Lieutenant von Haartman, who had considerable difficulty in speaking the language of which she, in common with most members of the Swedish-speaking "upper classes" of those days, had very little knowledge.

In June the Headquarters was moved to 27 Mikonkatu, the house of Baroness Valborg von Kothen, who later was to become a soldier and a *War Cry* seller. On the 8th of the month the first Army wedding was celebrated. Commissioner Railton had visited Finland for five days during Easter and had been much impressed by the progress that had been made in so short a time. A band of seven instrumentalists was formed. It is interesting to note here that Finnish Salvationists wear two letters—a crossed " P " and " F "—on their uniform, the " P " being for Pelastus and the " F " for Frälsning, the Finnish and Swedish words respectively for Salvation.

In the London *War Cry* for 27 December, the Christmas Number of 1890, Adjutant (later Lieut.-Commissioner) James Toft, who had arrived in the August from England, reports that " although Hell seems to have mustered all its black forces . . . yet God has very wonderfully indeed led things, so that our aim in coming here has been gained " ; but all open-air work was forbidden. The average sale of *Krigsropet*—the Swedish edition of the *War Cry*—and *Pelastusarmeija* (*The Salvation Army*) edited in Finnish, sold 1,500 weekly at Helsingfors corps. The second opening took place on 18 August 1890 at Borgå, a town of some 4,000 inhabitants ; the third, opened five weeks later, was at Hämeenlinna, a military town with a garrison of 1,000 Russian soldiers. This was the first Finnish corps. A Swedish corps at Åbo, a seaport of 25,000 inhabitants, one half speaking Finnish and the other half Swedish, was opened in October by women-officers. An unfrocked minister of religion was a capture here, and the policemaster thanked the officers for helping him with the drunkards. At Pori, another seaport, the first two Finnish lad-lieutenants were "making the salvation fire blaze." Here the officer was arrested, taken by prison-sleigh to Åbo and then to Helsingfors, but was soon afterwards set free by the Governor.

In November five corps with 19 officers and about 200 soldiers had been established and an auxiliary league [1] met

[1] Non-Salvationist friends

in the home of Baroness von Kothen. In 1892 Baroness Hisinger-Jägerskiöld, another auxiliary member, wrote: "The devil is attacking us in different ways; by discouragement, by making us think we cannot achieve anything; by putting apparently insuperable obstacles in our way." In June of that year Captain Glad, of Helsingfors IV, was imprisoned for fourteen days, as she was unable to pay the fines imposed upon her in Åbo for defying the ban on the holding of public meetings. A congress was conducted in September by Major Oliphant. Yet another auxiliary, Alma Forsblom, a promising young opera singer, was later to become an officer of high rank. The first distribution to the poor at Christmastime was made in this same year. Twelve corps had been opened by the spring of 1893, besides four slum corps and several outposts; the officers numbered 41.

Opposition was still very much alive in official circles and expulsion from the country of all foreigners belonging to the Army was insisted upon by the Governor-General. The law maintained that the organization was of foreign extraction; therefore, by removing the foreigners it was thought that the work would be extinguished throughout the country. It was while attending a congress in Copenhagen in 1893 that Major von Haartman received a telegram announcing the date when the first batch of alien officers under her command would be expelled. The only English officers were the Chief Secretary, Staff-Captain Jackson, and his wife. The other foreigners were Swedes. One policemaster declared that he would not lay a finger upon these foreign Salvationists until he was driven to it.

In September 1894 Colonel Sowton, upon arriving to conduct the annual congress, was informed by the authorities that he must leave the country; but at the end of its fifth year of work The Salvation Army in Finland had much for which to thank God. Work among children had been started, printed regulations issued, junior soldier local officers appointed and a Christmas feast held in Helsingfors. In 1895 the Helsingfors Temple was built. William Booth gave the work an appreciated stimulus when he visited the country in 1897, the same year that Brigadier von Haartman received marching orders for Switzerland, leaving 38 corps and the beginnings of the Social Work.[1]

A book in Finnish, *Kaikkea Pelastusarmeijasta* (All about The Salvation Army), was published in 1901 and in 1904 Mildred Duff's *Hedwig von Haartman* was translated into both Finnish and Swedish.

Chapter Ten

BELGIUM

Adjutant Charles Rankin, the Scottish principal of the Amsterdam training home, and Mrs Rankin, were appointed from Holland to open Belgium, which they did on Sunday, 5 May 1889, at seven o'clock in the morning. It was originally intended to commence in Ghent, but a friend in Malines consented to give the pioneers lessons in Flemish, and so this ancient city—the seat of the Archbishop-Primate —heard the first shots from the Salvationists in the " Frascati " concert hall, owned by the next-door publican, within twenty yards of the market square. The people of the city had the crudest notions about *Reddings Leger* (The Salvation Army), and the disappointing results of the opening battles, during which stinking chemicals were scattered on the floor, were not commensurate with the Rankins' expectations. Captains Haas and Veleema were

[1] *The History of The Salvation Army*, vol iii, p. 117

the corps officers and they, with the help of the Foreign Secretary at International Headquarters, Colonel (later Commissioner) A. M. Nicol, who had rented a hall in both Ghent and Malines during a prospecting visit in 1888, participated in this initial skirmish.

The first fortnight was a desperate struggle against the powers of darkness, and then came the "smash." The first convert was a prodigal son who soon began to wear a red guernsey and sell the newly-published *De Krygstrompet* (The War Trumpet) in the streets. A publican, his wife and son were also among the new converts. Within three months two cadets had been sent to the Amsterdam training home. One of them had been saved before the Army arrived in Malines through reading a copy of *En Avant*, the French War Cry.

Commissioner Railton was soon on the scene, as usual, and was greatly impressed by the possibilities presented. By the end of June the hall was being crammed to the ceiling almost every night, the order was splendid and the three biggest drunkards in Malines had knelt at the penitent-form together. The Commissioner conducted in Brussels the first watchnight service, which was attended by a few Salvationists and friends, although no barracks had yet been opened in the capital.

The opening of Ghent took place on 24 February 1890, and Adjutant Tuckwell was keeping up a most active campaign in Brussels. A private letter published in *All the World* for December tells of a splendid time in a great theatre, with a battalion of 24 policemen to keep order, which, apparently on this occasion at least, presented no difficulty. Testimony was given by a man who had been a frightful drunkard before conversion, when not a policeman in Ghent would dare to lay a hand on him for fear of being murdered.

In March Major and Mrs Lee were appointed to take command of operations in Belgium. These were now following the usual pattern for pioneers, for two officers had just previously been sentenced to prison for five days for leading a march through the streets of Malines, but an appeal to a superior court resulted in the sentence being quashed. This was the Army's first legal victory in Belgium. Within weeks Major and Mrs Percy Clibborn were placed in command of the country, they being assisted by Staff-Captain and Mrs Schoch, of Holland. The first swearing-in under the flag was conducted in September, the presentation of colours to the first French-Belgium (Walloon) corps taking place at Damprémy soon after. Although no halls were obtainable, by November 5 corps had been opened, 30 officers were at work, and 2 editions of *The War Cry*—one printed in French, *Cri de Guerre*, and the other in Flemish—had a united circulation of 5,000 copies. The *War Cry* could be purchased from public kiosks and was also sold by newsboys. Major Clibborn accepted the invitation of publicans to hold meetings in their halls, which were attached to the drinking saloons. The publicans hoped to do extra business by this ruse, but the Salvationists were successful in turning the tables, bringing about the conversion of customers and forming the nucleus of a fighting force for God. No fewer than 136,000 drinking saloons were operative in this little country at the time. The first headquarters, a disused skating rink, at 32 Boulevard Baudouin, in Brussels, was opened in January 1891, but under a great cloud of sorrow and mystery.

Major James Vint,[1] the Assistant Foreign Secretary, who had arrived in Brussels six months before to complete the purchase of the building, had been assassinated when leaving his hotel in St Josse. It was thought that a member of a

[1] See p. 10

secret society who had knelt at the mercy-seat in Rome, where the Major had begun operations in 1887, had divulged some of its secrets to him and in consequence another member of the society had been deputed to murder Vint when the opportunity presented itself.

About this time Major Clibborn had as his A.D.C. a young man in his early twenties, Adjutant Theodore H. Kitching, who was to become William Booth's almost indispensable henchman for many years, a Commissioner, and father of the Army's seventh General, Wilfred Kitching.

At Ledeberg forty soldiers were on the roll and a band of twelve, nearly all of whom had been Catholics, had been formed by September 1891. Marchienne was the scene of the wildest disorder—rowdyism, bomb-throwing, stone-peltings, and window smashings—from the time of its opening, but when the "Travelling Commissioners of General Booth" paid the town a visit the commissioner of police came to the hall to see things for himself. The result was that next evening four gendarmes were telegraphed for from Brussels; spurred, helmeted, armed and mounted before the hall, they kept perfect order. A young man here was sent to prison by his own father for being a Salvationist. The town being in the midst of the mining district, children were sent to work underground at the age of seven, women groaned under burdens too heavy for men, men were undersized and all seemed demoralized.

Among many remarkable conversions which took place in Belgium was that of Antomarchi, grandson of a military leader in Napoleon's wars. Because of his evil living, Antomarchi decided to end his life; but after meeting with two young Salvationists he entered an Army hall on 3 March 1892 and gave himself to God. Eventually he became an officer and served in France, Belgium and Italy. His old father also became a Salvationist and wore his

Legion of Honour star on his red guernsey. Later Antomarchi made himself a name in the French Protestant world as the author of a number of excellent books of Bible study.

Major Clibborn was a heavily-bearded officer, and even this fact was not without its significance for, upon rising from the penitent-form, a woman said that one of the things which made her believe in the Salvationists was " Que le Major avait une barbe comme le bon Dieu ! " (The Major had a beard like the good God). In May 1893 Major and Mrs Clibborn were succeeded by Major (later Colonel) Mary Tait and Staff-Captain Minnie Reid (later to become Mrs Commissioner Booth-Tucker). When Colonel (later Commissioner) McKie conducted a Congress in June a torchlight procession was allowed to march through the principal boulevards of Brussels, the band playing " The Marseillaise."

At that time Belgium was a separate command, but at the beginning of 1896 it was re-attached to Holland. Now it was given the status of a province, Major Palstra being appointed Provincial Commander, and Commissioner and Mrs Booth-Clibborn as Territorial Commanders for the two countries. In 1903 Belgium became a province of the French territory, Brigadier Fritz Malan being the Provincial Commander and Commissioner Cosandey the Territorial Commander.

Chapter Eleven

SOUTH AMERICA EAST

ARGENTINA

On the platform of the Exeter Hall, London, on 25 November 1889, Colonel and Mrs Henry Thurman—who had already served in Australia and South Africa—Captain (later Lieut.-Colonel) William Bonnett and Captain Frederick Calvert were dedicated by the General under the Argentine flag for service in the republic. They, with Sister Alice Turner, who eventually became an officer, left five days later. The Army had a few friends in Buenos Aires, the capital city, including John McCarthy, who was later to pioneer the work in Uruguay, some Swiss Salvationists who had emigrated, and some converted Spaniards known to an Army friend, Mr Armstrong, who was resident in Spain.[1] At that time Argentina held a considerable population of Englishmen, many of whom were employed on a railway being built from Buenos Aires across the continent to Chile.

Arriving on 22 December, the pioneers discovered Buenos Aires to be a city of 600,000 cosmopolitan inhabitants ; nationals and Spaniards formed the majority, and the remainder included a great body of Italians, French and Germans, but comparatively few English. Most of the men carried arms, and human life was cheap. Violent means were often used to settle disputes. The city was nominally Roman Catholic, but infidelity was abundantly rampant. A hall was secured at an excessive cost and was soon crowded with a curious but attentive Spanish-speaking congregation. A gang of roughs indulged in stone-throwing while the Salvationists held their open-air meetings. Nevertheless, converts were made. A *War Cry* printed in English and dated 25 January 1890 was the fore-runner of *El Cruzado*. Another hall was opened before the end of April, and there were prospects up-country.

Colonel Thurman was only a few weeks in Argentina before he asked for a change of appointment. He had been disillusioned. Headquarters had been given to understand that the 15,000 persons who comprised the British colony

[1] p. 66

were to be found in the capital, whereas they were scattered over an area ten times the size of Great Britain. Originally under the impression that the work could be established in the language of their homeland, and that officers raised from the converts could then be sent into every part of the South American continent, the pioneers had soon realized that this was not possible and that if they were to be effective they would have to learn Spanish and turn to the Argentines themselves.

The Colonel was succeeded by Major Barritt who, with Mrs Barritt, headed a fresh contingent of officers. The barracks were situated in Calle Cambaceres, in the centre of the city, and here the welcome meeting took place. Among the new converts was a policeman. Included in the officers of those days was Staff-Captain (later Lieut.-Commissioner) Stanley R. Ewens, who took with him a young fellow, Scribe Alfred J. Benwell, who spent fifteen years in Argentina and was to become a Commissioner. New premises were almost immediately afterward found in la Boca, a dockside district of Buenos Aires, so thickly populated by Genoese immigrants that Italian was spoken more commonly than Spanish. The officers in the capital were so poor at this time that they were glad to pick out for their dinner the best bits of scraps sent them in a can by one of the hotels.

It was not long before a revolution overtook the Argentine Republic. A corrupt government fell, discredited before the world. For two or three days civil war raged in all its horrors in Buenos Aires, and the principal streets were strewn with dead and dying. In the midst of the shambles Major Barritt and his little band of Crusaders—" Ejército de Salvación "—went to the rescue, although they had frequent and narrow escapes from death. The salvation war continued to make progress, and the *War Cry* was sold in the streets like a special edition of an evening paper full of fascinating news.

At the end of fifteen months it could be reported that although the fight had been hard, and to all appearances defeat had been inevitable for the Salvationists, " now we can daily and hourly report victory." Wars, rumours of wars, revolutions and internal dissensions continued to multiply ; the closing of the banks was a financial disaster, but " our work was never so flourishing." At meetings held in the summer of 1891, in one of the most influential churches in Buenos Aires, and at a lecture held in the rooms of the English Literary Society, university professors spoke of the good effected by The Salvation Army, and the first newspaper in the city reported the lecture in full. Some of the railway and tramway companies presented the leader and other officers with free travel passes. The largest of the meat factories sold meat for the soup kitchens at the equivalent of two pounds for a penny.

Nevertheless, the opposition made itself manifest. An officer was stabbed in the face, Benwell had the muzzle of a revolver thrust against his chest and later was imprisoned with his Captain, and doors, windows and shutters of halls were broken. The " vigilantes " (police) co-operated with the Salvationists. Alarmed at the progress being made, a Roman Catholic archbishop issued a pamphlet containing many of the charges and allegations made against the Army in other countries and disposed of years before. At Tala the priest threatened to excommunicate any of his people who attended Army meetings. For several weeks during 1890 four of the pioneer officers, including the seventeen-year-old Lieutenant Benwell, lay between life and death with smallpox and fever. By the end of the year four corps had been opened and twenty officers were engaged in the Salvation war.

SOUTH AMERICA EAST

URUGUAY

Almost as soon as Salvation Army operations were commenced in Argentina, news was received from some Swiss comrades who had been holding meetings at Cosmopolita, Uruguay. They were described as " a little troop of soldiers " who received the *War Cry* and had obtained " S's." Now they wanted officers to command them, but nearly a year went by before it was possible to comply with their request. However, on Sunday, 16 November 1890, The Salvation Army " took possession " of the Republic of Uruguay in the town of La Paz, near Cosmopolita. The pioneer officer was Captain John McCarthy who, upon arrival at the colony, was saluted by a man saying, " Where-ever you may go you are sure to meet The Salvation Army." The barracks was so full that many were compelled to remain outside the building. Disturbance was inevitable on the second night, but within weeks fifty-one people, including whole families, accepted Christ. An advance was soon afterwards made in Rincón, Cosmopolita and Sauce, and also in the Swiss colony. The Waldensian pastor defended the Salvationists against evil tongues.

Converts were speedily commissioned as sergeants and set to work to open outposts. When passing through Montevideo, the capital, Major Barritt found two Salvationists who were holding a weekly meeting in the name of the Army. On returning to Buenos Aires he immediately dispatched a group of six officers to form Uruguay into a division, with Staff-Captain Ewens as the leader. Within three months three corps were in operation in this city. The editor of the *Montevidean Times* published a long article about the Army's advent and headed a subscription list of donations toward its work.

Chapter Twelve

RHODESIA

A pioneer party, sent out by the Territorial Commander for South Africa, Commissioner Thomas Estill, and led by Major John Pascoe, and including Mrs Pascoe, their two children, a "nursemaid" and five men-officers, started from Kimberley for Mashonaland (Rhodesia) at midnight on Tuesday, 5 May 1891. They trekked in a wagon named "Enterprise," drawn by eighteen oxen, on what proved to be a six and a half months' very trying journey of one thousand miles to Fort Salisbury, which was reached on 18 November. Mr Cecil Rhodes was there to greet the Salvationists and to promise that a farm and two building sites in the town which he planned to build would be allotted to the Army. Two horses had been lost by sickness in one week on this journey and another had died two days after it had been exchanged for two oxen. Dr Jameson, the Administrator, carried out Rhodes' promise and granted the Army land for a barracks and a farm of 3,000 acres in the Mazoe Valley, some sixteen miles north of Fort Salisbury. This farm was, in 1892, given the name of Pearson, after Colonel William J. Pearson, who had recently passed away.[1]

Major Pascoe had a grand opening on Saturday, 21 November, parading the township with his wagon and sixteen oxen and holding crowded Sunday meetings in an unfurnished billiard-room lent for the purpose. The correspondent of the *Cape Town Argus* said of the pioneers that "their behaviour and presence here since their arrival would not be discreditable to the Archbishops of Canterbury and York, with a couple of deans and archdeacons thrown in. . . . Last Saturday their band turned out and proved

[1] *The History of The Salvation Army*, vol ii, pp. 43, 72, 107

excellent players. . . . Mrs Pascoe . . . has won the name of being the earliest public singer of Zambesia, as her brethren have that of playing the first brass band the Mashonas have ever heard." Soon after its arrival every member of the party was stricken down with fever. Fort Salisbury corps was formed with Captain David Crook and Lieutenant Theodore Seale, who came from St Helena, in charge. The first corps for nationals was established within the first twelve months in the Mazoe Valley, under the command of Captains Edward T. Cass and Robert H. Scott. This was something of an achievement because at first the people ran away in horror at sight of the white men. Indeed, it took a considerable time for the officers to get near to them and gain their confidence. The first white baby to be born in Salisbury, Mashonaland, was the child of Salvation Army parents, Major and Mrs Pascoe, who named him Frank Salisbury.

Toward the end of 1893 operations in the Mazoe Valley came to a standstill on account of the Matabele raids on the Mashonas. The officers were ordered by the authorities to leave all they had at the farm and take refuge in Fort Salisbury, which was under arms and expecting attack and bloodshed. Eventually they returned to their posts, but were not able to go out after dark owing to the presence of lions in the vicinity.

Fort Salisbury corps had to be closed because of the war in Mashonaland, but was re-opened later, in 1894, by Adjutant W. R. Taylor—the Pascoes having resigned—with whom was Mrs Taylor and Captain Charlotte A. Griffin, who went out to marry Captain Cass. *En route* on the three months' journey the Adjutant was confined to the wagon for four days with fever, and lions and wolves prowled unpleasantly near.

Another unfortunate setback to the work occurred in the

same year when the buildings on Pearson Farm were destroyed by fire, and the officers lost all their belongings, barely escaping with their lives. In March 1896, the Matabele rose in rebellion against the whites and the Mashonas sided with the rebels in June. While trying with other men to convey to safety a party of women, including his wife, in a wagon, Captain Cass was murdered in an ambush near Mazoe.[1] The work in Mashonaland was suspended following the death of the Captain and the breakdown in health of Adjutant and Mrs Taylor, who returned to South Africa with Mrs Cass. Work was restarted at the conclusion of the Boer War in 1901, Commissioner Kilbey visited the country and took with him Adjutant Fred Bradley, whose only companion for a long time was Lieutenant Joel Mbambo Matunjwa, the first Zulu convert.[2] Bradley, who afterward became a Lieut.-Colonel, and his wife laid the foundation of the successful operations that are now existent in Rhodesia.

Chapter Thirteen

INDONESIA

In the summer of 1894, a Dutch officer, Ensign Adolf van Emmerik, who, before being commissioned, had spent many years in Java, visited International Headquarters and gave much valuable information with a view to the Army commencing in that colony, which then had a population of 26,000,000. As a result of this visit Staff-Captain Jacob G. Brouwer[3] was appointed to open up the work and he

[1] A new road in a suburb of Salisbury was in 1957 named Cass Avenue in memory of this brave pioneer

[2] p. 134

[3] Afterwards Lieut.-Colonel, Order of Orange Nassau, O.F.

and the Ensign farewelled from Amsterdam toward the end of October. They arrived on Friday, 24 November, and the following day were both laid low with a heavy fever. Even before they had left Holland the Dutch East Indies Government had cabled the Home Government to prevent the invasion of Java by *Het Leger des Heils*, and a well-known Dutch missionary had advised the Governor-General not to allow the Salvationists to commence their work. "The Salvation Army is not wanted in this prosperous colony, with its idealistic conditions," declared the clergy and also a high government official. Nevertheless, the Governor-General received the pioneers with much kindness and wished them every success, although he advised them to go to a district away from the Europeans and from Mohammedan influence. The Dutch missionary later confessed his mistake and did some very useful translations for the Army, while his own daughter became sergeant-major of one of the native corps.

On the same steamer by which the Staff-Captain and Ensign travelled was a star in the musical world whom they often tackled about his soul. Within a very short time this man, on account of his dissipations, was banished from the country and at government expense sent back to his homeland. Upon arrival, he was met by a Salvation Army officer and taken to an industrial home ; here he made good.

In accordance with the Governor-General's advice the pioneers first took up their abode at Poerworedjo, in Central Java, in an open gallery belonging to a district head, but eventually found quarters in the home of an elderly couple who were Christians. Later the Staff-Captain and his second became convinced that the best place to begin operations was away from the town, at Sapuran, some fifty miles distant. Therefore, to this small centre in the mountains they walked, an eight days' journey. Here the first headquarters was set up, and the first corps opened among a few Christians, sheep without a shepherd, who used to hold a Sunday morning service, led by the eldest of them. The pioneers had attended this meeting on their first Sunday in the place, and had been asked to speak. The Staff-Captain found that drunkenness was unknown and thieving very seldom encountered. The people lived in peace with each other, but the false interpretation of religious duties by conscienceless so-called (non-Christian) religious leaders was "the curse of the land." As in India, the pioneers dressed in native garb and walked with bare feet. This made a great impression and Javanese, Chinese, Arabians, Negroes and Hindoos flocked to the meetings, but government officials resented this departure from custom.

In the second year re-inforcements arrived in the persons of Ensign Alice Cleverly, van Emmerik's fianceé, and Ensign Claydon, who had served in India. After the Emmeriks were married a corps was opened at Semarang. Work was started among military men, in prisons and in the open air. Toward the end of 1895 a police official in Semarang forbade the Salvationists to hold open-air meetings, and threatened them with imprisonment. He received the reply that they were not transgressing the law, but in accordance with Article No. 119 had perfect liberty to profess their religion and intended to continue doing so. Orders were issued to take proceedings against the Salvationists, but were withdrawn, and no more was heard of the matter.

The people were slow and cautious with regard to adopting Christianity ; but notwithstanding, within a year or so ninety-five had knelt at the penitent-form, and forty-six had become either soldiers or recruits. The first convert, a Manadonese military man, remained a Salvationist for nearly forty years until his death. Among the earliest converts were three opium slaves, one of them being in the

International Pioneers

1 Fritz Schaaff (Germany) 2 James B. Vint (Italy) 3 Gerritt J. Govaars (Holland) 4 C. F. Schoch (Holland) 5 Robert Perry (Denmark) 6 Alexander Alexander (British Guiana) 7 George Morris (St Lucia) 8 Albert Orsborn (Norway) 9 Christian Erickson (Iceland) 10 Baron Constantin A. L. Boije (Finland) 11 Charles Rankin (Belgium) 12 William Bonnett (Argentina) 13 John Pascoe (Rhodesia) 14 Jacob G. Brouwer (Indonesia) 15 Walter M. Powell (Japan) 16 John Milsaps (The Philippines)

International Pioneers

1 George D. Egner (Hawaiian Islands) 2–3 Mary and Annie Hartelius (Scandinavian Work, U.S.A.) 4–5 Captain and Mrs Dawson (Newfoundland) 6 Lutie DesBrisay (Bermuda) 7 James Osborne (Zululand) 8–9 George and Mrs Harris (St Helena) 10 Arthur Young (Newfoundland) 11–12 Hedwig von Haartman and Alva Forsius (Finland) 13 Fritz Malan (Italy) 14 Gunpei Yamamuro (Japan) 15–16 Major and Mrs Gordon (Italy)

habit of spending on opium seven guilders weekly (eleven shillings and sixpence), a hefty sum in those days.

For Salvation Army purposes Java was made a division of Australia under Major F. Cumming in 1898. Some little time before, Staff-Captain Brouwer had received permission from the Governor-General to visit the prison in Semarang and hold meetings with the prisoners. Later, permission was extended so that all prisons in Indonesia could be visited. The first Salvation Army hall was built in 1899 by the officers themselves, the Javanese population in the district providing the money. In the meantime the headquarters had been established in Semarang. The first *War Cry*, a monthly periodical, with three pages in Malay and one in Dutch, was published in 1900.

In 1903 Captain Annie Healey, an Australian officer, while ministering to the sick, was fatally stricken with small-pox. The Resident of Semarang sent a letter of sympathy to Major James Glover, who was then the officer-in-charge, which stated that the Captain's "too early departure will be a great loss for the sick and poor at Kajen." All the native chiefs of the district attended the funeral at dusk, riding on horseback in full official garb and carrying lances and flaming torches. Captain Julius Jessen, a German officer trained in Australia, also laid down his life while helping the sick during a cholera epidemic.

Chapter Fourteen

SPAIN

Interested in Spain from the days of his youth, George Scott Railton visited Barcelona in 1868, and twenty years later called upon an Army friend, Mr Armstrong, of Valladolid,[1] who had nine congregations under his care and who used Salvation Army songs in his meetings. On this occasion Railton himself conducted a few meetings, but it was six years, in the latter part of 1894, before he really got down to prospecting in Spain with a view to establishing the Army's work there. Early in the New Year he secured a small carpenter's shop in Madrid at 54 Calle del Olivar. Here he held regular meetings and distributed cheap meals to the poor, being assisted by Captain Venegas, a Spanish officer he had encountered in the Argentine. Several converts were made and soldiers enrolled before a new and larger hall was opened in the autumn. Later mat-making and hammock-making was started for the unemployed. The editor of one of the leading dailies spoke of the work in the highest terms and referred to the General as the Apostle of the Nineteenth Century. This paper, and another leading Madrid periodical, opened its columns to the Army for advertisements and reports free of charge. Another newspaper, however, came out with an attack, but Commissioner Railton managed eventually to get the reporter converted. In one meeting 27 persons sought salvation and 150 entered their names as desiring to become Salvationists.

Railton returned to England at the end of June in a serious condition of health and in the November Major and Mrs Stanley Ewens were appointed to Spain, the Army's statutes having received the government's sanction and a ten-roomed headquarters having been leased for twelve months. The Major was first to prospect in Barcelona before going to Madrid; but his appointment was soon cancelled. Captain Wirtz, a Spaniard trained in London, and Mrs Wirtz, were next appointed, and were followed

[1] p. 56

in the February of 1896 by a party of officers. What happened to them is lost in oblivion, but the work suddenly came to an end. It would appear that Commissioner Railton's early success was largely because it was thought he was the representative of a new military order of the Roman Catholic Church, for at this time he took to wearing a large yellow cross emblazoned on his red guernsey. When it became clear that The Salvation Army was not linked to the Church no freedom of activity was allowed and the position became impossible.[1]

Chapter Fifteen

JAPAN

With the hope of introducing The Salvation Army into his native Japan, Cadet Shinobu L. Nagasaka, a member of the Samurai Order, travelled from San Francisco to London in 1893 to lay the needs of his country before the General. Brought up in the Buddhist faith, he had eventually become a Christian, as had his wife, and hearing the call to engage in missionary service he had left her and their four children to work in the Hawaiian Islands. While in San Francisco he had encountered the Army, claimed the blessing of full salvation, entered the training garrison, and translated some 200 Army songs and other literature into both Chinese and Japanese.

Evidently the General was interested in the cadet's proposals, for in the autumn of the following year he

[1] Commissioner Catherine Bramwell-Booth gathered that this is what had happened from conversations she heard at home at the time

appointed Colonel Paynter to farewell from India to take command of the work to be established in Japan, despite the fact that war was being waged in the Far East. But the Colonel did not leave India, and Colonel and Mrs Wilson, at the head of a small contingent of officers, farewelled for Japan in the Royal Albert Hall, London, in March 1895. Mrs Wilson, however, could not make the long journey, as the doctors refused to give her a clean bill of health. Eventually Colonel and Mrs Edward Wright were chosen to be Japan's first leaders. The Colonel had been a pioneer in New Zealand,[1] following which he had seen service in Australia. The Japanese expedition sailed on 21 July after having been farewelled from the City Temple. In the party were Brigadier (later Lieut.-Colonel) Walter M. Powell and Captain (later Lieut.-Colonel) Matilda Hatcher.

The pioneers, attired in Japanese costume, arrived at Yokohama on Wednesday, 4 September. That night, when walking through the European quarter, the Colonel passed a public-house in which a piano was being thumped as the accompaniment to a man's lusty voice. He was singing:

The Salvation Army has come !
The Salvation Army has come !
O Lord, have mercy upon us !
The Salvation Army has come !

Learning of the Salvationists' arrival in Tokyo, where a headquarters was secured, and being impressed by their teaching, a property-owner resolved to order his 300 tenants to join the Army at once on pain of instant eviction. When it was explained that no such compulsion could be permitted, he said that he would give them a reasonable time to decide

[1] *The History of The Salvation Army*, vol ii, p. 293

for themselves and then, if they did not yield, he would raise their rents!

The Salvationists were known as the *Kyu Sei Gun* (Save the World Army), nearest equivalent to The Salvation Army. The principal Japanese newspapers welcomed them and a reporter, having collected the information he required, said, " Now I want to be saved ! " and was prayed with on the spot. The first meeting was conducted on the following Sunday in the large Young Men's Christian Association hall, which was filled. In smaller meetings held on the same day the first four Japanese penitents were recorded. The first corps was established in a building on the Ginza, the main street of Tokyo, and after a few weeks more than sixty seekers had knelt at the penitent-form.

One of the earliest captures in Tokyo—he was already a Christian—was a student, Gunpei Yamamuro,[1] who was employed by Colonel Wright as a hall-door coolie in order that he could study the Army more closely. Yamamuro had been greatly impressed by the aims of William Booth's *In Darkest England and the Way Out*, which he had heard read aloud, and also through his own reading of *Orders and Regulations for Soldiers*. Eventually he became a Salvationist and was appointed a Lieutenant, being the first officer of Japanese nationality in Japan. In course of time he was to receive the rank of Commissioner and become Territorial Commander of his native country.

The publication of *Toki-no-Koe* (The War Cry) was not at first a success as its language—as was that of all religious papers—was that of the classical and not the colloquial Japanese with which the poorer people were acquainted. Appointed editor by Colonel Henry Bullard,[2] who had followed Colonel Bailey, the successor to Colonel

[1] *Soldier of Peace*, by Cyril J. Barnes (Victory Book)
[2] *This Quiet Man*, by Catherine Sturgess (Liberty booklet)

Wright, Captain Yamamuro created an innovation by producing a paper in words that the most simple Japanese could understand. A young Christian woman-tutor, Kiye Sato,[1] became an officer and Yamamuro married her in 1899. During their honeymoon the bridegroom prepared the manuscript of *The Common People's Gospel*,[2] which was to become a classic in Japan and the means of innumerable conversions.

Upon arriving in 1900 Colonel Bullard found that, although the Army had been working in Japan for five years, it had as yet no buildings of its own; he thereupon secured halls in a number of cities during a very difficult period. The Army's indoor meetings then became much more popular. Open-air work had never been restricted in the country and considerable crowds attended the gatherings.

Chapter Sixteen

GIBRALTAR

Major George P. Ewens, the first editor of the *War Cry*, was appointed to start operations in Gibraltar, mainly because of his knowledge of Spanish, and he and Mrs Ewens left London on 10 January 1895. A Presbyterian military quartermaster, who had formerly disliked the Army, invited them to hold a cottage-meeting in his house, and eleven people sought salvation, three of them being

[1] Her brother, Kozo Sato, became an admiral and Commander-in-Chief of the Japanese fleet in the Mediterranean Sea, during the First World War

[2] This has now run into its 480th edition. Dr Toyohiko Kagawa considered it to be 'imperishable'

members of the family. This resulted in the Major being able to conduct Army meetings in the Presbyterian church. A home was later opened for sailors and soldiers[1] in the Ewens' rooms, which were situated in a "ramp," as the alleys of Gibraltar were called. In September, the pioneers' successors, Adjutant and Mrs Ellis, opened a four-roomed store in Engineer's Lane, the upstairs front room being a meeting-place by day and a shelter by night, the beds being moved in and out by the residents themselves.

Public-house visitation with the *War Cry* resulted in many servicemen being brought to the mercy-seat. A hall being unobtainable, the military authorities gave permission for the Salvationists to use their schoolrooms for meetings. A weekly gathering of servicemen was also held on board one of Her Majesty's ships.

Chapter Seventeen

HONG KONG

When the Japanese pioneer party under Colonel Wright arrived in Hong Kong harbour on Tuesday, 27 August 1895, it was met by Brother Joseph, formerly a soldier of the Great Western (Marylebone) corps, who informed the Colonel that about a score of Salvationists, mostly military men, were living in the city of Kowloon, and that a meeting had been arranged in a small room belonging to Brother Mears. Leaving the ship the party, singing lively songs, marched through the military quarters to this meeting-room, which was crowded with some fifty Europeans.

[1] *The History of The Salvation Army*, vol iii, p. 290

On the Thursday the Wesleyan chaplain offered the Colonel the use of his church for the evening, and 1,000 handbills were hurriedly printed and distributed. The flag was unfurled, Brother Joseph being installed as flag-carrier, the Colonel and Ensign Goslin played their concertinas, Lieutenant Hart "scraped away on the fiddle," and the rest of the party fell in behind for the first organized Salvation Army march in Hong Kong. Thousands of people "walked up" on either side of the streets to the church where a good number of military men were gathered.

In the early part of 1898 Staff-Captain Symons arrived in Hong Kong and, within two days of landing, found a house which he fitted up as a seamen's home.[1] Within a few months all the beds were full every night.

Chapter Eighteen

MALTA

When Malta was ceded to England in 1800 a rather curious treaty was entered into with the Maltese Government: no work of a religious nature should be attempted among natives of the island for one hundred years. Nevertheless, as far back as 1886 a friend of the Army living on the island was distributing copies of the *War Cry* sent him from London. Later, Sergeant-Instructor Evans, R.M.L.I., who had formed the members of the Naval and Military League into a corps, desired, with them, that an officer be sent to Malta. He dispatched a letter to the General, who responded

[1] *The History of The Salvation Army*, vol iii, p. 290

to their appeal by sending Staff-Captain John Henry Gordon to investigate the possibilities. When he arrived, in the latter part of 1895, he found the birthday of William Booth registered on a Maltese Roman Catholic almanac, and the Army already represented by some forty sailors and twelve soldiers.[1] The Staff-Captain and his wife led meetings in Valetta, the capital, in the San Lorenzo soldiers' and sailors' home and also in the schoolroom of the Presbyterian church. Ensign and Mrs Pike were appointed to take charge of the work in Malta and they arrived at Valletta on Sunday, 25 July 1896. Soon afterwards a 400-year-old building, which had originally been a palace but was then being used as a Methodist church, was taken over by the Army. Operations were begun among the children of the dockyard employees and numbers of servicemen were converted.

Chapter Nineteen

THE PHILIPPINES

As the first Salvation Army chaplain to be recognized by United States military forces, Major John Milsaps left San Francisco for Manila, capital of the Philippine Islands, on 29 June 1898, during the Spanish-American War. He arrived there just before the city fell to the besiegers. Major-General Wesley Merritt, first American Governor-General of the Philippines, had given him free transportation; Admiral Dewey had given him permission to hold meetings on vessels under his command; the jealously-guarded doors

[1] *The History of The Salvation Army*, vol iii, p. 290

of Bilibid Penal Prison swung open to him; and the first public meeting on the island was conducted on 3 September in the parlour of an old Spanish mansion at No 2 Calle Santa Elena. This became the Major's quarters. Six American soldiers and two Spanish boys constituted the entire congregation, which sat on the narrawood floor, there being no chairs or furniture. Song-books and Chinese candles were distributed to each person. Many meetings followed and more than one serving soldier found Christ. Other meetings were held in tents, under trees, on the top of the walls of Intramuros, the Spanish city within Manila, in the palatial homes of Spain's proud sons, here and there in the streets, under a theatre porch, and in the leper colony. Although the Salvation Army flag was not to fly officially in the Philippines until nearly forty years later, the work of Major Milsaps during this Philippino insurrection was remembered long after he had returned to the United States.

Chapter Twenty

WEST AFRICA

How The Salvation Army first came to be known in West Africa may forever remain a mystery, but in 1902 International Headquarters received a number of letters earnestly begging for someone to be sent there to open up the work, one of the correspondents signing himself "James Q. Napier, Captain." "Mrs Napier," he wrote, "has gone to bush to preach the Gospel and show them Christ and The Salvation Army." Evidently, too, *The Young Soldier* was known there. While the following story cannot be authenticated, it is not without likelihood: Some West Indian Salvationist-servicemen, when stationed in Sierra Leone, commenced Army meetings and gathered a large number of converts, from whom they appointed local officers, even giving them titles as Captains. Possibly "Captain and Mrs Napier" were left in charge of these unofficial forces, who were supplied with periodicals, books and insignia from the West Indies. In May 1903 the Army befriended and obtained justice in a London magistrate's court for six destitute young women from Sierra Leone, who had been participating in exhibitions in Europe and shamefully exploited by the showman. During the time they were under the Army's care all professed conversion.

Toward the end of 1903 Commissioner Railton was dispatched to West Africa on an important prospecting and pioneering tour—a tour that ended abruptly, for at Accra he suddenly became extremely ill and lay in an African hotel sick almost to death, with no one to attend him or even to bring a doctor. As usual, by preference, he was journeying alone. Eventually he was cared for by two African women with whom he had made friends and who had called to see him. Letters from various friends show that he had already visited Northern Nigeria, Kumasi, Elmina and Cape Coast; they testify to the blessing and inspiration they gained from contact with Railton and recalled with gratitude the earnest messages he gave in the open air.

Operations in West Africa did not commence officially until 1920 and then in Nigeria.

Chapter Twenty-one

RUSSIA

Although in 1888—during which year Major Rapkin visited the country—the censor in Russia approved of Salvation Army publications, in 1892 M. Paul Nardin, of the Department of Finances, St Petersburg, addressed official enquiries to local authorities throughout the civilized world requesting their opinion of the organization. M. Nardin had read *In Darkest England and the Way Out* and other Salvationist literature which, apparently, had impressed him, but he had also read some of the many accusations made against the Army, and he wanted to know the facts. Was it genuine and charitable ? If so, to what extent had it affected the moral and material welfare of outcasts ?

Two years later a Mr T. C. Booth, editor of *Timber and Wood Working Machinery*, who wished to visit Russia in connection with its wood-exporting trade, was turned back on the German-Russian frontier. No reason was given at the time, but when he returned to Königsberg he discovered that his " offence " consisted in his being suspected to have some connection with General Booth ! Despite his protestations to the contrary the ban remained, Mr Booth's only satisfaction being an expression of regret from the Russian Government.

Prince Nicholas Galitzin of Russia later closely investigated the evangelistic and social work of the Army in England, having previously seen something of its operations in Washington, D.C. and New York. He was a devoted Christian and accompanied the General on his campaign in Holland. Evidently misunderstandings had arisen in his country regarding Salvationists and he returned prepared to defend their work and methods ; but to the end of 1904 the Army was not represented in European Russia, with the exception of Finland,[1] which then had a constitutional government with the Czar as Grand Duke.

Chapter Twenty-two

CHINA, MALAYA AND WAYSIDE GLEANINGS

In a letter published in *All the World* for January 1888 Commissioner Tucker (Fakir Singh) stated that he had sent Staff-Captain Bradley (Yuddha Singh) and Captain Bailey (Johangir) to " survey China " in response to repeated invitations received from Mr Charles T. Studd and other friends. The officers were instructed not to commence work, but only to consult with friends and collect information. Operations in China were not begun until 1916.

* * *

Although work in Malaya was not established until 1935, two Indian missionary officers, Captains Sarah Byrne and Blanche Gearing, went reconnoitring in Johore in August 1892 from Singapore and called upon the Sultan, His Highness Abur Bakar, G.C.M.G., K.C.S.I., at his palace, where they were kindly received. The Sultan introduced them to his wife. They explained the nature of their work in India and referred to *In Darkest England and the Way Out*.

" Oh, I have the book," said the Sultan, " and am not unacquainted with the work of The Salvation Army. Who

[1] p. 45

has not heard of General Booth ?" His Highness sent back the lasses to Singapore on the following day in one of his carriages.

* * *

References were made from time to time in both the *War Cry* and *All the World* to people who became converted in various countries in which the Army has never been properly established. Born and trained as a carpenter in Nazareth, a young Arab was converted at Port Said largely through an open-air meeting conducted there by Commissioner Booth-Tucker, while the vessel in which he and the "Jubilee Fifty"[1] were travelling to India was awaiting her turn to enter the Suez Canal. This man, Geris Hanne, eventually found his way to London and later, in 1888, was commissioned an officer to work among Arabs in India, having as his first Lieutenant, Narayana Muthiah, who was to become the first Indian to reach the rank of Commissioner. It was hoped that Hanne would have prepared a pioneer party for an advance upon North Africa. A Greek was converted in Alexandria, Egypt, through reading a copy of the *War Cry* and journeyed to London to enter the training home in 1889. He was a native of Corfu, and spoke French, Italian and English in addition to his own language. A missionary in Smyrna, Asiatic Turkey, wrote to Headquarters asking that no more *War Crys* be sent to him. "I like the paper very much," he said, "but the Turkish authorities are all startled by thinking that there is going to be war. They have forbidden anybody in this territory to receive *War Crys*. People who are caught with one in their possession will be put in a dungeon for one hundred and one years." Staff-Captain Abdul Aziz, of India, was an Arab. "Paul of Tarsus," an Armenian, became a

[1] p. 119

Salvationist at Highgate, London. Visitors who came to London from Estonia stated that the influence of the Army had spread to that country. Work was commenced in Estonia in 1927, but was closed down when the Russians took over the country in June 1940.

II CONSOLIDATING THE WORK OVERSEAS

Chapter One

DISPATCH OF OFFICERS

WITHIN five weeks during the summer of 1886 no fewer than 110 officers were sent out from London to various parts of the world to consolidate the work already established, among them 65 for the United States and Canada and 40 who left on 18 August to reinforce the personnel in India and Ceylon. The latter group was under the leadership of Commissioner Tucker and Major Arnolis Weerasooriya, nephew of a Buddhist high priest, who had been visiting International Headquarters. These contingents of officers were no little tax upon a poor and comparatively small organization. Four months later twenty other officers sailed for India. In 1887, and to celebrate Queen Victoria's Golden Jubilee, fifty officers, three of them women from France, farewelled from the Exeter Hall on 29 June. This contingent was the largest ever sent anywhere. Each passage and outfit was secured for the absurdly low amount of £15 and the yearly support cost £5 each at the most, as against the £250 generally required for the upkeep of a missionary sent out by other organizations.

"Like a second Peter the Hermit, dear Tucker goes about preaching this Indian Crusade, and straightway scores burn with holy zeal and boundless enthusiasm," wrote the British Field Secretary. The General bade the party a final

The Zulu Contingent

The Contingent which attended the 1894 International Congress in London three years after operations commenced in Zululand. The Leader, Adjutant J. Allister Smith, is seated on the left of the picture, and by his side stands his first Convert, Mbambo Matunjwa, who was to become a Major and be awarded the Order of the Founder

The Salvation Army's High School, St John's, Newfoundland

farewell from the Great Western Hall, promoted Weera-sooriya—who had been summoned to London to help select the officers—to the rank of Colonel and appointed him as Second-in-command in India to Commissioner Tucker. Thus upward of 100 European officers were subject to national control, a thing that had hitherto been unheard of in missionary annals.

Yet another 50 officers, described as the "Wedding Fifty," farewelled for India from the Exeter Hall in August 1888 with the newly-wedded Mrs Commissioner Booth-Tucker,[1] about to enter upon her first term of missionary service. Staff-Captain Prema Bai (Nellie Smith), who was returning to Colombo, moved the audience as she recounted how her call from God to missionary work was received in the midst of a street riot in Stamford, Lincolnshire. The boots were trodden from her feet; and as she led the march in blood-stained stockings, God spoke to her saying, "Commissioner Tucker is doing this in India, and you ought to go and do the same and help save the heathen." When the party embarked at Genoa on ss *Dominico Balduino*, it numbered 61 persons. To commemorate the passing of Catherine Booth in October 1890 another party of officers, known as the "Memorial Fifty," left England on 22 November for "Darkest India," since when a constant flow of missionaries has been maintained.

[1] p. 118

Chapter Two

THE UNITED STATES OF AMERICA, MEXICO, THE HAWAIIAN ISLANDS AND ALASKA

Following his first visit to the United States of America, in September 1886,[1] the General decided to replace the ailing leader, Commissioner Frank Smith, a logical choice being Colonel Ballington Booth, the General's twenty-nine-year-old second son, who had made a very favourable impression during his North American tour earlier that year. So, with the new rank of Marshal, Ballington arrived in New York with his wife as joint commander on 21 April 1887, and they remained in charge until their regrettable resignation in 1896.[2] Ballington, six-foot-four in height and strikingly handsome, had been married on 16 September 1886 to the beautiful five-foot-tall Maud Charlesworth, daughter of an Anglican clergyman, the Rev. Samuel Charlesworth. She had been given away by her brother-in-law, the Rev. Samuel Barclay, husband of the authoress, Florence Barclay. Mr Charlesworth had objected to his daughter's becoming an officer, but Maud had already shown her independence and strength of character, especially in those Victorian days, by going to France at the age of sixteen in the company of Catherine Booth, William Booth's eldest daughter, and later being arrested and expelled with her from Switzerland.

Soon after their arrival in America the Ballington Booths set about healing old wounds, and Richard Holz (later Commissioner) and one of the pioneer officers, Emma Westbrook,[3] were among several who left General Thomas

[1] p. 143 [2] p. 355
[3] *The History of The Salvation Army*, vol ii, p. 231

E. Moore's army[1] to return to the international organization. Moore died in January 1896 at Harper, Kansas, where he was pastor of a Baptist church. In December 1887 William Booth's first grandson was born to Ballington and Maud Booth in New York.

By 1890 nearly 21,000,000 persons of foreign birth were resident in the United States, and three years previously The Salvation Army, through the efforts of Swedish Salvationist-emigrants, had commenced work among the Scandinavians, the first corps being officially opened as Brooklyn No 3 on 23 December 1887. Mary and Annie Hartelius, who had left the United States in March 1883 to help pioneer Army operations in Sweden, returned in 1887 to visit their widowed mother, and were appointed to command the corps. Thus they became, not only the first officers to leave America for an overseas appointment, but the first to open officially Scandinavian work in the United States of America. The venture quickly progressed, new corps were established and the first issue of *Stridsropet*, the Swedish-language *War Cry*, was published on 7 February 1891. The Scandinavian side of affairs was given an impetus in the following year by the visit of Commissioner Hanna Ouchterlony, who had pioneered Army work in both Sweden and Norway.[2] German work, commenced by Railton in 1880, was revived in November 1887, and on 29 October 1892 *Der Kriegsruf*, a German *War Cry*, made its first appearance. The German force did not flourish, however, and was disbanded, *Der Kriegsruf* being discontinued in January 1903. Work among Italian-Americans was begun in 1894, but no large numbers were "weaned from the Church of their ancestors." A Chinese corps was established in San Francisco in 1886. In November 1889

[1] *The History of The Salvation Army*, vol ii, p. 237
[2] *The History of The Salvation Army*, vol ii, p. 282 ; vol iii, p. 59

the Pacific Coast edition of the *War Cry*, edited by Captain John Milsaps,[1] became a weekly.

The first Self-Denial Week was observed from 6-13 October 1888. In 1889 Maud Booth, who was to become the first woman in The Salvation Army to hold a minister's licence legally to celebrate marriages, published her book *Beneath Two Flags*. Ballington Booth's *From Ocean to Ocean* appeared in 1891, in which year he was given the new title of Commander.

In order to reach places where ordinarily very few, if any, religious services were held, Major (later Colonel) Philip Kyle, the intrepid and aggressive divisional commander of the Pacific Coast, formed in June 1892 a cavalcade of twelve mounted officers and a wagon containing their provisions and equipment. Ten of the officers played instruments and when they entered a new district a sensation was created by the sight of a band on horseback.

In 1893 Captain McFee, of San Francisco, an ex-sea-captain, procured a steam launch, which was named *Theodora*, to cruise around the Bay and up and down the River. It was not only a mission-boat from which a religious meeting was held on some merchantmen in port, but also a floating labour bureau, procuring employment for working men at ranches along the banks.

At the great Columbian Congress held in New York at the end of 1893 Commissioner Railton represented the General. Officers came from all parts of the territory, and an impressive parade through the streets astounded the city. The Carnegie Hall was packed with 5,000 people two nights in succession, thousands being turned away. Railton described the Congress as " one of the most devil-terrifying and God-glorifying exhibitions of the power of Jesus

[1] pp. 73, 88

Christ in human hearts and lives ever displayed in this world."

William Booth was delighted with the welcome given him in 1894-5,[1] and at the conclusion of this second visit told reporters: "I found the Army here far beyond my expectations. I am more than satisfied with the spirit of the officers and soldiers."

The dedication of a new National Headquarters, built at a cost of $350,000 as a memorial to Catherine Booth,[2] took place on 3 June 1895. This was an eight-storey building at 120-4 West Fourteenth Street, New York, replacing the now much-too-small headquarters at 111 Read Street opened in 1888. The most bitter persecutions had ceased and occasional attacks by roughs were the unusual rather than the commonplace. Two important factors in winning public support were Maud Booth's drawing-room meetings, which attracted the attention of the major New York newspapers, and the activities of the auxiliary leagues begun by Major Moore in 1883 but made considerably more effective by Ballington and his wife. Subscribers to the league contributed $5 per year and were entitled to a year's subscription to the *War Cry*, a small badge and a ticket to all Salvationist functions. Members were asked to pray for the Army at 12.30 p.m. each day, to defend it when attacked and support it with gifts. By 1896 the auxiliaries numbered 6,000. While Maud Booth was raising money and winning friends she was at the same time directing the Army's slum work and visiting prisons. During Ballington and Maud Booth's leadership the number of corps more than doubled and the officer-force was increased two and a half times.

The first "official" convert of the pioneer party of

[1] p. 146
[2] p. 303

1880 had been James Kemp, better known as "Ash-barrel Jimmy." A policeman had discovered him lying head-first in an ash-barrel after a drunken spree. He served as a soldier until 14 October 1882, when he was commissioned a Lieutenant. He was a Captain at Boston when he died on 10 March 1895.

The beginning of 1896 saw the Great Schism in the Army in the United States, which is fully described in a later chapter. For a few weeks Evangeline Booth held temporary command of the territory and then, on 1 April, Commander Booth-Tucker and his wife, the Consul, took joint command. Booth-Tucker had not been in New York long before he was arrested for going about the streets in a disguise which he had used in order to get "inside" the slums. The magistrates discharged him. In April 1897 he was charged on the complaint of several residents near National Headquarters for keeping "an ill-governed and disorderly house." The long-suffering neighbours averred that in the course of an "All-night of Prayer" 2,000 persons with five brass bands had "caroused" throughout the night. The Salvationists, it was stated in court, had sung hymns to the tune of "We'll never get drunk any more" and "We won't go home till morning." The trial lasted three days. After five hours of deliberation the jury found Booth-Tucker guilty. He was released on $25 bail until receiving sentence, which was postponed, apparently indefinitely.

A great victory was secured in the Law Courts in Philadelphia where, in 1899, during a five months' tent campaign, 53 persons were arrested, most of them without warrants, and eighteen drums were confiscated by the police, who acted on their own initiative, no complaint having been made by any private person. Judge McCarthy, at the quarter sessions, concluded his judgment on this wise:

There was no emergency, present or prospective, which justified the seizure of the defendants without warrant. As the arrest of the defendants was not lawful the after-proceedings based upon it are void. The indictment is therefore quashed.

The press, without exception, condemned the police authorities, the *Philadelphia Press* writing: "The raiding of The Salvation Army was a great outrage and a disgrace to the city."

A training home afloat was the unique institution of the Commander, when, in the summer of 1900, he rented a one-time oyster-scow on the cooling waters of the Hudson River for the thirty cadets in New York who, with their instructors, were on the verge of prostration owing to the intense heat. On Sundays the scow was converted into a barracks to "carry the Gospel to those who inhabit the land as far up as Troy, N.Y." This was the first training ship to be used by The Salvation Army and, apparently, the last. "If the experiment is a success," announced the *War Cry*, "the boat may be purchased later on," but there is no record of the purchase.

At the Paris Exhibition in 1900 America's section included exhibits of methods for dealing with and reforming the poor and vicious classes of society, and the American Committee had requested Commander Booth-Tucker to furnish evidence of what the Army was doing in this direction. The Commander complied and the Paris Exhibition Committee awarded the Army a gold medal, the highest recognition of merit.

A disastrous fire at the Cincinnati Slum Nursery in the autumn of 1900 resulted in the death of seven persons, including Staff-Captain Elizabeth Erickson and Captain Bertha Anderson; and in the October of 1903 the Consul was killed in a railway accident.[1]

[1] p. 361

MEXICO

"Captain Harry Stedman with a party of Salvationists has already invaded Old Mexico and held an Army meeting with a good measure of success." So reads a report in the American *War Cry* for 10 June 1894. "We can report four precious souls this week." The *War Cry* for 23 November 1895 states that "Staff-Captain Thomas has left Southern California for a trip into Mexico. His mission is of a religious-social nature." Work in Mexico was not officially commenced until October 1936.

THE HAWAIIAN ISLANDS

Salvation Army operations in Honolulu commenced after Brigadier Keppel, who commanded the work on the Pacific Coast, had received a letter from a Mr Frank Cooke in which some rare old postage stamps were enclosed with directions that they were to be sold to a philatelist, the money so realized having to be used for defraying the initial expenses of the pioneer party. Further financial assistance was forthcoming from the same source and then the island's newspaper promised a donation. On 1 September 1894, therefore, the Hawaiian contingent, consisting of Adjutant and Mrs George D. Egner, their small son George, Captain Mary Zimmer, Lieutenant Jennie Jeffers and Candidate Viola Monroe, accompanied by Staff-Captain John Milsaps, editor of the Pacific Coast *War Cry*, left San Francisco for Honolulu, where they landed a week later. On the first Sunday, after visiting two Sunday schools and speaking to a class of boys from a public reformatory, they addressed a large company of Chinese in a Chinese church, finally speaking to an audience of both male and female prisoners in a gaol. A good hall, formerly a store, was secured on the following day ; on the Tuesday they held a Hawaiian meeting in the Chinese quarter " with a Brother Higgins acting as interpreter. A member of the late King Kalakaua's famous brass band played cornet for the meeting and a Hawaiian lady manipulated the organ."

The first real " attack " on the Hawaiian, or Sandwich Islands, as they were originally called, began on Thursday evening, 13 September, when a large congregation of whites and nationals gathered in the new barracks. Soon the platform became too small for the number of converts, for most meetings ended in seekers at the penitent-form. During the first five months sixty-one persons professed conversion. Within six months, on 13 November, a second corps was opened at Hilo, the meeting being conducted in a Japanese church. Later the officers acquired an old three-sided building, but this was demolished soon after and the Salvationists were left without a hall for several weeks ; then the lower part of an old Chinese joss-house was rented. Nevertheless, in the first eight weeks the conversion of more than sixty souls rewarded the efforts put forth. Meetings were held on Mondays for Hawaiians, on Wednesdays for Chinese, and on Thursdays for Portuguese.

Meetings for children in Honolulu were commenced in the spring of 1895 with an attendance of four, but in Hilo they were held almost from the start of the corps being opened. During the months of January and April 1895 the hall in Honolulu was closed owing to local disturbances. A correspondent, writing in the Pacific Coast *War Cry*, says :

We have felt quite lost the last few days, not being able to hold meetings because of the " Revolution," but it has done us good not to see the saloons opened and crowded with men drinking themselves into Hell. A few of us still meet together at 6.30 a.m.

ALASKA

Sometime during 1897-8 an Indian, John Darrow, having been converted in a meeting conducted by Consul Booth-Tucker in San Quentin Penitentiary, U.S.A., returned to his tribe at Wrangel, Alaska, wearing the uniform of The Salvation Army. In administering tribal punishment to an offender he had committed murder which, while in accordance with native custom, contravened the law of the United States. Now, an enthusiast for Christ's cause, he moved among his people with patience and perseverance and was successful in leading many of them to his Master. His flock grew larger and, finally, help arrived in the persons of Captain and Mrs Robert Smith, who officially established the work. Unfortunately, Methodists and Salvationists held differing ideas as to denominational boundaries and prerogatives, and some of the Indians, handicapped educationally, added to the trouble by their constantly-changing affiliation.

On 15 April 1898 Commissioner Evangeline Booth, who was then in command of the Army's work in Canada, left Toronto with a party of officers for Klondike, in the Yukon Territory,[1] which was at that time the centre of the famous gold rush. At Skagway, just inside the Alaskan border, they held stirring meetings, and here William Benson, a Klawock Indian, approached the Commissioner, pleading for officers to be sent to his tribe. He himself was commissioned to the task and returned to his people to represent The Salvation Army. The work in Skagway was consolidated in 1899 when Adjutant T. McGill and Ensign Fred Bloss, who were among the Klondike party, farewelled from Dawson City to take charge. Many Indians turned from their totem worship, the first convert being

[1] p. 108

young Jim Hansen, who three months later confessed to the murder of a white rancher and his wife. He was put on trial and sentenced to death. The Attorney-General of the United States of America declared the affair to be "the most remarkable criminal case in the annals of American jurisprudence." The judge, however, impressed with Hansen's sincerity and greatly admiring his courageous confession, wrote personally to President McKinley, who commuted the sentence to life imprisonment. For three years Hansen served in a federal prison, winning other prisoners for God before he passed away.

A paragraph appeared in the London *War Cry* for 14 March 1903 stating that a soldier from St Ives, England, had settled among the Indians in Alaska and had commenced to hold meetings with them, thirty-five having professed salvation.

Chapter Three

AUSTRALIA

An inter-colonial war council held in Melbourne in 1886, and presided over by Commissioner Howard, considered the advantages of a single control for Australasia, for at this period the Australian states were completely separate colonies, each with its own government. As a result the territory was re-organized into twelve divisions in the following year, Colony Commanders being retained in New South Wales and New Zealand. Major James Barker, who had been in charge of the work in Victoria and also of the growing social operations in the other colonies, was promoted to the rank of Colonel and assumed responsibility, in association with the Commissioner, for general affairs of the territory. He continued in this position until his return to England in 1889.

The first party of Australian missionaries, comprising eight officers and six cadets, under Captain (later Brigadier) and Mrs J. Foote, embarked on 25 June 1887 for India and Ceylon. Following a reconnaissance by Staff-Captain (later Colonel) Ernest Knight, thirty-four Australian officers assisted in the development of the work established in Indonesia by two Dutch officers,[1] one of whom, Staff-Captain Jacob Brouwer, married Adjutant Margaret Twyford. In the 1890's fourteen Australian officers served during the Army's pioneering days in Japan.

On 1 September 1888 the headquarters in Melbourne was removed from No 75 Stephen Street (later re-named Exhibition Street) to No 120, but in the following year all departments, including printing, were housed at No 187 Little Collins Street, No 185 being occupied later. The Young Men's Christian Association building, containing a hall seating 1,250, and situated at 65-73 Bourke Street, was purchased for £19,500 by Commissioner Thomas B. Coombs in 1894 only two years after its erection. Its original cost was £40,000.

To pioneer work among the aborigines of South Australia officers followed these nomadic people from place to place in an eighteen-foot boat known as the *Yammalative*, a native word meaning "the first." Within three years 100 aborigine Salvationists had been enrolled; Sergeant-Major Pantoni accompanied Commissioner Howard to England in 1888. Work was also established at Albury, New South Wales, for Chinese domiciled in Australia, and meetings in their own language were conducted for them

[1] p. 62

at the hall in Little Bourke Street, Melbourne, notorious for its opium dens. Efforts were made to improve the standards of the Chinese both educationally and spiritually. The spiritual needs of South Sea Islanders working temporarily on the sugar plantations in Queensland also received attention.

The inter-colonial training home for men was opened in Punt Road, Richmond, Victoria, on 14 March 1888, the first principal being Staff-Captain (later Lieut.-Colonel) Henry Gallant, who had been trained in London. Eighty cadets passed through the home during the first year. Long-distance marches of 200 and 300 miles by cadets known as the "Royal Guards" took place in the country areas of Victoria in 1889, among those who participated being William McKenzie (later Commissioner and known throughout the Commonwealth as "Fighting Mac"). General George L. Carpenter was a cadet in 1892. At 3 a.m. on Sunday, 1 October 1900, the old two-storied weatherboard structure was completely burned out. A training home for women cadets was opened in 1889 in the same district, but within the year a larger building had been secured in Erin Street. This was called "The Women's Garrison," the word "garrison" being used by the Army in Australia for the first time. Staff-Captain Mary Shackson was appointed from London to take charge. Plans for the erection of the Federal Training Garrison, Scottish baronial and castellated in style, for both men and women, came to fruition on a site in Victoria Parade, Eastern Hill, Melbourne, with the inauguration of the Commonwealth of Australia at the beginning of the new century. The opening was performed by the Countess of Hopetoun on 16 July 1901. Cadets from both Australia and New Zealand were trained here. John S. Bladin, who was a cadet in 1903, returned as a Colonel and Training Principal in 1935. He was the first cadet of the Melbourne Garrison to be its Principal and the first from the garrison to become a Commissioner and Principal of the International (William Booth Memorial) Training College in London.

Commissioner Coombs, who arrived in Melbourne from Canada at Christmastime 1889 to succeed Commissioner Howard, formed the Headquarters Brass Band, now the Territorial Staff Band, in 1890. General Carpenter, Commissioners John McMillan (who was to become Chief of the Staff), Benjamin Orames and Bladin, Lieut.-Commissioner Colledge and Colonel Robert Sandall (author of the first three volumes of this History) were numbered among the players under the baton of Staff-Captain Jeremiah Eunson. The League of Mercy was also established in 1890. This was, and still is, a body comprised mainly of women-Salvationists dedicated to regular visitation in hospitals, homes for the aged, sanatoria, asylums, and other public institutions.

Commandant Herbert H. Booth took charge of the territory in 1896 and continued to do so until his resignation in 1902.[1] During his command a new printing-house was acquired at No 508 Albert Street, Melbourne. Commissioner Thomas McKie followed, remaining in control for eight years.

Gold having been discovered on the Murchison Fields in Western Australia in October 1891, twelve officers were commissioned for service there by the General during his visit to Melbourne and sailed for Perth on 10 December, the leader being Staff-Captain Knight. Corps were opened in quick succession. Westralians welcomed the Army from the beginning. Miners, farmers and timber-cutters travelled miles to attend the meetings. When gold was found also in Coolgardie, in 1892, thousands of prospectors came post-haste from all parts of the world to seek their fortunes, and the Army opened up a corps. In the goldfields the officers

[1] p. 364

themselves constructed halls of gimlet-wood saplings from the bush, hessian and quarried stone or sun-dried bricks rendered with cement. Quarters were in keeping with the surroundings, "wattle and daub," or oat bags and hessian. Water cost the same price as beer, and was used for half a dozen purposes in succession. Soon, owing to unhygienic conditions in the fiercely-hot climate, epidemics of fever and dysentery broke out and many died, officers sometimes making the rough coffins and conducting the funerals. Two officers were among those who perished.

Persecution continued unabated in some parts of the island-continent. At Ballarat, Victoria, in 1891, several women-officers were included in the five groups of Salvationists who suffered imprisonment for breaking the 66th bye-law by marching in Sturt Street. When the General visited the city Mayor C. C. Shoppee,[1] in reply to a routine request for permission to march through the streets, said: "I have made a search of the Military List, but fail to discover any name such as that mentioned, and therefore permission cannot be granted." In February 1892 seven Salvationists were fined £5 each with costs, or one month's imprisonment in default. All served the full sentence, including Ensign (later Brigadier) Charles Dennis, Captain (later Commandant) Maggie Harper and Lieutenant Eva Le Cornu (later Lieut.-Colonel Mrs McLeod) who, ironically enough, became the first woman in South Australia to be appointed a Justice of the Peace. Bishop Thornton headed a deputation of protest to the Mayor. Commissioner Coombs offered to come to an arrangement with the city council, but his overtures were at first refused. Eventually he met the council in open conference, with the result that an agreement was arrived at whereby Salvationists could march through the streets on three evenings during the

[1] p. 270

working week and on Sundays between certain prescribed hours. Mayor Shoppee and the councillors later signed a petition to the Minister of Justice praying for the release of those who were still serving their sentence on the eve of the conference.

By 1891 the circulation figures of the Australian *War Cry* had become the third highest in the Army world. *Power for Witness*, later re-named *Full Salvation*, a monthly magazine devoted to the teaching of holiness, was again changed in name in 1897 to *The Victory*. Mrs General Carpenter, as Ensign Minnie L. Rowell, was for some years its editor in addition to being editor of *The Young Soldier*, which was first issued in April 1890. *The Local Officer*, now incorporated in *The Musician*, a fortnightly magazine, commenced publication in 1902.

In November 1891 the Calvary Forts scheme—designed to reach people in areas remote from townships—was launched by the General in the Melbourne Exhibition Building, the forts being named "Warrior" and "Australia." Soon forts "Aggressive" and "Benalla" were also on the roads. These forts were actually vans equipped for work in the outback, with tents swung below. From 1899 and for fifty years Frank Seaton, an intrepid and fearless officer, travelled an average of 10,000 miles each year by "push-bike," motor-cycle and car successively in the vast north-west of the Western States, the most isolated region of the continent, cut off by deserts, having no railways or through roads, and with many people living as far as 300 miles inland. Several of the station-owners he visited possessed holdings of from 150,000 to 1,000,000 acres in extent. Seaton made his meetings a community effort. At one isolated township the doctor rang the bell to announce the meeting, the schoolmaster acted as organist and the publican took up the collection. A group of specially-chosen men-officers, called the "Salvation Horsemen," was commissioned in Brisbane in 1892 to ride forth to evangelize sparsely settled districts in North Queensland.

Among the miracles of grace "captured" by the Army in Australia was Edward Trickett, who was converted in 1894 in Sydney and became the corps colour-sergeant at Echuca. He was the first Australian oarsman to be three times champion sculler of the world. He remained a Salvationist until he died under tragic circumstances at Uralla, New South Wales, in 1918.

Outstanding officers not yet mentioned were Commissioner Robert Henry, who was to become Territorial Commander for Southern Australia in 1936; his brother, Colonel Ambrose Henry, for many years Financial Secretary in Melbourne, both of whom entered the training home from Brisbane in 1893; and Colonel and Mrs Allen G.Fisher, of New Zealand, who were transferred to Melbourne in 1896. As Financial Secretary the Colonel laid the foundation of a sound financial system, and Mrs Fisher (formerly Captain Nellie Barnard) held the position of Women's Social Secretary.

An important advance in October 1888 was the inauguration of a system of thorough training for young people. Ten years later, on 24 August 1898, the corps cadet brigade was established in Melbourne by Commandant Herbert Booth.

That the first photo drama produced in any part of the world was "Soldiers of the Cross," is today freely acknowledged by research experts. The film, 3,000 feet in length, took more than twelve months to complete, and was prepared, during 1899-1900, by the limelight department in Melbourne for use with a lecture of that title by Commandant Booth, then Territorial Commander for Australia. It was dedicated by him to the seeking of 200 cadets for the new federal training garrison. The initial showing of "Soldiers of the Cross" took place in Melbourne Town

Hall on 13 September 1900. Incidents in the lives of outstanding witnesses for Christ, beginning with first-century martyrs, were depicted, and included the heroic efforts of the women-officers on board the *Wairarapa*, which had been wrecked on Great Barrier Island, New Zealand, a story fresh in the public mind.[1] Great pains were taken to ensure that every detail of the script was historically correct. Officers produced the period costumes, cadets dressed as Roman soldiers rehearsed their parts at the Punt Road training home, and a " studio " was rigged up at the Dandenong Road property then known as the " Murrumbeena Girls' Home." Large back scenes painted on canvas were thrown over the high fences surrounding the tennis-court. The *Australian Photo Review* has declared that the Army was the pioneer of visional education in Australia. The limelight department, which existed from 1892 to 1909, filmed several important public events associated with the inauguration of the Commonwealth Parliament in 1901.

Many songs which have reached world-wide popularity in the Army originated in Australia during the period under review, chief of the composers being Colonel Arthur Arnott, son of a Sydney biscuit manufacturer. From 1902 and for thirty-three years, the Colonel conducted the singing at the annual congress young people's demonstration in the Melbourne Exhibition Building.

Chapter Four

CANADA, NEWFOUNDLAND AND BERMUDA

" By the fall of 1886," says Arnold Brown in his history of The Salvation Army in Canada, *What hath God wrought ?*

[1] p. 141

" the salvation fires had grown so hot that only a slight further breath of enthusiasm was needed to fan them over Ontario's western boundary and into the youthful Province of Manitoba." The first Sunday's meetings there were conducted in the Victoria Hall, Winnipeg, by the North-West Brigade under Staff-Captain Young, the Divisional Officer. Hundreds were unable to obtain admission. The work continued to spread and on 25 June 1887 had reached the Pacific Coast, the first far-west corps being opened in Victoria, British Columbia. Six months later, on Sunday, 18 December, Captain Hackett and Lieutenant Tierney " assaulted the wickedness of Vancouver." Meanwhile, the old Albert Street Church, adjacent to the Toronto Temple, had been purchased and turned into a printing office to produce the *War Cry*, the *Little Soldier* and *En Avant*, the last-named being printed in French for distribution among French-Canadians; its first editor was Mrs Staff-Captain Simcoe. Five training homes were in operation in the territory including " L'Ecole Militaire " at Quebec, which was afterward transferred to Montreal.

Strangely enough, not until five years after the establishment of the Army in Canada did a swearing-in of soldiers take place, and this aroused considerable misunderstanding both inside and outside the organization, some thinking that enrolment was a form of oath to a secret society, and others questioning the doctrines to which they were expected to subscribe. There were some losses, but the storm was weathered. During the last months of 1887 and into the early part of the next year a series of fires caused a lamentable loss of Army buildings, beginning with the deliberate burning of the Mechanics' Hall, Montreal. " Devilment " resulted in two young men setting fire to the new building at Kingston in October 1887, the first hall also having been destroyed by fire. A third case of fire in the one week occurred at Thornbury. In January 1888, two days after its opening for operations among the French, fire-bugs attempted to destroy the Theatre du Champ de Mars in Montreal. Within a month the London barracks were destroyed by fire.

"The French Work"—for which the General himself had dedicated the pioneers in a public meeting in Toronto during his 1886 visit—not only included fires, but also violent mob scenes, the actual bombing of a citadel and what was known as "The Battle of the Basilica." One of the officers described the opposition from French-Canadians in Quebec City as: "Paris over again; but it is a religious Paris instead of an infidel Paris." No women would dare attend the meetings, nor could they be contacted in their homes; a strict ecclesiastical edict forbade. Nevertheless, the seed was sown and a remarkable harvest was forthcoming. The first anniversary celebrations were conducted by the Territorial Commander, Commissioner Thomas B. Coombs. On the evening of Thursday, 25 August 1887 a grand march processioned along the Rue St Jean, one of the principal streets of Quebec City, and as it was about to pass the Basilica a mob suddenly rose from behind the cathedral fence and attacked the Salvationists with stones and clubs. Twenty-one of them were seriously injured, an officer was stabbed in the head with a knife, and the drummer's eye was gouged out on to his cheek, driving him to madness. Two Salvationists were escorted to the barracks by two friends with loaded revolvers. The press described this terrible affair as a "baptism of blood." Organized attempts to exterminate the "Salutistes" began on 24 November, some 600 university students marching to the scenes of the open-air gathering. General disorder resulted. The chief of police and thirty of his constables tried to quell the disturbance, but the 600 swelled to nearly 5,000 and the police were practically powerless. Three nights later 3,000 people attended a mass meeting and were inflamed by speeches to settle the " to be or not to be " of the Salvationists once and for all in a physical encounter on the next evening. As they dispersed the crowds sang until they were hoarse : " We'll hang The Salvation Army to a sour apple tree." The clash was averted by Mayor Langelier's action in submitting a test case to the courts. He stated that if it were found that the Salvationists were entitled to march the streets he would protect them ; if not, they would be suppressed. The courts deferred the case again and again and the Salvationists waited patiently. Eventually Captain Bryce and his comrades were found guilty of " making a noise upon the streets." Despite all the opposition, however, the work of the Lord made steady progress.

Little soldiers' meetings were commenced in Canada in the summer of 1887, and by 8 October the Toronto Temple little soldiers' drum and fife band was featured on the front page of the *War Cry*. Annual campaigns under canvas were commenced in 1888 and maintained for many years at Wells' Hill in the suburbs of Toronto. In the year which followed, a group of twenty officers left Toronto for India, having been inspired to offer themselves for missionary service by the visit of Major Musa Bhai and his Hindu contingent. The Household Troops Band, just arrived from England, participated in their leave-taking. En route the missionary party introduced many new songs to the British Territory, two of which have remained great favourites, " O the peace my Saviour gives " and " Saviour, lead me, lest I stray."

Among the musicians of those days were the " Welsh Minstrel," Staff-Captain Tom Griffith, father of Lieut.-Commissioner Richard Griffith, who used to wear a quaint uniform of his own design, including a fur cap, red stockings, and gaiters; and Professor Wiggins, writer of many popular songs. The Household Troops Band created so much interest that a similar combination was formed in Canada under the leadership of Staff-Captain McHardy, Captain Leonard being appointed bandmaster. The band began its first tour on 13 August 1889. A staff band was already in existence, and now corps bands began to be formed at a number of centres. Commissioner Thomas Adams was then in command, and was succeeded for a short period by Commissioner David M. Rees.

The year 1892 saw a break in the ranks which centred around Brigadier Peter Philpott and caused much mental and spiritual suffering. Although described as a "split," this deflection did not result, as in the United States of America,[1] in the formation of a rival organization, for most of those who left joined other denominations. Canada was passing through a period of economic depression, and thousands of its people were crossing the border into the the United States in the hope of finding employment. Some well-meaning folk actually agitated for the annexation of Canada by the United States in the hope of assuring financial stability, and some Salvationists began thinking along similar lines regarding the administration of the Army. A number of corps had to be closed down and it was felt that the glory of the Lord was departing from the Army. Officers were either drawing a very small salary or none at all. Philpott, first to hold the rank of Brigadier in the dominion, and others issued a complaint against Territorial Headquarters. In order to alleviate the distress of their comrade-officers they transgressed against orders and regulations. At the Wells' Hill camp meetings Philpott was interviewed by the then Territorial Commander, Commandant Herbert H. Booth, and, not being satisfied with the course of events,

[1] *The History of The Salvation Army*, vol ii, p. 237

resigned, despite the efforts of the Commandant and his wife to avert such a calamity. The next morning a protest meeting was held in the Yorkville barracks, with the result that several highly-placed officers arraigned themselves on the side of the highly-regarded Philpott and also resigned. The soldiery was naturally affected by the actions of officers whom they respected and many followed their leaders out of the ranks. For some years the controversy smouldered, being fanned into flame every now and again by the press, but eventually the whole unfortunate business died down. The misunderstanding, it was no more than that, has long since been forgotten, and though some of those who left never returned, they became, Philpott included, among the Army's warmest friends.

Under the leadership of Mrs Commandant Booth, the league of mercy[1] was constituted in Toronto in December 1892 for the purpose of prison and hospital visitation.

In connection with the General's jubilee in 1894, fifty years having passed since William Booth dedicated his life to God's service, fifty schemes were inaugurated as part of the Canadian celebrations. Two of them were novel. One was the opening of a salvation farm of 100 acres of excellent land near Little York, then a suburb of Toronto, which was purchased "for a most reasonable sum." This farm was (i) to provide honest employment for any willing to labour; (ii) to provide a lovely and healthful spot where sick officers might recuperate; (iii) to supply the commissariat needs of Army institutions in the city; and (iv) to make a monetary profit to help support the Army's increasing social work. The farm was successful for a time, its name eventually being changed to "The Industrial Colony."

The other of the two unusual schemes was the expansion

[1] p. 94

of The Salvation Navy. The *Glad Tidings* was already working among the Newfoundland fishermen off the coast of Labrador. The new scheme called for the launching of a larger vessel for similar service in Newfoundland waters. Soon the 32-ton *Salvationist* put out from St John's. Another idea developed in connection with The Salvation Navy and the ss *William Booth* was bought for service on the Great Lakes. On its second voyage, however, the vessel struck a reef at Selkirk on the shores of Lake Erie and was ordered into dock for repairs. Here it caught fire, but money was quickly forthcoming to cover the cost of the repairs. It was this same vessel on which the General sailed from Brockville during his 1894-5 visit.[1]

NEWFOUNDLAND

The unofficial beginning in 1885 of Salvation Army work in Newfoundland, then known as "Britain's oldest colony," was the happy result of a happy event—a honeymoon! Mrs Captain Dawson (Emma Churchill), accompanied by her husband, went from Ontario to visit her parents at Portugal Cove. During their stay the newly-married couple conducted meetings in the Temperance Hall in Victoria Street, St John's, the capital, and, though this building had been condemned, it was so crowded that Mrs Dawson had to be carried into it over the heads of the congregation. Here, and in the Orange Hall, where subsequent gatherings were held, hundreds of seekers were recorded and they formed the nucleus of the work officially opened on Sunday, 1 February 1886, by Divisional Officer Arthur Young and a small pioneering party.

The first open-air meeting was held on the Parade Ground. A large crowd was attracted but, eventually getting

[1] p. 144

beyond control, it was dispersed by the police, the officer escaping with minor injuries. A hall was secured in Springs dale Street, but street marches were limited to one on Sunday mornings and the Salvationists were given police escort because of the confusion caused. Opposition of a particularly violent kind was encountered in those early days and for many months both officers and soldiers were severely harried. When officers left a house they had visited they were sometimes met by a crowd armed with hatchets. Women would attempt to stab the officers with knives, scissors and darning needles, and time and again only police intervention saved them from serious injury and perhaps death. One night a woman-Salvationist was attacked by a gang of three hundred ruffians, thrown into a ditch and trampled on. She managed to crawl out only to be thrown in again. Women shouted "Kill her! Kill her!" She was so badly injured that it required three policemen to take her home. The hall doorkeeper was seized by roughs and trampled on so angrily that he became a permanent cripple. Pieces of rock were thrown through hall windows and when these were barred with woodwork heavier missiles were used to smash it; but through all this fierce persecution fishermen and their families were being soundly converted, and new corps were opened in the same year at Brigus and Carbonear. Among the first converts was Jonas Barter, a hard drinker and gambler, who five years later married Amelia Reed, a convert of Captain and Mrs Dawson. Theirs was the first Salvation Army wedding in St John's and it was attended by the Prime Minister, Sir Robert Thorburn.

In course of time, and after a revival at St John's in the spring of 1888, as things gradually settled down and corps grew in size and multiplied in number, the question of schools arose. The Education Act provided for grants for educational purposes being made to religious denominations on the basis of the membership recorded at a periodical census; but the Act stipulated that each denomination must provide its own qualified superintendent, inspectors and teachers. For a considerable time this barred the way to the general establishment of Salvation Army schools. The spread of Salvationism in Newfoundland was strongly opposed by prejudiced individuals, and attempts were often made to use the schools to check the growth of the organization. The need for separate schools, however, made itself so acutely felt that at several corps the commanding officer set up a school without government aid, and bravely endeavoured to meet the necessities of the position.

In 1892 the Legislature passed a bill providing for the setting up of a Salvation Army Educational Board, with the provision that until the Army had established its own schools the funds granted to it would be distributed to those schools of other denominations which the children of The Salvation Army were attending. The Legislature of 1898 approved a bill for the setting up of a Salvation Army Board of Education to establish and operate schools, under the supervision of the existing Church of England and Methodist superintendents, who were to supervise in alternate years the schools of other nonconformist groups. In actual practice this supervision was given by the Rev. Canon W. Pilot, D.D., Superintendent of Church of England schools, in the early years. In 1901 representations made to the government were sympathetically received, and the conditions upon which grants were made so altered that outside help could be employed. The Education Act of 1902 gave the Army authority to set up five educational districts with a board in each district, and the right to appoint a person to supervise its own schools. Three years after the amendment of the Act twenty-five schools were in operation.

BERMUDA

Work in the sub-tropical coral islands of Bermuda was opened on 12 January 1896 by Adjutant L. Des Brisay, Captain Johnson and Lieutenant Forsythe, who were sent there from Canada by Commandant Booth. A coloured Lieutenant was actually the fore-runner. He had secured a hall and quarters and held meetings on his own account with the help of two or three naval and military leaguers.[1] A service of song, followed by a supper and watchnight service, resulted in sixteen seekers. Within the first five years halls were opened in several towns and more than 1,500 persons sought salvation.

During the command of Ensign (later Colonel) Gideon Miller the Army was praised as an important factor in the decrease of crime throughout the islands. St George's Gaol was rendered unnecessary, and the suggestion was made in the Legislative Assembly that it be turned over to the Army as a barracks. In those days Bermuda was a highly-important outpost of Empire and as such was strongly fortified. The 2nd Worcester Regiment arrived with as hard-bitten a personnel as any that had preceded it, but when the regiment left for participation in the South African War the tone had completely changed, for a religious revival had taken place through the Army's ministrations and hundreds of men had claimed salvation. The famous West India Regiment also produced a crop of converts.

* * *

It has been declared that the year 1896 was the dawn of a golden decade in Canada, the Army moving forward

[1] *The History of The Salvation Army*, vol. iii, p. 289

rapidly under the leadership of Commander Evangeline Booth, who was to guide its destinies for the next nine years. During 1897-8 a Tsimpsean Indian, William Young, and his sister, both of whom had become converted in Seattle, commenced meetings in their own district on the Skeena River in Northern British Columbia, and then went further afield, arriving among the Kispiox Indians about Christmas time, when a great revival broke out. Trouble ensuing among certain nationals who resented the Army's intrusion, the Agent for Indian Affairs gave a portion of land to the Salvationists on which they established their own completely Salvation Army village, Glen Vowell.

By 1900 the Canadian Territory included the whole of Canada, Newfoundland, Bermuda, Alaska, North Dakota, Montana and the northerly portion of the State of Washington, Vermont and Maine.

Chapter Five

FRANCE

While the press was ringing with the rumours of the advance of the French army toward the Prussian frontier at the beginning of 1887, and all Europe was thrown into a state of intense fear and trembling, " L'Armée du Salut " was " taking up important strategical positions in the very midst of the enemy's territory," under the vibrant leadership of the Maréchale, Catherine Booth, eldest daughter of the General. Since 1 December 1886, fire had been opened, among several other places, in St Etienne, one of the largest mining towns in France, and Calais, a Catholic town in which a large dancing-saloon had been taken. Thirty-five cadets had been commissioned as officers and thirty had entered the training home to replace them.

On 8 February 1887, the Maréchale, commanding both in France and Switzerland, was married to her Chief-of-Staff in France, Colonel Arthur Sydney Booth-Clibborn, who five days earlier had altered his name by deed poll to include that of his bride. The wedding was conducted by the General in the Congress Hall, Clapton. Booth-Clibborn, a former Irish Quaker and thirty-two years of age, was a man of great physical stature ; the Maréchale was twenty-eight.

An outstanding event took place in April 1889 when a new headquarters with a central hall and extensive office and printing accommodation was opened at No 3 Rue Auber, in the heart of Paris. Present at the ceremony was M. Albin Peyron, of Nîmes, who was to become a Brigadier and the author of *Reflexions et Experiences d'un Salutiste* (Reflections and Experiences of a Salvationist). He was the father of Commissioner Albin Peyron and the grandfather of Commissioner Irene Peyron and Mrs Commissioner Wycliffe Booth. A theatre holding 600 people in the Rue Belleville was also secured.

Considerable progress was now being made in the country, but the work remained hard and difficult in many places. The Maréchale had a most trying time, for instance, when conducting meetings in the Eldorado Theatre, Marseilles, and in describing French scepticism on this occasion she stated that well-dressed ladies sat and screamed with laughter at the simple Army uniform, so absurd did any sort of religious dress seem to them. The most solemn Bible passages struck them as purely comical. " The Hebrew emblems and phrases which are familiar to the roughest English audiences are nonsense in this land where teachers are forbidden even to mention the name of God in the schools of the state."

Although open-air gatherings and street processions were not allowed by law, by the summer of 1890 only two departments of the nineteen in which corps were operating denied the Army full liberty to hold indoor meetings—Tarn and Ariège. Splendid work was in progress at Mas d'Azil in the last-named department, but the Roman Catholic mayor of the village ordered the closing of the meetings. The prefect of the department was then appealed to, and he at once sent a strongly-worded letter of remonstrance to the mayor, instructing him to protect and not to persecute the Salvationists. His closing of the meetings was quite contrary to the spirit of the liberty of the French *régime*, and the mayor was to post the prefect's letter to him on the door of the town hall. In the Tarn Department an appeal to the Ministry of Justice, signed by resident Salvationists, resulted in the Commissioner of Police receiving instructions that the decree forbidding the Army's public meetings had been withdrawn.

In the same year the General's *Orders and Regulations* were translated into French. Miss Blundell, formerly editor of *Ami de la Maison* and other French papers, and who had become a Salvationist, helped with the translation. These *Orders and Regulations* were also circulated in Switzerland and Belgium. *Des Chants du Salutiste* (Songs of the Salvationist), a monthly magazine, very well produced by a competent musician, had been issued in 1887; in the following year *Vainqueur* (The Conqueror), a book by the Maréchale, appeared. *Dans les ténèbres de l'Angleterre*, a French translation of the General's *In Darkest England and the Way Out*, was published in 1891; and "the most engaging book that has yet issued from our Continental press," *Liberté* by Commissioner Booth-Clibborn, appeared in 1893. This gave the true facts of the relation of the Army to the government of the country and showed that religious liberty includes the right of people to meet in private or public places for the worship of God.

At the beginning of 1895 the Army acquired a "petroleuse," the name given to a carriage driven by a gasoline or petroleum motor, and it was "not an uncommon thing now to see one of these horseless carriages buzzing along the boulevards." The "petroleuse" was used to make a spiritual attack upon the fairs of France—a new kind of work. Automotor road conveyances had arrived at a much greater state of perfection in France than in England, largely due to the fact that in France there did not exist the very stringent laws in force in England, such as that which required all road engines to be preceded by a man on foot carrying a red flag. The "petroleuse" could climb hills at the rate of three miles an hour, but it could run on the level at the alarming speed of ten miles an hour. It cost the equivalent of 10d per mile for fuel and upkeep.

A *War Cry* report states that the Maréchale conducted a campaign comprising twenty conferences at Rouen in January 1896. The "Salle Philharmonique," one of the finest halls in the city, was engaged, and she was accompanied by the Flying Brass Band, a combination of twenty-one cyclists, including nine officers, which campaigned mainly in French-Switzerland. In March 1896 it was announced that after having pioneered the work in France from its commencement in February 1881, the Maréchale and her husband, Commissioner Booth-Clibborn, were to farewell from their joint command to take charge of the work in Holland and Belgium. They were succeeded by Commissioner and Mrs Emanuel Booth-Hellberg from India. Mrs Lucy Booth-Hellberg was the youngest sister of the Maréchale.

Commissioner Railton became Territorial Commander in 1901, this being his last responsibility in such a capacity. He was followed at the beginning of 1905 by Commissioner Ulysse Cosandey, when France, Italy and Belgium were united under one central direction from Paris. Lieut.-Colonel (later Commissioner) Albin Peyron was appointed Chief Secretary, Lieut.-Colonel Minnie Reid and Brigadier Fritz Malan remaining as Provincial Commanders for Italy and Belgium respectively.

By this time " L'Armée du Salut " was being acclaimed by ex-President of the French Republic M. Casimir-Perier ; by the important and high-class Catholic magazine *Le Correspondent* ; by *Le Signal*, the only Protestant daily paper in France ; by the Socialist writer, M. Urbain Gohier, who attained great publicity in the Dreyfus case ; and by many other distinguished Frenchmen.

Soul-saving work among French residents in the West End of London had been commenced in the early part of 1887, and a corps had been opened in a room in the Prince of Wales' Theatre in Tottenham Street, off Tottenham Court Road.

Chapter Six

SWITZERLAND

Although Salvationists were still being fiercely attacked in Switzerland, particularly in Geneva, Neuchâtel, Basle and Herisau, young hooligans being largely responsible, a review by the Maréchale and Colonel Booth-Clibborn at Gressy Sawmill on 19 May 1887 brought some 1,200 fully-uniformed troops from both French- and German-Switzerland. Many in that procession had been leaders of the cruel persecutions of a few years previously, which have already been recorded.[1] Opposition was continued, however, accompanied often by great violence, for a further ten years. In October 1888 Major Percy Clibborn, immediately following the opening of the new hall at Neuchâtel, was expelled and conducted to the frontier of the canton by a gendarme.

One of the most outstanding cases was that concerning a young Englishwoman, Captain Charlotte Stirling, who was condemned in the same month to a hundred days' imprisonment in the Castle of Chillon. She was charged with inviting a few children to a Saturday afternoon meeting without their parents' consent, despite the fact that each of the children had given an assurance of parental permission. The action was taken under an old law of the Canton de Vaud, passed in 1834, against proselytizing. An appeal was made to the Federal Tribunal and after serving 55 days of her sentence the Captain was released on bail (£40) to await the result. During the interval she returned to England and spoke of her experiences in the Exeter Hall, London. When her appeal was lost the Captain travelled back to Switzerland, surrendered herself to the authorities of the canton and re-entered the prison. On 29 May 1889 the General, then visiting the country for a five-days' campaign, was permitted to see her. When she had completed her sentence the Captain was expelled from the canton.

A moral, but unfortunately not a legal, victory was achieved in the summer of 1890 when President Ruchenot—who compared the opposition made to the Army with that made to Christ—and the Swiss Federal Council dismissed a petition with which they had been presented by

[1] *The History of The Salvation Army*, vol. ii, ch. 45

a small section of the Canton of Appenzell to prohibit the Army's operations on the grounds that they were dangerous to the state and Jesuitical in practice. Two years previously, when the petition was first organized, a counter-petition was presented by the Army, asking for the appointment of a committee to examine these accusations and pleading for the withdrawal of all the illegal decrees that had been issued against Salvationists. The Federal Council refused to answer either of these petitions until the first of June and in the meantime scores of godly people were beaten and imprisoned. In a review of the Army's work during 1890 the *War Cry* recorded :

> The persecution in German-Switzerland has been brutal. . . . The most unheard-of embargoes have been put upon our efforts, and in one canton no meetings are allowed to be held after 6 p.m., and the officers directing there are liable to imprisonment should any person under sixteen be found in the congregation.

The " Message " of the Federal Council, as it was called, said in effect that (1) the accusers were in error, (2) The Salvation Army had a high aim and object, (3) not being supported by the state it was necessary for the Army to make appeals for funds, (4) the Army was not a religious order like the Jesuits, but a movement which had liberty of conscience within itself, and (5) the Army being within its rights the Federal Council refused to make restrictive legislation. The Army had hoped (1) that the Council would have stated that the decrees against Commissioner and Mrs Booth-Clibborn, Major Percy Clibborn, Captain Stirling and others were to be cancelled, (2) the action of the cantonal authorities was both illegal and severe, (3) the brutal and rowdy conduct of the " Armée du Salut's " opponents should be summarily dealt with in future, and (4) the restrictions upon the right of meeting in Geneva, Neuchâtel and elsewhere were to be abrogated. The findings were somewhat of a disappointment, but the Army on this occasion was thankful for small mercies.

Within a few weeks Captain J. Beau, a sick girl-officer in charge of Essertes corps, was imprisoned for taking part in a meeting at Rolle some months previously when Major Cosandey had played his cornet.

When Major and Mrs Percy Clibborn were appointed to Belgium in June 1890, the then Staff-Captain and Mrs Ulysse Cosandey succeeded them in command of the French side, the Staff-Captain being the first Swiss officer to have charge of the work in his own country. Major (later Lieut.-Commissioner) Fornachon followed Major and Mrs Buller on the German side during the year.

Despite all the opposition the *Cri de Guerre* had at this time a circulation of 8,000 copies weekly, training garrisons were firmly established in Geneva, and pioneer field officers were sent to Belgium, Germany and South America. November 1891 saw the publication of Commissioner Booth-Clibborn's book, *Ten Years' War in the French and Swiss Republics*, described by its reviewer as "one of the best shilling's-worth we have ever seen."

Notwithstanding the fact that the Commissioner had time and again visited Geneva since his expulsion and had held public meetings to the knowledge of the authorities he, with the Maréchale, was forcibly dragged—they refused to walk, on principle—to a police cell by gendarmes on the termination of a welcome gathering in November 1892. In the same summer they were expelled from the canton. The newspapers, two days later, contained a telegram from Berne stating that the Federal Government was exceedingly annoyed that the Geneva authorities had expelled the Commissioners. The State Council had known nothing about the affair and all but one of the councillors were against the arrest and expulsion. Three officers in Liestal, in the Basle Canton, were sentenced to imprisonment for holding meetings after 9 p.m. in their own hall in the November of the following year. In December 1894 the Federal Tribunal of Switzerland gave a judgment which stated that the decree issued by the Cantonal Government of Basle-Campagne during the preceding summer was unconstitutional. This decision also cancelled all decrees that restricted the Army's rights issued by eight other cantons.

Thenceforward interference with the Army and its work became less and less. When in 1896 the General visited the country the *War Cry* was able to record that a fortnight before his arrival in Basle the government of the canton withdrew all bye-laws and restrictions against The Salvation Army. Among these was one that forbade the holding of meetings in any building in the town other than its own. The General's campaign was conducted in the largest public hall. At all the places he visited he was given an enthusiastic welcome by crowds of people, and it was made abundantly evident that the long-drawn-out and bitter attempt by vested interests to destroy the Army had utterly failed. Commissioner and Mrs Booth-Hellberg were then in charge of the country. An interesting paragraph in the *War Cry* of this period states: "Princess Ouchtomsky, of Vevey, Switzerland, has been promoted from a soldier to be a sergeant." The princess was among those who had accompanied Captain Stirling to the gate of the Castle of Chillon in 1888.

No fewer than seventy-five corps were opened between 1886 and 1904, among them Basle I, Vevey, Winterthur, Schaffhausen, La Chaux de Fonds, Lausanne, Reinach, St Gallen, Berne I, Amriswil, Berne II and Aarau; and they are still among some of the best today. From 1882 to 1901 the French and Swiss territories were under the same control and cadets were trained in Paris, with the exception of the years 1888, 1890, 1892 and 1893, when the French-Swiss cadets were trained in Geneva, Neuchâtel, Lausanne, Tramelan and Morges. These sessions lasted from two weeks to four months. Training work started for German-Swiss cadets in 1887 in Zürich and continued until the end of 1901, when all cadets of the territory were trained in Berne.

CHAPTER SEVEN

INDIA

A review of " the past year's fighting and victories " published in the *Indian Salvation Calendar* for 1888 reported that of the thirty-seven Christian missions working in the country, some of them since 1793, only the Church Missionary Society had a greater number of missionaries, both foreign and national, than The Salvation Army. Its soldiership placed it twenty-first in the rank of missions. The chief event in January 1887 was the arrival of Major Jai Bhai, after his tour in Canada and America, with a party of twenty officers from these countries. Captain Musa Bhai commenced a six months' campaign in Australia which resulted in fourteen officers volunteering to accompany him back to India. The marriage of Major Eshwar Das (F. Grundy) to Jeevee Raijee, daughter of Captain Gulab Bhai, is described as " probably the first thing of the kind in the history of Indian missions, and marks another bold departure from the ordinary traditions." The influence of Salvationist-missionaries was such at this time that a company of strolling players, although having obtained permission from the government to act in a town in Gujerat, were told by the inhabitants that they must also apply for permission from the Salvation Army officers. This being refused they were obliged to leave without acting !

A prison-gate home[1] was opened in Bombay in 1888, some 200 criminals passing through its doors within the first eighteen months. Many were converted and some accepted as officers. Commenting on the prison-gate work, to which it gave several columns, *Kaisar-i-Hind*, a leading Gujerati newspaper, said :

We may be ever so amused and grieved at the ways of The Salvation Army in converting the natives, and we may say as much as we like against them, but upon one subject we must say words of praise for these soldiers ; that is, concerning the praiseworthy endeavours which The Salvation Army is making towards the improving, and making honest, and setting to work, of the poor fallen people released from the jails. . . . We have a natural aversion for thieves, rogues, drunkards and villains ; but God has created them also, men like us, and in their fallen state it is our duty to do all that we can to reform them and keep them from their evil ways. This duty The Salvation Army is performing in a most honourable manner, and is giving a perfect lesson for others to follow.

Colonel Wilson, Commissioner of Police in Bombay, also praised the prison-gate brigade work in June 1890. During the previous month 550 tea-boxes made in the home were sold to tea-planters.

The first Indian Staff Council was held in Bombay during March 1888, and in the absence of Commissioner Tucker, who had gone to England to marry Emma Booth,[2] its meetings were presided over by the Second-in-command, Colonel Weerasooriya. Detachments came from all parts of India and Ceylon. Within a couple of months the thirty-

[1] *The History of The Salvation Army*, vol. iii, p. 3
[2] p. 81

year-old Colonel had passed away with cholera, which he had caught from officers whom he had been nursing. Booth-Tucker, who had changed his name by deed-poll, returned to India at once. His bride, now co-Commissioner and taking the name of Raheeman, followed him in the autumn. During the same year the Bombay territorial headquarters was purchased with part of an unexpected gift of £5,000 sent by C. T. Studd, the famous English cricketer, who was serving as a missionary in China. Tucker often said that this gift was the foundation, humanly speaking, of The Salvation Army in India, for it had also enabled the General to send out the "Jubilee Fifty."[1]

Booth-Tucker constantly and indignantly replied to the charge that the Army's method of evangelizing India was more costly in the lives of white workers than the more usual European plan of living, and in 1889 he published figures to prove that the death-rate among the officers was actually considerably below that of the workers in other missions. Of 192 officers brought to India in two and a half years only four had died and nine had returned to England as unsuited to the climate.

Commissioner Raheeman, who had been absent from the Indian Field from April 1889 until after the death of her mother, whom she had nursed, left London in November with her husband, Fakir Singh, her sister Lucy (Colonel Ruhani) and sixty other officers and arrived in Ceylon on Christmas Day. But Raheeman was stricken with illness soon after and had to return immediately to England from Bombay, almost at the point of death. She never again saw India.

The divisional commander of the southern field had decided in May 1892 to apply to South India a novel system of warfare which had been introduced with remarkable

[1] p. 80

success during the previous two years in Gujerat for the opening up of new and hitherto untouched districts. This was the Boom March. The plan was briefly as follows: The leaders ascertained which of the neighbouring districts and castes were the most approachable and likely to surrender to a concentrated attack. An experienced pioneer officer was then selected to visit these districts along fakir lines without, however, wearing Salvation Army uniform. He interviewed the leading people of the caste and, after explaining the aims and objects of the Army, said that it was proposed that a party of Salvationists should visit their district—would they send him an invitation and help with the food arrangements? The composition of the party was carefully considered. Some members were mounted on horses and camels, and included the best of the sergeants and soldiers. Music and flags with appropriate mottoes were a tremendous attraction and brought many visitors from villages not included in the programme. The boom march lasted for three or four weeks and proved an exceptional success.

During the month of March a series of such marches in Gujerat had produced no fewer than 13,328 seekers, including many devil-dancers, but in Travancore the march gave rise to bitter opposition on the part of the high-caste Hindu population. Barracks were burnt down and false charges made in the courts. Adjutant (later Lieut.-Commissioner) Yesu Ratman (William Stevens) was ambushed, brutally assaulted and left for dead on the road near to Cape Comorin, Travancore. Later the attackers smashed everything in the barracks. Lieutenant Manikam, a Tamil, entering a caste street in Thalakudi during a festival, was seized and carried off to the police-court. He was released on bail for the sum of Rs 500 and an appeal was made to the Diwan of Tranvancore and to the British Resident, but while they were considering the case the lad was dragged to court sixteen times, put into prison twice and forced to travel more than 200 miles. Eventually he was sentenced to twenty days' imprisonment. Several South Indian newspapers spoke out strongly against the sentence and pointed to its injustice. A telegram was sent to His Excellency the Governor of Madras, and Lord Wenlock gave instructions that in future all such cases must be dealt with by the district first-class magistrate only, but the Lieutenant had to serve his twenty-days, and was very harshly treated in gaol. Despite the persecutions and prosecutions, invitations to open up new villages poured into headquarters. The success of the boom march system in Gujerat and Travancore led to an effort being made in 1893 to apply it to the Marathi Country, where the work had hitherto been of a very struggling and discouraging character. Staff-Captain (later Commissioner) Sukh Singh (Arthur Blowers) was appointed to superintend the march which, as in Travancore, engendered considerable antagonism but nevertheless resulted in the formation of two new districts.

It was not until 1895 that a small party was dispatched to attack the Punjab villages on the boom march plan, but in the course of a few months sixty-one corps and outposts were opened and about 100 officers and cadets raised. The work continued to make rapid progress under Staff-Captain (later Colonel) Yuddha Bai (Catherine Bannister).

Commissioner Ruhani had remained in India for a short time after Commissioner Booth-Tucker left and then returned home, but farewelled for India again in July 1892. On 18 October 1894 she married Colonel Emanuel Hellberg and they jointly commanded the territory until 1896. Following the General's visit that year[1] a change was made in the system of supervision. India was divided into four

[1] p. 161

separate commands: Northern India under Colonel Jai Bhai (Paynter), the North-west Provinces under Colonel Eshwar Das (Grundy), Southern India under Colonel Musa Bhai, and Ceylon under Brigadier Nurani (Clara Case). A Resident Travelling Secretary was also appointed to represent International Headquarters and to form a link between the different territories. Colonel (later Commissioner) Jai Singh (Henry Bullard) was the first to occupy this post, and he was succeeded by Commissioner Edward Higgins, whose son was to become General in 1929.

Chapter Eight

CEYLON

The numerous conversions—some 400 were recorded between 19 September 1886 and the beginning of 1887—which took place in Ceylon following the arrival of the forty officers brought from England by Commissioner Tucker and Major Weerasooriya, after the first International Congress, gave rise to considerable opposition from the Buddhist community, and in some places a Buddhist "Salvation Army" was formed. This innovation attracted large congregations to its gatherings. The doctrines of Buddhism, however, did not lend themselves to its success and the imitation army found it difficult to maintain interest and soon faded out.

Not infrequently a shower of stones would greet the Salvationists when they appeared in the streets, and on one occasion a stone actually bounced from Tucker's head, although he was wearing nothing more to protect it than an Army handkerchief; he was not even bruised. When, during an open-air meeting in Angulana, a Buddhist struck him across the back with a heavy stick which ought to have felled him to the ground, he scarcely felt the blow, so marvellously was he preserved. The conversion of the young son of a Mohammedan priest in Kandy caused a sensation in the town and a crowd of angry Mohammedans besieged the Army hall in an attempt to seize him. To save him from capture he was secretly, as it was thought, taken to Colombo, but the news of his presence in the city was noised abroad. Believing him to be taking part in an open-air procession, a mob of Mohammedans began to throw stones and brandish staves until the Buddhists heard of the attack upon the Galavima Hamudava (Salvation Army), whereupon they surprisingly championed the Salvationists, turned upon the Mohammedan rioters and cleaned the streets of them. No love was lost between the rival religionists of Ceylon! A number of converted Buddhists eventually became officers. Solomon S. Perera, son of a Christian planter, was nominally a Christian himself although actually he would be better described as "a man about town." Converted in an Army meeting at Gampola in May 1887, he entered the training home ten weeks later with his wife and two small children. On more than one occasion during his early officership he was kidnapped by Buddhist relatives; Perera, however, was to become a Lieut.-Colonel and one of the Army's outstanding leaders in the East.

Disturbances continued on the island throughout 1887, but the magistrates acted with admirable firmness in punishing the rioters. Pavistina, a Cingalese, was stabbed no fewer than eleven times while returning from a meeting at Angulana, and her assailant, to whom she had been engaged prior to accepting Christianity, escaped. Pavistina recovered, became an officer and visited England, but upon her return was threatened by her former fiancé who was discovered, arrested and sentenced to five years' imprisonment.

Prison-gate operations were commenced in Colombo at the personal request of the Governor of Ceylon, who had learned of the success of the work established in Australia, and Captain Dev Kumar (John Lyons) was appointed in August 1888 to take charge of the home, the first to be opened in the East,[1] with Captain Perera as his assistant. The government contributed a monthly grant of 50 rupees which, after three months, was increased to 100 rupees. Lyons conceived the idea of holding what he called "Thieves' Dinners," to which all the thieves in Colombo were invited. A large number turned up for the first meal and "Thieves' Dinners" became a regular feature of the home. Many criminals, and even Buddhist priests, confessed conversion, some seventy passing through the home during the first five months. To his surprise Lyons found Pavistina's would-be murderer in the prison. He had then but one mad desire: to kill the girl as soon as he was released. An hour before his departure from the prison, however, he suddenly fell dead although he was apparently in perfect health.

During the South African War Brigadier Jeya Kodi (Johnston), who was then the Territorial Commander in Ceylon, conducted meetings among the Boer prisoners at the Dyatalawa camp. Some of the Boers were Salvationists and led meetings among their compatriots. There were about eighty soldiers and recruits of The Salvation Army in the camp and 400 adherents. Boer prisoner-of-war camps were also established at Mount Lavinia and Reyana.

[1] *The History of The Salvation Army*, vol. iii, p. 3

Chapter Nine

SWEDEN

The pioneer of The Salvation Army in Sweden, Major Hanna Ouchterlony, was promoted to the rank of Commissioner on 6 August 1887, thus being the first woman outside of the Booth family to be so recognized. At Christmas time, when the Temple in Stockholm was dedicated, the cadets, whose number had increased each year since the first four were trained in 1883, were accorded a dining-hall, a lesson-room and about thirty cubicles. A branch training home was also opened in Göteborg in the following year, when the depot system was introduced. Five or six cadets were attached to several corps and were taught by the commanding officer. When this system was discontinued the course was divided into three periods: six weeks of theory at the Stockholm garrison, one year on the field and a final two weeks in the garrison.

In the issue of the *War Cry* of 2 February 1889 the General, signing "In the war for the extermination of evil," writes "To the officers and soldiers of the Swedish *Division* of The Salvation Army," regarding his recent visit. In the same issue is a report concerning the imprisonment of Captain Augusta Harnström and Lieutenant Kristina Petterson, of Askersund, for continuing with indoor meetings after 9 p.m. "Now I suppose we are rid of those screech-owls," said Mr Otto Setterberg to the burgomaster, Mr H. A. Waldenström, as they stood on the railway station to watch the offending Salvationists depart for Örebro Prison.

A bill affecting The Salvation Army was brought before the Swedish Parliament in the early part of this year and was opposed by a large majority. Its purpose was "to lessen the right of holding public meetings and give the police authority, whenever they think proper, to interfere with the holding of any public meeting." Mr C. O. Berg protested that "the Salvationists have been greatly annoyed; these blameless people have been punished as transgressors by a law which has been brought into force, but was never intended for religious bodies"; and Mr P. Waldenström said: "I do not agree with all the methods of the 'Frälsningsarmén,' but I know sufficient to convince me that they are a good-meaning, sacrificing band of people, who do far more for the outcast and unhappy multitudes than any others will or can." Later, three women-officers were each forbidden by magistrates in Linköping, Kristinehamn and Köping, respectively, through especially-produced bye-laws, to continue their meetings after a certain hour. The Army appealed to the governors concerned, but lost two of the cases. All three cases were eventually brought before King Oscar II and his Cabinet, who reversed the decisions of the magistrates and governors and stated that these authorities had no legal right to make such restrictions. This was hailed as a great legal victory.

An interesting appointment was gazetted in the London *War Cry* for 20 April 1889: "Lieutenant Herman Lagercrantz to be Staff-Captain." Two months later he and his wife returned to Stockholm from London to be publicly welcomed as Salvationists. Several officers attached to the regiment in which Lagercrantz had served were present as also were reporters from Sweden's most important newspapers. Carriage after carriage containing members of Sweden's much-displeased aristocracy stopped at the door of the Temple, for Lagercrantz was the son of a civil and military governor in His Majesty's service and an officer in the King's Guards. The father of Mrs Lagercrantz had a seat in Parliament. Subsequently promoted Major, Lagercrantz became a Colonel in July 1893 and was appointed Chief Secretary, but within a few months continued illness—the King's physician diagnosed galloping consumption and said that he must die soon—forced him to leave this position, which was filled in January 1894 by Colonel (later Commissioner) Charles Sowton. However, after some months, Lagercrantz was appointed to develop the General's Settlement Scheme in India, but again ill-health dogged him and he had to return to Europe after a comparatively short stay. Eventually he resigned his officership but continued as a Salvationist. He lived to be nearly ninety years of age and was Sweden's ambassador in both Copenhagen and Washington.

A review in the London *War Cry* for 27 May 1893, of Colonel Hellberg's *History of Ten Years' War in Sweden*, stated that the circulation of the weekly issue of the Swedish *War Cry*, which had been commenced in 1886, had risen from 5,000 to 40,000 copies within the year. Twenty-one officers and seven soldiers had suffered imprisonment for conscience's sake. From 1886 to 1890 the progress of the Army into all parts of the country was steadily remarkable. Commissioner Ouchterlony, feeling a special calling to do something for the people in the islands off the west coast, had secured a boat in 1890, and put a converted sailor in command, with three officers as his crew. The work was most successful and International Headquarters presented Sweden with a more suitable and comfortable vessel, the schooner *Vestal*. In the following year a smaller boat, *Glory*, was added. There were then 225 corps and outposts and 527 officers. It is of considerable interest to note from this book that " The War has cost England comparatively nothing in men or money. There is scarcely a mission or dissenting body in Sweden that can exist without American or English subsidies. All along our Swedish War has been self-supporting. . . . If there ever was a poor man's church, paid, kept and sustained by his earnings then it is The Salvation Army of Sweden," for Commissioner Ridsdel, who in 1892 succeeded Commissioner Ouchterlony—she was conducting a spiritual campaign among Scandinavians in the U.S.A.—" would find it a problem to discover a friend who would cheerfully part with £50 to further the prosecution of the War," despite the fact that the Army was gradually winning the sympathy of the ruling classes. In addition to being practically self-supporting, Sweden had sent some of its best officers to India, pioneered the Army's entrance into Denmark and Norway and generally helped Finland with officers from time to time.

Work among the deaf and dumb was first commenced by The Salvation Army in Sweden in 1894.

At the close of his command in 1901 Commissioner W. Elwin Oliphant was granted an audience with King Oscar and allowed to attend at the palace in full uniform. The King's face, said the Commissioner, was " suffused with visible emotion," as he spoke in graphic detail of the Army's work among the poor and needy. Previously His Majesty had contributed 500 kröner to the Self-Denial Fund and, for a nominal sum of money, had given a piece of land for use as a woodyard. This recognition of the Army amazed many in high court circles, for although violent opposition had died down by this time—nearly all the older officers had served prison sentences for Christ's sake—official favours had not been forthcoming. The privilege of processioning in Sweden was not granted until 1903.

CHAPTER TEN

SOUTH AFRICA, ZULULAND AND ST HELENA

Rapid progress was made in South Africa during the latter half of 1886 and the first half of 1887, no fewer than 60 corps having been established by that time; 150 officers were at work and some thirty candidates ready to enter the field. Thirty corps had been opened for Europeans, 18 for the coloured races, 10 for the Dutch and 2 for Africans. Brother J. Franklin, who had been an officer in the 45th Foot Regiment, was converted at Maritzburg, Natal, and appointed editor of the *War Cry* in December 1886, receiving the rank of Lieutenant.

A definite spiritual attack upon the African tribes began in 1887 when a party, headed by Staff-Captain Charles H. Lewis, left headquarters in Port Elizabeth for King William's Town, where hundreds of Africans lived in squalor. After holding a meeting there, and leaving a Lieutenant to consolidate the work, the party trekked on in the *Conqueror* wagon in the direction of Ncera. Another wagon was soon put into commission and officers known as "Salvation Riders" were later appointed to spend their whole time in visiting isolated farms on horseback. The farms were mostly worked by the Dutch.

It was hoped to have begun activities in Zululand in the early part of 1888, but Staff-Captain Jim Osborne, who was accompanied by Captain Isaac Marcus, could find only a few natives and no suitable centre, so thought it best to get a start at Umvoti in Natal until Zululand, then in a state of considerable unrest, had quietened down sufficiently. Soon after being appointed to the position of Provincial Officer for the Western Province, Major Osborne, "the most popular Salvationist in South Africa," died a victim of typhoid fever in January 1897. He had been in charge of native work in Zululand[1] for three years, after which he had been Divisional Commander for the Transvaal and Orange Free State.

A training garrison was opened in January 1891. The first issue of *Kriggskreet* was published in March, and in August 1893 a monthly magazine, *Banier des Heils*, appeared. Work among the 6,000 Indians resident in Natal was commenced by Staff-Captain (later Colonel) Harry Millner in 1892, and a number of Tamils were converted and enrolled as soldiers. A territorial headquarters was opened in Cape Town in November 1893, but the work grew so quickly throughout the country that it was found necessary to build a new territorial headquarters and citadel in Loop Street, and the foundation-stone was laid by Sir David Tennant, Speaker of the House of Assembly, on 11 August 1894. Commissioner Thomas Estill was then in command, Commissioner David M. Rees following him soon after; Commissioner William Ridsdel succeeded Rees in the summer of 1896. A territorial brass band was formed at Cape Town in 1894. In September 1899 Commissioner George A. Kilbey became Territorial Commander, and he was succeeded by Commissioner Railton, who was dispatched to Cape Town posthaste in January 1900, although he had only recently arrived in London from the West Indies. The Boer War was still in progress[2] and The Salvation Army had never had, perhaps, so great a triumph as during this lamentable conflict, for it was acknowledged to be the only organization capable of holding men of opposing forces in perfect union. Officers served among the wounded of British and Boer. No sooner were the

[1] p. 131
[2] *The History of The Salvation Army*, vol. iii, pp. 291–2

sieges of Kimberley and Mafeking ended than Salvationists recommenced their open-air meetings in each of these towns, speaking in both English and Dutch. Said the Chief Rabbi in the Metropolitan Hall, Cape Town, on 2 July 1900 : "The work of The Salvation Army recognizes no distinction of colour, sex, nationality or religion." It was his earnest prayer that the blessing of their common Father might continue to rest upon that work.

A few months after the Boer War, and while Martial Law Regulations still prevailed in Cape Town, The Salvation Army's shipping agents there received an invoice from the London Trade Headquarters for 20,000 cartridges. The agents were astounded and informed the Territorial Headquarters that the M.L.R. forbade the introduction of ammunition. What were they to do ? The agents were satisfied when the Commissioner explained that the cartridge[1] represented nothing more formidable than small envelopes in which Salvationists put their weekly contributions to the corps funds.

ZULULAND

A letter dated 9 April 1888, to the editor of *All the World* and written by the editor of the African *War Cry*, stated that Captain Isaac Marcus had left the Cape for Natal to work among the Zulus, with whom he had been brought up. Nothing further seems to have been recorded until the October issue of *All the World*, in which one reads that :

> The Zulu Expedition, after being driven about from one place to another, have at last found a resting, or rather fighting, place, having been granted the privilege of settling on the farm of a friend in Natal, close to the borders of Zululand. There are plenty of Zulus there. Staff-Captain [Jim] Osborne and his comrade have commenced fighting, and the latest news to hand

[1] *The History of The Salvation Army*, vol. ii, p. 82

states that they have had *ten converts*, the first of them being the chief of the location [Ntshibonga.] Fire a volley for the first Salvation Army Zulu chief! The Staff-Captain states that there are many locations or villages around, and begs for some more officers immediately. There has been a good capture of a young Zulu in Kimberley who, I think, will make a fine officer.

It would appear that a renewed attack upon the Zulus, which occurred as the Staff-Captain arrived in Natal, had involved a refusal of permission for him to go beyond the colony. Allowed by a chief to reside in his village fourteen miles from the nearest missionary station, he built himself a hut in African style in which Captains Marcus and Fred Clark (later Colonel) slept on one side, the Staff-Captain and his wife on the other side, Captain Ada Griffin—who subsequently married Captain Ted Cass, murdered in the Mashona rebellion[1]—at the back, and Lieutenant Stephen Nikelo in the wagon. The hut was round, twenty-two feet in diameter and was divided by three curtains. It had no windows and the door was but four feet three inches long and two feet ten inches wide. Marcus and the women slept on three stretchers, Clark on a mattress and Osborne himself on the floor. "I hope," he wrote to headquarters, "that you will not send any male officer who is not willing to sleep on the floor." By April two corps had been "firmly established among the Zulus."

The Army was still on the doorstep of Zululand in 1891, and in order to open up more effectual opportunities Staff-Captain Morgan, who had succeeded Osborne, decided to pay a visit to Eshowe, to interview Colonel Carlew, the Acting Commissioner for Zululand, travelling there by horse and cart. The Staff-Captain was accompanied by his A.D.C., Captain De Rot, and Captain Clark. The Commissioner received the Salvationists with Christian courtesy

[1] p. 62

and promised to facilitate their efforts. At Stanger, on the way home, they met two well-educated Zulus who requested them to preach at the church of the mission station at Grantville, so at half-past six on the Sunday morning a knee-drill was attended by a congregation of fifteen. An eleven o'clock meeting was followed in the afternoon by a "real free and easy," and twelve cases of conversion were registered. Another meeting followed at 7 p.m.

Later in the year, on 29 October, an expedition set out from Pietermaritzburg to take possession of and settle ten acres of land granted by the Government of Zululand at Amatikulu, on the bank of the river of that name. This gift was in fulfilment of the acting-Commissioner's promise of help and the party was dispatched by Commissioner Estill, commander of South African operations. In the party were Ensign Marcus, the "driver-in-chief," a sturdy colonial born in Natal of British parentage, who spoke the Zulu language fluently and was an experienced builder; Captain Sovereign Bang, a young Norwegian; Lieutenant Richard Joslin, an Englishman; Captain Nikelo, a Fingo by tribe and a school-teacher by profession; and Adjutant J. Allister Smith,[1] a former Scots compositor and leader of the party. They had received a solemn charge—"Take Zululand for Jesus!"—from William Booth under the flaring lights of a large circus in Kimberley, in a meeting he conducted in the August at the end of his first campaign in South Africa. The expedition finally arrived at Amatikulu on 11 November. The Zulus welcomed the party on the following Sunday.

The first meeting was held under the precarious roof provided by the wagon-sail, some thirty Zulus crouching and shivering there in shelter from the cold and heavy rain. The next Sunday, 22 November, was regarded as the

[1] *Zulu Crusade*, by J. Allister Smith, O.F.

pioneers' real start to their soul-saving work. The weather was blisteringly hot and a great crowd gathered for the morning meeting under the shade of a mimosa tree. During the meeting the adult members of the congregation had frequent recourse to the snuff-boxes which they carried in the slit lobes of their ears, passing pinches of snuff to one another. Two young men in all the finery of war responded to the first appeal. "Thus," says Allister Smith, "was The Salvation Army born in Zululand." One of these converts, Mbambo Matunjwa, was to become a Major and receive the Order of the Founder; the other, Mosisi Mapumulo, became the first Zulu local officer. Allister Smith introduced the first plough, thus affording the Zulus a better system of food cultivation, and his wife and other officers taught the women the use of the needle and the art of cutting out garments.

ST HELENA

A nucleus of active Salvationists had sprung up in the lonely island of St Helena[1]—which Napoleon described as "an inaccessible rock surrounded by a melancholy ocean," more than 1,000 miles from the mainland of South Africa—and had been without an official leader for more than a year, when Captain and Mrs George Harris were sent from England to take command. They arrived at Jamestown on 26 November 1886, and almost immediately conducted an open-air meeting in Napoleon Street. On their first Sunday night three times as many people as occupied the hall had to be turned away from the meeting, so great was the interest created. Within four months five corps had been opened on this small island with its population of only 5,000, and 100 seekers for salvation had been recorded. On one

[1] *The History of The Salvation Army*, vol. ii, p. 292

occasion a large vegetable market was taken for a Sunday campaign and it was estimated that no fewer than 1,300 people listened to the night meeting.

In the following year a band of fourteen was formed. Brother Thomas Woodman, who had opened his house for cottage meetings a year prior to the official commencement of the work, later became the first corps sergeant-major, and had the oversight of the corps at Half-Tree Hollow. Ensign (later Lieut.-Colonel) and Mrs Albert J. Mayers, Adjutant (later Commissioner and Chief of the Staff) and Mrs Alfred G. Cunningham, and Adjutant and Mrs Widdowson were among the early-day officers in charge of the activities on the island. Captain Wilcox and Lieutenant Evans were the only women-officers to be appointed; this was for a short period during 1888-9.

Chapter Eleven

NEW ZEALAND

Numerous court cases and imprisonments are recorded in the history of the Army's work in New Zealand from the latter part of 1886 and onward. Two converted drunkards were imprisoned in 1888 for testifying in the street at Rangiora, but the case that caused the greatest public interest in the 80s arose from the Napier Borough Council's bye-law. Early in 1886 the officers and some soldiers were summoned for conducting open-air meetings, but Magistrate G. A. Preece dismissed the case, ruling the law *ultra vires*. The council thereupon appealed to the Supreme Court and Mr Justice Richmond upheld the appeal. The council, now feeling confident of its position, proceeded to invoke the bye-law, and in August summoned Lieutenant Joseph Hildreth and thirteen of his soldiers for marching in the streets without its permission. The magistrate appeared to be sympathetic to the Salvationists, but had no alternative to their being convicted and fined them five shillings each. On principle they refused to pay and in default were imprisoned for forty-eight hours. Indignation meetings, sponsored by non-Salvationists, were held urging the repeal of the bye-law, and a petition signed by several hundred Napier residents was sent to the Governor of New Zealand, Sir William Jervois. The council did not repeal the bye-law, but no further summonses were issued, and the Army continued to hold its street meetings.

Two similar cases were fought out in Gisborne in July 1888 and Hastings in July 1889. The officer imprisoned in the Hastings case, Captain Gibson, later married Lieutenant Hildreth, of Napier. Both cases aroused the righteous indignation of Richard John Seddon, who protested strongly in Parliament against the restrictions on the liberty of the subject. Seddon advocated the introduction of a bill that would declare the troublesome bye-laws *ulta vires*, and said that it was shameful that The Salvation Army should be so persecuted when it was yearly saving a large amount of money to the State, and redeeming persons that no other sect, nor the State itself, was able to deal with. The Minister of Justice, Mr T. Fergus, replied that there was considerable difficulty in the way of interfering with the right of local bodies to pass their own bye-laws, and the government could not, therefore, consent to bring forward a bill. However, he hoped that public opinion would make itself so strongly felt that local bodies would be dissuaded from invoking the obnoxious bye-laws. There the matter rested for a while, although there were to be even greater struggles ahead.

The series of events that took place at Milton in the latter half of 1893 had wide repercussions throughout the country. Late in 1888 the borough council had passed Section 60 of Bye-law 2, a restrictive provision regarding open-air gatherings apparently aimed directly at the Army. The corps continued to hold its usual open-air activities, and the bye-law was not invoked. However, in July 1893, at the corps anniversary celebrations, a disturbance took place at an open-air meeting held close to the Commercial Hotel, the outcome being that five Salvationists were each fined five shillings and costs, or in default, four days' imprisonment. They refused on principle to pay the fines and were prepared to go to prison, but an anonymous sympathizer paid their fines. In August Captain James Kerr was charged with playing a cornet in a public street. Magistrate R. S. Hawkins, in a lengthy judgment, repudiating the decisions of Mr Justice Hawkins and Mr Justice Cave in similar English cases,[1] fined the Captain £3, or in default, one month's imprisonment. Kerr elected to go to gaol. The magistrate's decision provoked protest meetings all over the colony. Questions were asked in Parliament and Premier Seddon was deluged with telegrams of protest, to one of which he replied :

The Government does not intend the sentence to be served. In my opinion bye-laws such as the one in question ought to be *ultra vires*, seeing that freedom of speech and religious liberty are thereby jeopardized.

In reply to questions in Parliament Mr W. Pember Reeves, Minister of Justice, said that it would be grossly unfair to restrict the activities of The Salvation Army, whose good works all members appreciated. Captain Kerr, after serving only two days of his sentence, was released after the Cabinet had advised the Governor to exercise his

[1] p. 273

clemency. The Milton councillors, however, were not over-awed by what they regarded as unwarrantable governmental interference, and in the September Captain F. Matthews and seven other Salvationists were charged for taking part in an unlawful procession. The defendants were fined, and on refusal to pay were given a week's imprisonment, their departure for Dunedin under police escort being described as " the liveliest scene that has ever occurred on the Milton railway station." A further spate of protest meetings and resolutions resulted up and down the country.

Colonel Bailey, Commander of the Army's work in New Zealand, and Major Robinson, Commander of the Southern Division, conducted meetings in Milton to welcome Captain Matthews and his comrades back from gaol, whereupon both Bailey and Robinson were charged with unlawfully playing a cornet and a concertina in the street, fined 2s. 6d. and costs and, on refusal to pay, were committed to gaol for seven days. Again an anonymous sympathizer paid the fines and the defendants were released after three days. On 6 November Colonel Bailey addressed a letter to the Milton Borough Council inviting it to bring foward another case against the Army, so that appeal could be made to the Supreme Court to test the validity of the bye-law. The mayor, a prominent publican and a bitter opponent of the Army, said that he regarded the Colonel's letter as a piece of impertinence ; nevertheless, it caused the council to take stock of the situation for, although the Salvationists continued to hold their gatherings the bye-law was never again invoked against them. It must be recorded that Mr Hawkins' magisterial impartiality was demonstrated several times when he brought convictions against people who had disturbed the Army's indoor meetings, one of the occasions being at the height of the bye-law dispute.

The Milton affair did not close the question of open-air meetings in New Zealand. There were at least two further cases of imprisonment: at Patea, where the defendant was Captain M. Milligan (later Mrs Lieut.-Colonel Gunn) in 1896; and at Ashburton in 1897. Cases brought by local bodies were dismissed by magistrates at Ashburton in 1895, when one of the defendants was the Colony Commander, Brigadier Hoskin; at Wellington in the same year, when Sir Robert Stout ably defended the Army; and at Oamaru in 1896.

A notable venture in Colonel Josiah Taylor's term of command was the official beginning of activities among the Maoris, and at a meeting held in Wellington in June 1888 Captain and Mrs Ernest Holdaway, who were known as Kapene (Captain) Enata and Hiro Horowe, and three Maori converts were commissioned to pioneer the work of "Te Ope Whakahora" (The Salvation Army) among the Maori peoples. Within a short time they were working among the "pas" of the Wanganui River area. Mrs Holdaway died of typhoid fever within twelve months. The financing of the Maori work was always a difficulty, and in 1891 it was decided to make a regular monthly levy of a penny from every soldier in every corps in the colony in order to build up a Maori Fund.

Since August 1889 New Zealand had been a separate command, the Colony Commander being responsible direct to International Headquarters. In the *War Cry* of 1 December 1894 appeared a letter from the General announcing that he had reluctantly decided, after consultation with leading officers in Australia and New Zealand, that the colony was to become again part of an overall Australasian command. This was in some measure a blow to New Zealand's pride, but the advantage accruing from a closer and more frequent interchange of officers was considered ample compensation. In January 1895 Colonel Bailey and his wife left for Australia, the Colonel's position as Colony Commander being taken by Brigadier W. T. Hoskin who, under the new administrative arrangement, was responsible direct to Commissioner Coombs, the Australasian Commander, whose headquarters were in Melbourne.

Prior to 1890 there was little organized training for full-time service as officers. Colonel Taylor set up a training garrison for women-cadets at Sydenham, and one for men at Christchurch. Later other training establishments were opened in Auckland and Wellington. Young people's work was not taken seriously until this year and in 1891 Ensign and Mrs Hoare arrived from London, being especially commissioned to organize it. In January 1896 it was decided that the training garrisons should be closed and all the cadets be trained in Melbourne.

As a means of alleviating the unemployment problem, the Army set up in 1891 a labour bureau and free registry in Christchurch. All officers throughout the colony acted as agents of this bureau for the purpose of putting unemployed workers in contact with employers. William Pember Reeves, the Minister of Labour, cordially approved of the bureau. When government labour bureaux were set up they incorporated some of the ideas pioneered by the Army, which closed its institution in 1894.

New Zealand was stirred with deep sorrow when on 1 November 1891 it was announced that the ss *Wairarapa* had sunk off the Great Barrier Island with great loss of life. Four Salvationists were on board, including Staff-Captain Annette Paul and Captain Flavell, who displayed a fine courage as they clung to each other on the deck of the steamer, the Captain in a clear voice shouting: "If you have not trusted Him before, the Blood of Jesus Christ can save you now ! " They hung on to the ship's rail for twelve hours, and eventually a line was got to the shore. Captain Flavell was the second person to make the attempt to reach land, but failed to maintain her hold and was lost. Staff-Captain Paul next made the attempt and reached the rocks safely.

In the late 80's most corps of any size had some sort of musical combination. A marked improvement in efficiency and evangelical effectiveness took place in the 90's, when bands became properly organized with their own *Orders and Regulations* and *Band Journal*. A landmark was the formation of a lasses' band in February 1892 under the conductorship of Ensign Wilson. This band visited nearly every town in New Zealand during the year it was in existence, and attained a remarkably high standard of efficiency that was commented on by many newspapers. Later other lasses' bands were formed. The Federal Band from Melbourne toured the colony from March until August 1899.

One of the best-known of the devoted band of women-officers engaged in rescue work during the period under review was the survivor of the ss *Wairarapa* disaster, Staff-Captain (later Major) Annette Paul, who in 1894, gave a portion of land in Cuba Street, Wellington, where the people's palace now stands, for the erection of a more up-to-date rescue home.

Commandant Herbert Booth toured New Zealand in 1897-8-9, making a great impression with his oratory and musical ability. He had a remarkable gift for raising funds and gaining influential support for his ambitious schemes of social and evangelical advancement, and his six-year term of command of Australasia was a period of dynamic leadership and all-round progress. When he resigned in 1902 his place was taken by Commissioner Thomas McKie.

III WORLD-WIDE CAMPAIGNER

WILLIAM BOOTH was one of the world's greatest travellers in his day, and one of the first to use motor transport in connection with evangelistic campaigns. What his record would have been had air travel come into being before his passing in 1912 one can only conjecture. As it was he was ceaselessly employed one way and another here, there and everywhere. In the earlier days of his voyaging wireless communication with ships at sea was unknown, and this may have had its reflection in the quantity of literary work he was able to get through when on lengthy voyages. He was an indefatigable worker when travelling as at any other time, sending out a constant stream of letters, articles and topical calls to his forces in all parts of the world. On his way to Australia in 1895 he wrote no fewer than thirty-five articles for Salvation Army publications. In rough weather on board ship he would have himself strapped to a chair and use his special writing desk, which remained stationary despite the rocking of the vessel.

But the General was more than a traveller in the ordinary sense of the word. He undertook his journeys for far more weighty reasons than sight-seeing, for which he used to say he had no time to spare, or even in pursuit of knowledge, or health or wealth, or the many other reasons of personal interest or profit for which men "go down to the sea in ships." His journeyings were all undertaken in pursuit of his supreme mission: to bring men to God through Jesus Christ, the world's Redeemer. On 12 March 1904, Evangeline Booth wrote to her brother Bramwell regarding their father's restless activities:

I think with you that it is a disastrous thing at his age [he was seventy-five] for him to have so *little* freshness or variety, and do hope that what I have said may help him to think of the necessity of taking a change now and then.

But with the one exception of 1905 he travelled every year of his evangelistic life, visiting nearly every country in the world.

Chapter One

CAMPAIGNS IN THE WESTERN HEMISPHERE

The 1886 Congress had hardly closed before the General crossed the Atlantic to see at first hand the work which had been represented by the delegates from the United States of America and Canada. This campaign was opened at Toronto on 28 September and was concluded at New York on 11 December. Ten of Canada's most important cities were visited, and twenty-two in twelve of the States across the border. Although the Salvation Army flag had been unfurled in Canada only four years earlier, thousands of Salvationists took part in William Booth's campaign "as if to the manner born." Owing to "splits"[1] that had hindered progress in the United States, the numbers were fewer, but the recovery that had already been made was very much aided by the General's presence and a considerable increase of public confidence followed. In both countries evidence was abundant that The Salvation Army had become "a native agency."[2]

At Fredericktown, Maryland, a meeting was held for

[1] *The History of The Salvation Army*, vol. ii, pp. 237-8
[2] *The History of The Salvation Army*, vol. ii, p. 225

coloured folks only. This corps had been opened about six months previously with coloured women-officers in charge. At Brunswick, N.J., the General spoke of a hurried visit he had been able to pay to the Reverend James Caughey, by whom, when the American minister had preached in Nottingham some forty years earlier, he had been greatly stirred. The first black baby to be dedicated under the Army's colours was presented to God by the General at Boston, Mass.

The General went to his ship from an all-night of prayer in New York and returned to London on Christmas Day. He was first given a tremendous welcome at Euston. This was followed by a procession to Exeter Hall, in the Strand, and the holding there of three crowded meetings. In the thirteen weeks of his absence he had travelled 6,000 miles by sea and 10,000 on land, and had addressed audiences totalling 200,000.

In 1894-5, 1898 and 1902 William Booth again crossed the Atlantic for campaigns in Canada and the United States, and, as on former occasions, his return to the international centre was marked by enormous demonstrations—in 1895 and 1903 at the Royal Albert Hall and in 1898 at the Crystal Palace.

Commandant Herbert Booth, the Territorial Commander, bought a steam yacht, *Blandina*, for use on the lakes and rivers of Canada, and re-named her *William Booth*. F. W. Fry's[1] diary for Friday, 12 October 1894, reads :

Sailed in our steam yacht *Blandina* up St Laurence between "Thousand Islands" to Gananoque. She went splendidly till within 7 or 8 miles of our destination, then pipe leaked and we could not get up steam. Tug came and ignominiously dragged us in. This was the General's first trip in her.

Previously Fry had written :

Some paint caught fire and all her inside was burnt out, the hull

[1] *The History of The Salvation Army*, vol. ii, p. 122

and engines only being left. We bought her for $1,500. Her repairs cost $1,600.

During this campaign the General paid his first visit to Newfoundland where, at St John's, he was given a midnight reception by a great crowd, which included the Premier, Mr A. F. Goodridge, and a former Premier, Sir Robert Thorburn, with whom he stayed.

Much was done toward laying the foundation in Canada for the subsequent development of the migration work of the Army when on 3 January 1895 the General met the Premier, the Hon. T. Davie, of British Columbia, and his Cabinet at the Parliamentary Buildings, Victoria. A few days later the General addressed a Y.M.C.A. Sunday afternoon meeting in London, Ontario, when fully 2,000 men were present in the Opera House. It was the first of its kind he had conducted and he hoped, he said, it would be the last! Nevertheless, he "seemed greatly drawn out towards the audience." Later still he was received by the Governor-General of the Dominion, the Earl of Aberdeen, at Government House, Ottawa, where he talked to an audience comprising the Prime Minister of Canada, Sir Mackenzie Bowell, the members of the Cabinet and other prominent people, on his proposed oversea colony. When the Earl of Aberdeen brought his Countess to say goodbye to William Booth, she told him that she had often attended Salvation Army meetings. On 20 February the General gave his first address to an audience of students, 1,200 being gathered when he visited Harvard University. The special correspondent on this tour, Captain (later Lieut.-Colonel) Henry L. Taylor, wore a band around his cap bearing the words "War Cry Staff" instead of "The Salvation Army." A great welcome-home meeting held in the Royal Albert Hall on Monday, 11 March, included a band of 350 musicians and a songster brigade of 1,000.

Writing in *All the World* concerning this 1894-5 visit, the General said :

I have been further impressed by the great influence for good exercised by the Army on the Christian workers outside our own ranks. . . . The Army has started any number of Churches and Philanthropic individuals on the same or similar methods of labour . . . all more or less of the same character and having the same object. . . . If imitation is the highest expression of approval, then The Salvation Army is being endorsed throughout Canada, the United States and the entire world. . . . Only let our friends always bear in mind that . . . our methods are of little practical service to the world without the living soul thereof.

To this he could have added, no doubt with the twinkle of humour so often seen in his eyes, that one man in America had told him that he was going to start a new Salvation Army which would avoid what he considered to be the mistakes of the old, and be bigger and better in every way. In conclusion the General wrote :

The Army has revived faith in the power of the Holy Ghost to regenerate the hopeless classes of the community. It will not be questioned that a spirit of helplessness has more or less come over Society with respect to what have now come to be known as the " Submerged Classes." The Tramp, the Pauper, the Drunkard, the Lost Woman, the Casual, the Criminal, are all alike spoken of all round the world in accents nearly akin to despair. Government Authorities, Legislatures, Christians and Philanthropists are at their wits' end as to how they are to be dealt with. It had been hoped that the influences of Universal Education, Free Libraries, Temperance Societies, Picture Galleries, and all other agencies and outcomes of our modern civilization, would have met the difficulty ; but, by general confession, they have failed. Now, it seems to me that a light is breaking on the darkened mind of the Community that perhaps, after all, some Super-human, some Divine Power may be needed for their regeneration. The wonderful trophies of deliverance effected through the Army's agencies scattered all over the world are making men think that there may be some need for active interposition of God Himself in order to [effect] the breaking of the infernal shackles, the opening of the prison-doors, and the bringing out of the poor slaves so long confined therein.

When in Washington, D.C., in 1898, the General was honoured by being requested to act as Chaplain to the Senate and to open the proceedings with prayer. A *War Cry* report described the occasion, on Thursday, 10 February:

Promptly at twelve the Vice-President of the United States, and, by virtue of that office, President of the Senate, enters. He walks to his desk, gives two knocks and steps aside. The General advances toward the President's chair. The entire body of Senators rise. Many in the gallery do the same. At once ensues a profound silence. . . . The General . . . with his hands behind his back, begins . . . as he proceeds a solemn feeling steals over the august assembly. The blind Chaplain of the Senate, Dr Millburn, draws near to the steps. . . . The General's . . . language is simple, and reaches the heart. . . . He beseeches the Great Ruler of all to continue His favour to those there gathered for the ruling and regulation of that great nation, and that all might be done to His honour and glory. . . . He asks that the country may be more forward in the march of Christianity, and an example to all other nations of the earth.

Of the second occasion, on 12 February 1903, it is recorded :

The marble corridors and spacious stairways of the Capitol were thronged . . . all present being intent to witness the unique spectacle of the illustrious visitor walking to the discharge of the sacred privilege. . . . As the voice of the General broke into prayer, it seemed as if each soul was carried into the presence of God. So simple was the petition, so suitable that not one seemed left out ; and so tender that every heart seemed touched.

The Senate unanimously voted that the prayer should be included in the Congressional Record of the day's proceedings. The rules that ordinarily exclude " strangers " from the floor of the House were suspended and for nearly an hour the General remained conversing with Senators and

Congressmen. A few days later, on 8 March, the General writes to his Chief of Staff:

> You will understand these proposals [regarding his forthcoming visits to the Continent, Africa, Australia and India] are made altogether independent, and almost I might say, in spite of my inclinations. As I write this morning I feel it would be Heaven to get away somewhere, where my poor brain and body would rest themselves for a month or two, or anyway only have some literary work to employ them, but I must go on, and the interests of the concern are paramount.

While in Washington on these American visits the General was also invited to meet Presidents McKinley (1898) and Theodore Roosevelt (1903) at the White House.[1]

From the ss *Philadelphia*, on which he sailed in the fall of 1902, he sent to International Headquarters the first wireless telegram the Army had received. On a later trip he was to have Marconi as a travelling companion.

As an introduction to the General's campaign in Washington in 1903 Senator Marcus A. Hanna, of Ohio, arranged a formal dinner, inviting to meet the Army's leader what was described as "a gathering of national celebrities such as had seldom taken place." Senator Hanna was one of America's foremost statesmen, of whom it was said, "He carries the Presidency of the United States in his pocket." He died in April 1904.

Of the 1903 campaigns in Canada and the United States it is recorded that the General visited 52 cities, held 200 meetings, addressed 300,000 people and travelled 16,000 miles. To his great delight more than 2,500 persons knelt at the mercy-seat in those gatherings. He was most favourably impressed by what he saw of the United States and its people. A summary of his impressions printed in *All the World* for May 1903 prophetically stated:

[1] p. 312

As passing through an almost uninterrupted chain of thriving and influential cities, reaching from New York to San Francisco, from Chicago to New Orleans, I have gazed upon their thronged thoroughfares, making ever-increasing inroads upon even the desert and arid portions of the West. I have pictured to myself the well-nigh hundred million of the present population multiplied by two, by three, by four in the not distant future, and from this standpoint alone I cannot fail to grasp something of the mighty destiny that must await the youngest of nations, in shaping the future counsels of the world. Again, what wealth, what science, what commerce are to be found within her borders! . . . Here are men and women with ability, education, means, and daring sufficient to conquer the world. . . . Easy of access, quick in perception, courageous in acknowledgement, and open-handed in response, surely they present a remarkable field for the crusaders of the Cross. . . . From the Bowery tough and slum Arab to the Governors and Senators, from Church and Legislature, from tenement attic and stately White House, intelligent interest and practical sympathy have mingled in a manner such as perhaps would have been embarrassing but for the realization that it was directed towards the cause I advocated rather than its representative. . . . In the face of untold difficulties and innumerable misunderstandings, she [The Salvation Army] has not only maintained her position, but . . . from East to West and from North to South she has marched, winning her way into the hearts of people . . . gaining the confidence of authorities . . . and, better still, creating a force of Officers and Soldiers with souls aflame to help Jesus Christ to win the world. . . . I have been equally impressed by the unquestioning conviction that The Salvation Army is exactly the kind of agency required to deal with this ocean of sin and woe.

On each of the General's visits to the West increasing public interest was shown. Appreciation of his life-work and character, enhanced by personal contacts with him, mounted with each occasion. One writer shrewdly remarked that great as had been his triumph over the calumny and opposition which he had faced in the early days of his career, he had shown even greater strength of character, and proved his honesty of purpose and devotion to his cause, by allowing in no way the popularity he had won to affect him adversely.

Among those present in the Royal Albert Hall on 30 March 1903, when he was welcomed from America, were Mrs Asquith (later Lady Oxford and Asquith), Sir George Newnes, Mr (later Earl) Lloyd George, M.P., three Metropolitan magistrates and several Metropolitan mayors in their official robes. Two boxes were occupied by members of the Stock Exchange.

Chapter Two

ON THE CONTINENT OF EUROPE

Before the end of 1887 the General had paid his first visit to Sweden, Norway and Denmark. In 1888 Holland was added to the list, and in 1889 Belgium and Germany. Visit after visit to these Continental countries and to France followed. Italy was included in 1896 and Finland in 1897; here the visit was, of necessity, without public demonstration. His visits to Sweden in the earlier years stand out in marked contrast to those of later date, and it was more or less the same elsewhere in Europe. Official reserve melted before appreciation which came with knowledge, not only of the General's personal charm but of his service to the community for which he and his followers stood.

His reception on 29 October 1887 at Stockholm railway station is a case in point. The *War Cry* report of the occasion read:

Telephone messages were sent during the day to our headquarters from the police office, that no demonstration of any description would be allowed, and so great care had to be taken to prevent collision with the authorities. Being forbidden to march in rank from the different barracks to the station, the soldiers mustered and walked as much in rank as they dared, and upon arriving at the railway station found at least 200 police with a reserve of mounted force, waiting to receive them. Our plan of drawing the soldiers up in line was frustrated, and the police took the control of the whole proceedings, and assembled them as they would. We noticed the chief of police, police commissioner and others of every grade amongst the force, who were on the alert to receive the forces as they arrived, and place them in the positions they deemed advisable. Now came the cadet lasses, led on by Mrs Major Whatmore . . . these last-named were walking too orderly, and were at once reprimanded by a police official and their names taken. . . . The order to have *no* demonstration that we received earlier in the day, meant also no " volley firing." . . . A few minutes before the train arrived, Lieutenant Lagercrantz (an officer of the Swedish army and a good friend of The Salvation Army)[1] desired the police commissioner that Major Whatmore and Lieutenant Buller might accompany him on the platform. That high official was very condescending, and made the way clear by saying to the nearest constable, " *Let this gentleman and these two men on the platform.*" . . . The General drove off, and good naturedly the crowd attempted to follow, and then the mounted men . . . were immediately reinforced by a score of constables.

With regard to the reception of the General by his own people, Mildred Duff (later Commissioner, then beginning her service in Sweden) reported :

The General—*our* General. They looked at him with reverent awe. The General who stood in London years ago alone. The General to whom indirectly they owed their salvation. The General whose books and letters they have read over and over again, and now more than ever " Our " General—when he has

[1] p. 126

journeyed all this way to visit us. . . . "Ah, he does love us. You see what a heart he has for us," say the soldiers to each other, and feel more than ever linked on to the one glorious Army of the redeemed that is fighting and conquering in Jesu's strength.

As the General passed from country to country Mildred Duff's verdict upon the character of the reception given to him in Sweden everywhere stood true to fact.

In 1888 the General paid his long-promised visit to German-Switzerland and for meetings which included the Ascension Day gatherings at Gressy. When he again visited Switzerland in May 1891 it had been hoped that the Reformation Hall in Geneva would be rented for the Ascension Day meetings, but the authorities put up so many impossible restrictions as to make it evident that his presence in the city was not welcomed. He was to appear as *Mr* Booth and out of uniform. The Salvation Army was not to be named in the announcements, neither were the meetings to have any " Salutist manifestation." A large tent fitted up at Renens, a few miles from Lausanne, where the work had began only six months previously, was then made the venue for the Ascension Day gatherings, a theatre for the previous day's afternoon lecture in Lausanne itself being used for the first time in Switzerland. Count Rorf, of Russia, and Professor Bovet, a well-known Hebrew scholar, were among the speakers at Lausanne.

In December 1888 the General conducted the first dedication service held in Denmark. The child, Maud Dagmar, was the daughter of Staff-Captain and Mrs Lee, temporarily in charge of the Army's work in the country during the furlough in England of Major and Mrs Perry.

An outstanding event was the holding of a North-European Congress in Copenhagen in the April and May of 1893. Such a get-together was rendered necessary by the remarkable growth of Salvation Army operations on the Continent. In the three years which were completed by the date of the Congress, in the nine commands concerned—France, Switzerland, Belgium, Holland, Germany, Denmark, Sweden, Norway and Finland—the number of corps had been increased from 287 to 896 ; officers from 500 to 1,800 ; social institutions from 1 rescue home to 3, and 19 other centres, including food depots, shelters, factories and labour yards had been established. Copenhagen was chosen as the place of meeting because of its geographical position. The Congress lasted five days. The General was assisted by the Chief of the Staff (Bramwell Booth), a staff council being the central engagement.

The public side of the Congress commenced in the Concert Palace and is vividly described by the *War Cry* reporter :

> Ladies came in evening dress, provided with fan and opera glasses. In fact, the grandeur and swelldom of the city of Copenhagen were surely never more richly represented at a *salvation* meeting pure and simple. . . . When the first song, " Victory for me," was given out, not a score of people in the gallery or floor of the hall rose and took part. They had come to *see* the performance.

The fascinated crowd stayed through the prayer-meeting until eleven o'clock, however, after which came a " break," ten seekers being registered during a re-commenced prayer-meeting. This Congress was the occasion of Colonel Lawley's first visit to a country outside the British Isles ; he was later to travel many thousands of miles with both William and Bramwell Booth as their A.D.C. It was stated at the Congress that it was quite likely that the Army would not have been granted the use of the railway station for the General's reception, had it not been for the good influence of a Salvationist servant-girl. A second North-European Congress was held in April 1901. There were 140 staff officers present from Sweden, Norway, Denmark and Finland who represented a total of 429 corps and 1,474 officers. The Chief of the Staff again accompanied his father.

The *War Cry* reporter of the Midsummer Day campaign the General conducted in Sweden in 1893 says, somewhat extravagantly it must be confessed :

Had I the eloquence of the world, could I command the language of the nations and the descriptive powers of all men, I should fail to make you understand or see the blessedness of this 24th. Give me a pen from Paradise, the speech of the skies, the ability of an archangel, a hand from heaven, and the power to put glory into cold type, I might then be successful in making my readers understand something of the grandeur, blessing and glory that came to the hearts of thousands on this particular Saturday.

The day commenced with no fewer than thirty-eight steamers conveying thousands of Salvationists across the thirty miles of lake from Stockholm to Södertälje, where the camp meetings were to be held, and in pelting rain. Thirty-four souls were converted on board these steamers *en route*. A few days later the General conducted " A Day of Heaven in Holland " with a congregation of 5,000 in the woods of Middachten, the property of Princess Gravin Bentinck, who entertained him at the castle. When he had visited Holland in the April of the previous year 3,000 people, controlled by from thirty to forty policemen, greeted him as he stepped from the gangway of the ship that had brought him to Rotterdam in the early morning. 15,000 people waited to welcome him in the station square in Amsterdam later in the day, and it was estimated that another 50,000 lined the streets.

Writing to Bramwell from Kiel on 9 July 1894, William Booth gives expression to his sense of loneliness on these Continental tours :

I am terribly lonely at times. I ought to find more comfort and companionship in God. Pray for me.

And Bramwell writes a note of warning to his father from Zürich :

It seems to me that the devil is scheming to kill you by persuading you to do these awful rushes. A few hours' pause here and there would be an untold blessing, but I am tired of suggesting it.

The spring of 1895 saw him again in Holland, at Amsterdam, Rotterdam, and Utrecht, where at the last moment it was decided to march from the station square, in which the General had addressed a crowd of some thousands, to the mansion of the Baroness von Wreveed, where he was to be entertained. Nothing of this kind had ever previously been attempted owing to the restrictions of the city authorities, but on this occasion the police cleared the way, others formed a bodyguard beside the General's carriage, and between 3,000 and 4,000 people brought up the rear.

Scandinavia was visited again during the summer of this year. It is estimated that a crowd of more than 18,000 assembled to greet the General at Stockholm railway station. In Copenhagen he was given, for the first time, an escort of some thirty Salvationist-cyclists, but the General completely collapsed after three days of intense campaigning ; nevertheless he recovered sufficiently to resume his activities after missing only a few appointments. The year 1896 saw him yet again on the Continent, visiting Norway, Sweden, Denmark, Germany, Holland and Switzerland, where 1,074 seekers were recorded in twelve days. In the May of 1901, after again conducting Ascension Day meetings in Switzerland, the General visited Italy, speaking in the Olympia Theatre in Milan where, although some of the city's best people were present, the crowd was not as large as had been hoped. In Turin he spoke in the National Gallery. The police authorities in both cities afforded him the kindest attention.

In Berlin in 1902, following the end of the Boer War, for the outbreak of which England was bitterly criticized by Germany, the Army's international leader did what was considered at that time to be a most delicate, difficult and daring thing, when he stood before a large congregation of Germans and asked them to pray for the restoration of King Edward VII, who was seriously ill with appendicitis, and to sympathize with Queen Alexandra—and William Booth succeeded.

Back again in Norway in 1904 he writes to Bramwell on 21 April to describe his previous night's meeting in the Calmeyer Hall, where some 4,000 people had gathered despite the day being one of the worst in the whole year.

The great mass of the people stayed until after 11.30 p.m., and they had 22 out, which 22 I attribute not to my sermon but to the pulling and hauling the poor things had to suffer at the hands of the pertinacious fishers! So far as making the people hear in this building I could so do as easily as in the Stockholm Temple —I was going to say *more* easily.

And this long before the days of the microphone. He mentions the time he needs in preparation for the third International Congress, and says that almost immediately after this is over he will have to start off again for Switzerland.

I have been tempted this morning to think that my lot is rather a hard one, but I suppose I must go on to the finish.

His officers' councils in Germany in November 1904 he told the Chief of the Staff in a letter from Berlin, "were certainly the best Councils I ever held in the country by a hundred miles." On this occasion he was interviewed by a newspaper-man from Vienna who wanted to know "why we had passed by Vienna; that the people were saying 'Why is The Salvation Army working in every important city except ours?'"

CHAPTER THREE

UNDER SOUTHERN SKIES

When the General sailed from Southampton on 25 July 1891 for his first campaign in the Southern Hemisphere he was given a tremendous send-off. The R.M.S. *Scot*, making her maiden voyage, was escorted down the Solent by eight steamers carrying more than 4,500 Salvationists, including playing bandsmen. The voyage set a pattern after William Booth's heart. His book, *In Darkest England and the Way Out*,[1] was prominent in—and out of—the ship's library. Everywhere he went after its publication he explained his Scheme in detail to the people he thought could help its fulfilment, but always his campaigns were dominated by the spiritual issue, and this with evident success.

Having accepted the invitation of Mr Smart, a missionary, to conduct a midnight meeting with a handful of friends, the General left the boat at Madeira to fulfil his promise, returning to the *Scot* at one o'clock the next morning. Lord Carrington (later to become Marquis of Lincolnshire) presided over a lecture the General gave in the saloon at the request of a passengers' committee, and the General wound up his activities on board with a salvation campaign on the forecastle.

One of the great benefits that have come in the wake of the discovery and application of wireless communication is seen in today's marked contrast to the old-time uncertainty as to the arrival of vessels at the end of a lengthy voyage. The *Scot* had been held up by engine trouble, so that instead of the General arriving in time for meetings at Cape Town

[1] *The History of The Salvation Army*, vol. iii, part 2

on the Sunday, it was Monday morning before he landed, nothing being known of the delay *en route* until the *Scot* reached Table Bay. His further voyaging from Cape Town to Hobart, Tasmania, was likewise prolonged without any indication of the trouble, so that at his destination, in order to enable his engagements to be fulfilled, special trains and boats had to be called into service, in the arrangements for which the Tasmanian Government and the Union Steamship Company of New Zealand were most helpful.

Interest in the General's visits to South Africa, Australia and New Zealand was considerably increased by the publicity given to his book. At each large centre "select meetings" were held at which official representatives, including the governor, chief justice, premier and leaders of the country's thought gathered to hear him describe his Scheme.

South African nationals and the work carried on among them received special attention. At the General's farewell to Kimberley, expeditions were dedicated for service in the Orange Free State, Swaziland and Zululand.[1] William Booth was welcomed upon his arrival in Melbourne after the style of his farewell from Southampton. Upon landing he was given a reception which, in the words of one of Melbourne's leading newspapers, for "boundless enthusiasm, and frantic, almost hysterical, warmth of welcome, showed him to be the most popular public man that had ever visited Australia," and that it was "indisputable that his adherents constituted a following the like of which, in mere point of numbers, no distinguished visitor had ever before found ready to greet him."

The attendances at meetings held in the Exhibition Building are stated to have been more than 50,000, one of the most largely-attended and impressive being a memorial

[1] p. 133

to Catherine Booth. At the General's final farewell the Territorial Commander, Commissioner Thomas B. Coombs, presented to him a cheque for £10,000 for missionary work, this being the year's Self-Denial Fund total, roughly double that of the previous year and a record up to that date.

In all the other Australian and New Zealand capitals commensurate enthusiasm was shown and huge crowds gathered. Among the famous public men who took part in the proceedings were Sir Henry Parkes, G.C.M.G. (New South Wales), the Hon. Alfred Deakin (Victoria), Father of the Federation, and Sir George Gray (New

Sir Henry Parkes contributes to 'The Darkest England Scheme'.

BOOTH: 'Brothers and Sisters, we will now take up a collection.'

This cartoon by 'Hop' of the Sydney *Bulletin* shows the Premier of New South Wales, 'The Grand Old Man of the pre-Federation period', placing an I.O.U. in William Booth's cap during his visit to Australia in 1891. To people of that generation, who knew of Sir Henry's supposed impecuniosity, there was a subtle touch in the contribution of an I.O.U. The artist has drawn a caricature of himself in Salvation Army uniform.

Zealand). At Invercargill, New Zealand, the town took a half-holiday in the General's honour. Other special events of the General's programme were the commissioning of officers to begin operations in Western Australia, then coming into prominence as a goldfield ; the conducting of six weddings of officers on the same occasion ; the shaking of the hands of 3,000 Salvationists at a levee ; and the dedication of vans to travel in up-country districts. Although it is true, of course, that the earlier interest evoked by the General's first presentation of his Darkest England Scheme became less enthusiastic in regard to the setting up of the overseas colony in the Australasian countries, it never waned in respect to the application of the principles of the Scheme to local needs.[1]

On his way back from the Antipodes the General conducted a campaign in Ceylon, where he spent ten days, with Kandy and Colombo as the chief centres visited, and South India, where he stayed a full month, with Madras, Bombay, Ahmedabad and Calcutta as the principal places of call. Keen interest was evidenced everywhere by both the visitor and the visited. Great pandals, roofed but open-sided, were erected for the holding of meetings. Representatives of the Brahmo Samaj[2] were among early callers on the General in Calcutta. Again leaders of all classes flocked to the special gatherings at which he spoke on his Social Scheme. The Viceroy, the Marquis of Lansdowne, received the General in audience at Government House. The Maharajah of Tagore not only welcomed him to his palace, but was so interested by his philanthropic proposals that he later paid an official visit to the General at the local Salvation Army headquarters, and there again went into the *pros* and *cons* of the social amelioration of the poor of

[1] *The History of The Salvation Army*, vol. iii, part 2
[2] *The History of The Salvation Army*, vol. ii, p. 275

General Booth's Welcome Home

Salvation Army hosts cheering the General off Calshot Castle, Southampton Water

(From the front page of *The Penny Illustrated Paper*, 20 February 1892)

1 John D. Allan 2 Albert E. Webber 3 James Bateman 4 John Lawley 5 Edward H. Hill 6 George S. Smith 7 Elizabeth Rumsby (Mrs McKenzie) 8 'Blind Mark' Sanders

India, emphasizing at the end of the interview that, in his opinion:

They can be only induced to improve themselves, General, by such men as yourself—of sympathy and possessing the organization behind you for giving effect to your wishes.

On his way back to the United Kingdom the General addressed two meetings in Rome—one for Italians in the Sala Dante and another for English-speaking residents and visitors. Both were crowded.

The General's welcome home on 12 February 1892 was after the fashion of his farewell. Eight steamers, with more than 5,000 Salvationists aboard, met and escorted him through Southampton Water to the docks. Next day, Saturday, a long procession marched through London from Hyde Park to Queen Victoria Street. At Marble Arch the General took the salute in an open carriage from the 6,000 or 7,000 Salvationists estimated to pass by the saluting base. Tens of thousands of Londoners, Lord Rosebery and Lord Wemyss among them, witnessed this splendid spectacle. The following two weeks were occupied with welcoming demonstrations. At the Agricultural Hall, Islington, a subscription "banquet" was held, the tickets being one shilling each. It was said that more people—5,000—sat down to a meal together than ever before in the country's history. Two days of meetings in the crowded Exeter Hall were succeeded by a day each in Cardiff, Birmingham, Manchester, Leeds, Glasgow, Sunderland, Sheffield and The Congress Hall, Clapton.

That a few days later the second reading of the Eastbourne Repeal Act was given a two to one majority in the House of Commons[1] was undoubtedly influenced by these tremendous gatherings. The General conducted another "down under" campaign in 1895-6 when he visited South Africa,

[1] p. 277

where he met President Paul Kruger and the Hon. Cecil Rhodes; New Zealand, where he was accompanied by Commissioner Pollard, who had pioneered the work there; Australia, Ceylon and India. At Shahgunt the Chief of Police, forming a bodyguard for the General, respectfully presented to him his sword as a sign of full surrender on his entrance to the city. Upon his return to London he was welcomed at the Crystal Palace on the evening of 16 March by an audience numbering 20,000 assembled in the nave. Again in 1899 Australia and New Zealand were the scenes of memorable meetings when the General re-visited these countries.

IV THE PEN AND THE PRESS

Chapter One

THE GENERAL'S WRITINGS

THE General's bulky fountain-pen never ran dry and all that he wrote was in vigorous vein. Prior to his first visit to America in the autumn of 1886 he had this to say in the *War Cry* to his " Comrades and Friends " :

I have lived with many of you so long, and loved you so much, that I have been in some danger of coming to consider myself essential to your happiness and success. While some have said, " What shall we do without the General ? "—the General may have been thinking, without saying it, something after the same fashion. Now God is giving us an opportunity to break the snare. He can do without the General, and with God The Salvation Army can do without him also. The next three months will prove, in this country, at least, what the Army will do after the General has gone to Heaven.

In November 1889 he writes a lengthy article on how to win 100,000 souls :

If a man has a money-making spirit, he will probably make money. If a man has an ambitious spirit, he will possibly vault to some higher grade of life than that in which he was born. If a man has a soul-saving spirit, he will certainly save souls. It matters little what his circumstances may be. Therefore, the business of every one of us is to come into the possession of an absorbing passion for the salvation of men.

The first issue of *Orders and Regulations for Soldiers of The Salvation Army*—" 64 pages of red-hot truth and wise counsel"—was published in May 1890 at one penny per copy. It was prepared by the General himself, and in the Preface he wrote :

These regulations are issued in order that all soldiers of The Salvation Army may know what manner of persons they ought to be and what duties they ought to perform.

Every possible phase of a soldier's life and work—secular as well as religious—was dealt with clearly and definitely. This unique publication attracted considerable attention and criticism throughout the entire press. *The Sunday School Chronicle* said :

General Booth has done a brave thing which will surely test the loyalty and obedience of many members of the Army. He has ordered that no *smoker* shall hold office in any of the Corps.

The Star wrote :

We heartily endorse General Booth's indictment of fashionable funerals. His objection to the ungodly and barbarous customs are absolutely unanswerable.

From time to time these Orders and Regulations have been revised and re-issued. No soldier of The Salvation Army needs to have the slightest doubt as to what he should be in character and performance, or to what doctrines and pledges he is committed.

The two centre pages of the *War Cry* for 30 June 1894 were entirely given up to the General's Jubilee Message, which was printed in a facsimile of his own very bold and clear handwriting. It was addressed to "My Comrades throughout the World." Among other things he wrote :

I want you to stand up boldly for Jehovah. Everywhere you will find a growing disposition in favour of shutting Him out of His own world, especially when it comes to the business of mending it. Perhaps, we have not just now so many loud, open-mouthed attacks upon the existence and laws and government of the Almighty as in bygone days. In our time men simply turn their backs upon Him treating Him and His claims with indifference, if not with contempt. Jehovah, the Jehovah of the Bible, did very well for the world in its infancy, they will say, but in this stage of keen scientific research and high-class culture, with our heads reaching to the very stars, the world can dispense with the fable of an all-powerful, all-governing, all-wise and benevolent Sovereign. That is the notion of sadly too many, my Comrades, but *you* must stand up for Him wherever you go.

A Postscript to another long *War Cry* article, published in November 1896, reads :

There is one thing I would certainly like to see in Nottingham, and that is a Barracks that should be worthy of the opportunity presented in the Town.

That wish was not granted him, but on 12 July 1915 the splendid William Booth Memorial Halls, erected by the citizens of Nottingham as a memorial to her illustrious son, were opened in his native city by the Duke of Portland.

In April 1900 the General began writing in the *War Cry* a series of papers to be read in soldiers' meetings. Two years later they reached the extraordinary number of 115. In addition were four addressed especially to bandsmen. These letters to soldiers were eventually published in two volumes with the titles *Religion for Every Day* and *Love, Marriage and Home* (1902). At about the same time the General published, in question and answer form, a statement of the doctrines of The Salvation Army. In *The Prophet of the Poor ; the Life-Story of General Booth* (Hodder and Stoughton, 1905) T. F. G. Coates said :

The people who do not know the inner life of the Army, who only know it because its flag, its processions, its bands are in evidence in the streets of every town and almost every village, will be surprised to find how detailed are the beliefs of the Army as set out by General Booth. The Thirty-Nine Articles of the Established Church are a small matter in comparison with the hundred and nineteen closely-printed pages which are required to set out in detail the Salvationist doctrines, although the words of these extensively-described doctrines are simple.

The actual doctrines[1] of The Salvation Army are few and simple, but being fundamental are capable of full application to every detail of life.

FAITH-HEALING

"Runaway" teaching with regard to Faith-healing had become a great danger, and so, in the absence of a direct statement of the attitude of The Salvation Army toward this false teaching the General prepared a memorandum on the subject for the guidance of officers.[2] This was later printed in serial form in the *War Cry* from 12 November 1904 to 1 April 1905. The final instalment was accompanied by the General's own summary of the views set forth.

Chapter Two

BOOKS AND PERIODICALS

An unceasing stream of books, periodicals, pamphlets and leaflets was flowing from the Army's printing presses in every country in which its work had become established. In May 1887 a new training home book, *Called out!* was advertised, price sixpence. It contained chapters by Mrs

[1] *The History of The Salvation Army*, vol. i, Appendices F and R

[2] *Faith-Healing* (Salvationist Publishing and Supplies, Ltd.) 1903. Now out of print. Appendix A, p. 382, Faith-Healing.

General Booth, Miss Emma Booth, Commandant Herbert Booth and Major Oliphant. Saints, sinners, friends and foes should read it, said the *War Cry*, for it "gives interesting accounts of many different kinds of work done by the cadets in training. The narratives of the journeys taken by the men on the march, and the women on the omnibuses and waggonettes will interest all." A set of penny books printed on "blazing red paper," and bearing such titles as *Salvation in the Convent*, *The Saved Clergyman* and *A Presbyterian Salvationist* were also cast off the press, as was *Addresses to Business Gentlemen* by Catherine Booth. *The Life of Catherine Booth* (F. de L. Booth-Tucker) was published in 1892; the first volume of the *Red-hot Library*, *Brother Francis of Assisi*, by Staff-Captain Eileen Douglas, in 1895; *Orders and Regulations for Social Officers* in 1898; *Servants of all*, *On the Banks of the River*, *Books that Bless* and *Social Reparation*, being Personal Impressions of Work for Darkest England, all by Bramwell Booth, in 1899; *Bible Battle-axes* (Bramwell Booth) in 1900; and the first volume of *The Warriors' Library*, which was *Catherine Booth* (Brigadier Duff) in 1901.

A series of eighteen eight-page tracts was advertised in May 1887. These contained "true stories of salvation, and are suitable for enclosing in letters or for general distribution.' They were priced at 3d per dozen or 2s for 100. Among the numbers of pamphlets produced from time to time was *What doth hinder?* (1889), a reprint of Elizabeth Swift Brengle's articles from *All the World*. In 1889 several penny tracts were translated into the Welsh language and were obtainable from "Publisher Braine."

In the mid-eighties a *War Cry* printed in Welsh was published once a fortnight, twenty-one editions of the *War Cry* were being produced throughout the world, and important articles and items of news dispatched from London to each of their editors. *All the World* had been enlarged to thirty-six pages in 1887, commencing with the March number, and the price raised from a penny to two-pence. The circulation was then 22,000 copies, but the first month's figures showed an increase of 5,000 copies, and before the year was out the circulation figures had nearly doubled.

Owing to the rapid extension of the printing and publishing department, it was found necessary to obtain additional premises, and a large warehouse at 56 Southwark Street in S.E. London was secured on exceptionally good terms. The editorial offices of the *War Cry*—the circulation of which was now 260,000 copies weekly—the *Young Soldier* (101,000 copies) and *All the World* (40,000 copies), the cashier's and accountant's departments, the Special Commissioner's (John A. Carleton) offices, and the central *War Cry* depot were transferred in March 1888 from No 96.[1] While the *War Cry* and the *Young Soldier* were made up on the top floor at No 56, they were still being printed on three Marinoni machines at Fieldgate Street.[2] The Commissioner made himself *solely* responsible for selecting, revising, and "making up" eleven pages of the *War Cry's* sixteen, and also kept a hand on the other five. A mother and her three daughters—all artists—were constantly employed in the department, furnishing innumerable illustrations for the various periodicals, annual reports and appeals. Every address delivered by the General or Mrs Booth in or near London, and the more important ones given by them in the provinces, with many of the Chief's addresses, had to be taken down verbatim and transcribed for future publication.

The three periodicals moved their editorial offices yet

[1] *The History of The Salvation Army*, vol. ii, p. 75
[2] *The History of The Salvation Army*, vol. ii, p. 71

again in February 1890 to 98 and 100 Clerkenwell Road, E.C., and after eleven years of work in connection with the Army's publications, Commissioner Carleton was succeeded in April 1894 by Colonel Brindley Boon, but the literary and editorial officers were brought under the more direct guidance of the Chief of the Staff. An important re-arrangement was announced by the General in August 1896, when the trade and newspaper departments were separated. In the previous November Bramwell Booth had suggested this to the General, who was then campaigning in Australia :

The London newspapers [he wrote] are so important to the spiritual efficiency and general tone of the whole Army throughout the world that they ought to be far more international than they are, and everybody connected with them removed from the petty-fogging bothers which naturally arise in an ordinary trading institution.

Colonel (later Commissioner) Randolph J. Sturgess was appointed secretary of the newly-organized printing department at Clerkenwell Road. The editorial offices, however, were transferred to the fifth floor of International Headquarters, 101 Queen Victoria Street, in the September, and were accommodated there when the building was razed to the ground in the "blitz" of 1941. Commissioner Alex M. Nicol was the editor-in-chief, he having been appointed to this newly-created position in the previous year, 1895

During a great Celebration Day at the Crystal Palace on Tuesday, 15 July 1890, to commemorate the Army's twenty-fifth anniversary, the General announced that "The circulation of the *War Cry* has doubled, trebled, within the last four years. We are now circulating 300,000 *War Crys* per week in this country alone." In April 1891 Mrs Commissioner Carleton was gazetted as organizing secretary of the War Cry and Magazine sergeants' department at

International Headquarters. The then Colonel Nicol, who for some time had been the General's secretary, was appointed to the editorship of the *War Cry* in September 1892 with "Plain Brother Taylor" (later Lieut.-Colonel) as sub-editor; Captain G. Clutterbuck, and "a diligent shorthand" forming the entire staff. Theirs was indeed a colossal task, for the type was small and the wood-engravings few and far between. In the June of 1893 special correspondents were appointed for every section of the Army's warfare. They were the fore-runners of the present corps correspondents, who report the latest news of local happenings.

In February 1894 Staff-Captain (later Colonel) Alfred E. Braine, who had been the manager of the publishing department for the past six years, was appointed secretary for the Salvation Army literature of the United Kingdom, and became universally known as "the oil-can man," a sobriquet conferred upon him in a *War Cry* write-up which stated that "there was no man more suitable to oil the wheels of this vast literature machine." His task was to push the sale of all Salvation Army literature, books, newspapers and magazines. *War Cry* sergeants, with the rank of ward publisher, were appointed at every corps and made responsible for the canvassing of each house in their ward—a district comprising so many streets. The chief ward publisher of the corps was the publication sergeant-major. The British Commissioner (Commissioner T. Henry Howard) inaugurated a special spring campaign commencing in February 1895, "with a view to further extending the interests of the Kingdom of God by increasing the circulation of Salvation Army literature."

The summer of 1895 brought an attack from the Printers' Federation upon the Army's printing department, which was to be emphasized by a demonstration held in Hyde Park on Sunday, 7 July. The Army's printer and publisher,

Colonel Ernest A. Bremner, asked for an independent investigation of the matter in question, and a deputation from the London Trades' Council undertook this duty, issuing the following declaration :

London Trades' Council,
East Temple Chambers,
2, Whitefriars Street,
Fleet Street, E.C.
July 5th, 1895

The result of the Enquiry by the Printing Trades' Group was submitted to our Executive last night, and the Resolution which I append herewith was adopted.

Yours faithfully,
(signed) George Shipton,
Secretary.

P.S. You can use this in any way you think fit.

The Resolution read :

That the Printing Trades' Group of this Council, after investigating the wages and conditions of employment in that industry by The Salvation Army, having reported that they are convinced that there is no foundation to the statements made against The Salvation Army, this Executive determine not to take any part in the Demonstration of the Printing Trades' Federation on Sunday next, and that the result be sent to all persons announced to speak who are members of this Council.

The Hyde Park demonstration (?) came to naught.

About the same time, Edwin Evans, a licensed victualler and the proprietor of a place of public entertainment known as the "Winter Gardens," situated in Railway Street, Chatham, sued the *War Cry* for libel, claiming £2,000 damages. The Chief of the Staff had visited the town to conduct a midnight march and meeting, and the reporter commented strongly upon some aspects of Chatham life to which Evans objected. Called upon to withdraw the comments and make a public apology the *War Cry* had refused, with the subsequent issuing of a writ by the High Court of Justice against William Booth and Ernest Bremner. The words complained of were :

But there is in Chatham, as elsewhere, an appalling degree of public apathy on the drink and prostitution matters, and while we sleep the enemy is making progress, threading his way by newer and more refined tactics. I consider, for example, that what are described as " Winter Gardens," near to Military Road, are cleverer death-traps to the morals of the young of Chatham than a score of drinking saloons of the " Duchess of Edinburgh " type, and how it is tolerated with two flaming saloons on the opposite side, is more than I can understand.

An appeal for " tanner " (sixpence) subscriptions to cover the expenses of the action was started in the *War Cry*. Before the case was heard the police authorities, without any knowledge of the impending libel action, made sweeping and startling charges against Evans for " allowing his premises to be the habitual resort of prostitutes or reported prostitutes, and allowing them to remain longer than necessary for the purpose of obtaining reasonable refreshment." The Queen's Counsel for the defendant directed particular attention to the section of the Act under which the prosecution was instituted : " If any licensed person *knowingly* permits his licensed premises to be the habitual resort or place of meeting of prostitutes. . . ." The Bench recognized the fact that the case turned entirely on the word " knowingly." Evans was therefore given the benefit of the doubt and the case was dismissed. Evidently Evans saw that his chance of obtaining £2,000 from the *War Cry* had now faded, for through his solicitor he pleaded leave, before the Master in the Law Courts, to withdraw his action on the ground that the police case had cleared his character! The Master completely vindicated the *War Cry* by ordering that the record be withdrawn and the action discontinued, the plaintiff paying costs.

The first and only number of *The Coming Army*, which was to have been the monthly magazine of the Junior Soldiers' Movement, was published in December 1888[1]—twenty-eight pages for a penny. This magazine was especially suited to officers, parents, junior soldiers' sergeants and elder junior soldiers, and told how to get the children saved, how to keep them saved, and how to make them into soldiers. The frontispiece contained a Meisenbach portrait of the Chief of the Staff. The first week in January 1888 saw the title of the *Little Soldier* changed to the *Young Soldier*[2]. In the following year the General decided that the *Young Soldier* which, like the *War Cry*, carried a page of congregational songs, should be used for singing from at least once on each Saturday night and Sunday afternoon in every corps. Roll-book regulations were published in May 1889. This gave full instructions with regard to the use of the soldier's roll and cartridge book.

The first issue of the *Darkest England Gazette*, "the paper to silence critics," was published on 1 July 1893, it being "a thoroughly representative organ of the great Scheme whence its title comes."[3] The price was one penny for twelve pages weekly, and its purpose was, according to the editor, to "wake you all up to your duty to these millions of white slaves who were cradled in misery and want, who are huddled in dens and rookeries of squalor, held fast by the chains of devilish habits, cruel oppression and the lusts and passions of wicked men." In June 1894 its name was altered to the *Social Gazette*. An interesting new departure at the beginning of 1895 was the change in shape—four

[1] p. 343 [2] p. 340
[3] *The History of The Salvation Army*, vol. iii, p. 76

large pages, 23″×17″ of six columns each—and price—reduced to a half-penny. "The *Gazette*," said the *War Cry*, "will voice the wails and needs of the submerged." By October its circulation was 42,000 weekly.

Another new magazine, but for private circulation, made its appearance in January 1893, the *Officer*, the first editor of which was Commissioner F. de L. Booth-Tucker. Its object, among other things, was "to place within the reach of every Officer the best and newest plans for saving the world." Yet another new journal, the *Local Officer*, made its debut in August 1897, for the edification and instruction of the 45,000 local officers in the British Territory "in all that pertains to the General Order of the War Section," as the editor-in-chief described its function. This monthly magazine was of the same size as the *Officer*, octavo, contained thirty-two pages, and was priced at a penny. The cover was white, but printed in two colours—red and black. The General had "The First Word" in which he expressed appreciation of the services of his corps sergeant-majors, treasurers, sergeants, bandmasters, secretaries, and so on :

> Your General is proud to know that in devotion, in sympathy, in Self-Denial, and in capacity for the fight to which God has called you, outside the Army you have no parallel on the face of the earth.

Assurance a new monthly magazine, also for private circulation, appeared a year later, the *raison d'être* being explained by its sub-title : The Official Gazette of the Life Assurance Department of The Salvation Army.[1] Commencing as a monthly letter to members of the Naval and Military League[2] *Under the Colours* eventually became a magazine.

[1] p. 226

[2] *The History of the Salvation Army*, vol. iii, p. 289

The Chief of the Staff, in the absence of the editor-in-chief, Commissioner Nicol, devoted considerable attention to the *War Cry* at the beginning of 1898, and one result was the formation of a news department, the special and exclusive work of which was to put the paper in possession of all that was taking place on the British battlefield and that was worth knowing. "The news department," it was stated, "will get on the war trail immediately after being acquainted with the news of any successful event that has taken place." Staff-Captain H. L. Taylor was placed in charge.

The *War Cry* celebrated the twentieth anniversary of its beginnings during the December of 1899, being described in the issue of 30 December as "The greatest thing in religious literature" and "one of the wonders of the Century." A year later the *War Cry* gives an account of the work of the editorial department. Commissioner Nicol was still the editor-in-chief, Brigadier Fred J. Moss filled a long-felt lack in the editorial system and had recently been appointed to the general management and direction of editorial duties. Major Eileen Douglas was the *War Cry*'s sub-editor, Staff-Captain Alfred G. Cunningham—who became Chief of the Staff in 1939—being temporarily in that position during the Major's absence. Major John Bond was editor of the *Social Gazette*, Brigadier Mildred Duff editor of the *Young Soldier*, Major Forward the sub-editor; Adjutant Ruth Tracy, who was to become one of the Army's outstanding song-writers, was also on the *Young Soldier* staff. Major V. F. Ward edited *All the World*, Adjutant E. P. van Norden, an American woman-officer, the *Deliverer*, and Major H. L. Taylor edited both the *Officer* and the *Local Officer*, his "sub" being Staff-Captain Brindley Boon, who only a few years before had been a colonel, the head of the department, and before that, the Army's first chief secretary. He had resigned from the oversight of the International Trade Headquarters to devote himself to the advancement of various social and political reforms, but had returned not long afterwards, much disillusioned.

The front page and three other full pages of the Christmas Number of the *War Cry*, dated 20 December 1902, were printed in colour on a newly-purchased Augsburg machine. This innovation was referred to as marking "an important departure, and, perhaps, the most interesting and attractive in its history." It was not until 7 February 1903 that another coloured front appeared. The coloured fronts, with but twelve pages to the issue, continued intermittently until the Easter of 1904, after which they were discontinued, evidently the venture not being as successful as had been hoped.

In April 1904 Commissioner Nicol was appointed to take charge of the newly-instituted literature department, which included the editorial department, Brigadier Moss becoming its chief secretary.

Newspapers being unobtainable in many villages the inhabitants depended upon the *War Cry* for their knowledge of passing events in the outside world, hence the column giving such information was eagerly read.

Chapter Three

MUSIC AND SONGS

Much of the congregational music and many of the songs that are in constant use in the Army today were written and published during the period with which this volume

The Band of the Great Western Hall (Marylebone) Corps in 1888

Fifth from the left on the second row from the back is Corps Sergeant-Major Edgar Hoe, who became a Lieutenant-Commissioner, and next to him is Corps Secretary Albert E. Powley, who became a Commissioner. Seated on the ground next to the drummer is Bertram Mills, who became proprietor of the world-famous circus bearing his name

Regent Hall Corps Band in 1889

The boy standing third from the left on the back row is Herbert W. Twitchin, who was for many years the Bandmaster, and who received the M.B.E. for his activity as such—a unique honour in Salvation Army history

The Salvation Army's Bands

(*Above*) An early-day impression, 'The Salvation Army' by William S. Strang (*Below*) The Household Troops Band (Bandmaster Caleb Burgess) playing on the sands at Margate in 1892, which it did twice a day for three months

is concerned, either in the *War Cry* or the *Musical Salvationist.*[1] The type for this magazine of songs, which contained both words and music, was set up almost unaided by the entirely uninitiated but ingenious Fred W. Fry,[1] who also was responsible for the printing on a second-hand press installed in the basement of the Clapton Congress Hall. Following the production of the *Musical Salvationist* came a volume in the tonic-solfa notation under the title, *Songs of the Nations.*

The prolific Colonel Pearson's " I'm set apart for Jesus " appeared in the *War Cry* for 6 November 1886, in which year a General Order was published drawing attention to the regulations concerning Christmas singing, when it was suggested that such tunes as " You must be a lover of the Lord " and " Prepare me " should be used to " call up to the minds of the guilty who hear them, solemn thoughts, and so probably lead to conversion on the following day." The words and music of the Army's first Christmas carol were written by Richard Slater,[2] " The Saviour chose a lowly place," and this appeared in the first volume of the *Musical Salvationist* ; but the first of all Slater's songs to be published appeared in the first number in July 1886. It was entitled, " While in my Lord confiding," and was written to an operatic melody by the French composer, Daniel Auber. The music of many another great composer was also to appear in the *Musical Salvationist* to words by Salvationists, and in due course was arranged for brass bands in the band journals. " Nothing but Thy Blood can save me " is considered by General Orsborn to be the greatest of Slater's hundreds of songs.

Klaus Östby, who had been a clarinet player in the Norwegian Royal Guards Band, having become converted

[1] *The History of The Salvation Army*, vol. ii, p. 124
[2] *The History of The Salvation Army*, vol. ii, p. 122

and commissioned an officer in Oslo, began in 1890 to write music for The Salvation Army, and subsequently was appointed head of the music editorial department in Sweden, during which time he sat at the feet of Richard Slater.

> Of the songs that were composed during the earlier years of The Salvation Army [he wrote], there is hardly anything that can be compared with Slater's songs. They have a lasting value, and as a composer there is nobody who can be compared with him.

An interesting glimpse of Slater's efforts to influence for Christ, by his songs, a former atheist colleague is shown in a diary entry of 30 January 1891, which reads :

> Took family to Wheeler's.[1] Wife sang several of my early songs [to her husband's organ accompaniment]. Wheeler had been to Bradlaugh's house to see if he could be of service. Bradlaugh [2] died at 6.30 this morning. . . . W. gave me the confession that in his judgment B. had been much of a despot and self-seeker.

William Booth did not write many songs, but " O boundless salvation!" published in the Christmas double number of the *War Cry* for 1893 and given a whole illustrated page, is by far his most popular song. Bramwell Booth's contribution to the songs of the Salvationist include " My faith looks up to Thee, My faith so small, so slow." As a song-writer his younger brother, Ballington, is best known for " The cross is not greater than His grace," and his eldest sister, Catherine, " The Maréchale," for her words to a French melody, " O Lamb of God, Thou wonderful Sin-bearer." Emma, the Consul, achieved song-writing success with " I'm climbing up the golden stair to Glory," to music by her husband, Commissioner Booth-Tucker. Words and

[1] James Mazzini Wheeler, sub-editor of the *Free-thinker*, with whom he had continued to remain on the friendliest terms after his conversion.

[2] Charles Bradlaugh, M.P., the agnostic, and a bitter opponent of the General.

melodies of songs that are widely known throughout the Army world appeared under the name of Evangeline Booth, among them "The wounds of Christ are open." The youngest child of the General, Lucy, claims a place among the Army's song-writers for "Keep on believing."

But Herbert was considered to be *the* song-writer of the Booth family. "The penitent's plea," written for the Christmas number of *All the World* for 1889 is, perhaps, chief among the many songs that bear his name and that, it is safe to assume, will live long. On the occasion of his marriage to Cornelie Schoch in September 1890 Herbert's songs were collected, with a few by his bride, making a total of eighty-six, and issued in a volume under the title *Songs of Peace and War*. When Mrs General Booth passed away in the following month Herbert was credited with the words and music of "Promoted to Glory," a funeral march which competent judges consider to be equal to any other, even those composed by some of the Great Masters. It is only fair to state here that, in the carefully-considered opinion of those who knew him best as a composer, and who served with him for many years, Fred G. Hawkes and Arthur Goldsmith, themselves composers and arrangers of no mean order, Richard Slater purposely subjugated his original music to the needs of The Salvation Army in its earliest and formative years. He had, however, the potentiality to write music that would have vied with that of some of the Great Masters. It is also significant that when Herbert Booth left the Army[1] and thereby cut adrift from the head of the music editorial department, as Slater pointed out to the author of this volume of the History, his name was never again heard of as either a composer of words or music.

Other authors and composers of this period "whose

[1] p. 364

works do follow them" are J. D. Allan (he became a Congregational minister) who wrote "Saved and kept by the grace of God" and "Blind Mark" Sanders,[1] who wrote "He loved me I cannot tell why." Alfred E. Braine composed the melody of "Whosoever will may come" to which William McAlonan put the words. Charles Coller, a household trooper,[2] wrote scores of songs, his first to be published being "Three bidders for the soul." W. G. Collins, of Guildford, gave the Army "I'm bound for Canaan's shore." Fred William Fry wrote many a well-loved song, among them, "To Thy cross I come, Lord." Alec Greig is remembered for "Why did He love me so?" One of Canada's best-known early-day Army song-writers, Professor Wiggins, passed away in July 1900. His most popular song was "Swing those gates ajar." Canada gave the Army another song-writer in William A. Hawley, whose contributions include "Shall you? Shall I?" One of Slater's many "discoveries" was Cadet Agnes McDouall (later Mrs Staff-Captain Heathcote), a Scottish minister's daughter, whose song, "Jesus came with peace to me," is a great favourite. Other still well-used songs are "Thou art enough for me" (W. Elwin Oliphant); "Storm the forts of darkness" to the melody of "Here's to good old whisky, drink it down" (Robert Johnson, a Scottish officer); "The Light of the world is Jesus" (Bandsman Alec Knight, of Clapton Congress Hall, a converted boxer); "My sins rose as high as a mountain" (John Lawley, the General's A.D.C. for many years); "We're the Army that shall conquer" (T. C. Marshall); "My sins went rolling away" (Tom Plant); "Speak once again, Lord" (William Ebbs, a British corps officer); "The path is very narrow" (Bandsman H. Allen, of New Brompton); "Eternity eternity, where will you spend

[1] p. 27 [2] p. 202

eternity ? " (Tom Robertson, " the one-legged prophet ") ; " Holy Spirit, come, oh, come ! " (Words by Richard Slater ; music by Thomas Emerson, of Darlington, who claimed to be the first commissioned bandmaster) ; " Love divine, from Jesus flowing " (Mrs George A. Mackenzie) ; " Thou art a mighty Saviour " (Bandmaster G. S. Smith, of Kingswood) ; " Lord, I come to Thee beseeching " (Ruth Tracy) ; and " Jesus came down my ransom to be " (Immanuel Rolfe). Major Alexander T. Smith, of the U.S.A., who died in 1895, was the author of the well-known chorus : " Oh, yes, there's salvation for you."

Song-writers who must also be mentioned as having made their mark between 1886 and 1904 were Bandmasters E. H. Hill (Southall), and A. E. Webber (Boscombe), Bandsman (later Colonel) E. H. Joy (Folkestone), Bandmaster Laurence Halcrow (South Shields 11), Deputy-Bandmaster Herbert W. Twitchin (Regent Hall), Mrs H. A. Beavan (Cardiff), Major (later Brigadier) Ernest Holdaway (New Zealand), Staff-Captain (later Colonel) Arthur Playle, John Bruce (Jarrow), Alice Purdue (Notting Hill), who later became Mrs Major Robert Edwards, and Deputy-Bandmaster Souter (Chalk Farm). Private (Major-General) Martyr, of Upper Norwood, one of the several military officers who became Salvationists in those days, also wrote the words of a song.

Captain James C. Bateman[1] passed away in June 1888 just a month before his song, " O the Blood of Jesus cleanses white as snow," was sung in the Spanish language by the boys of a Catalonian college, the master of which, captivated on hearing the song some time previously, had asked permission to use it in connection with an examination. Bateman had been a music-hall singer and a heavy drinker before conversion in his native Hull. Becoming an officer

[1] *The History of The Salvation Army*, vol. ii, p. 110

he commanded some of the largest corps, achieving great success as a soul-winner. Among his other songs is "Down where the living waters flow."

A new scale sheet was published for bandsmen in 1887. "The sheet not only gives some of the elementary matters connected with music, but indicates the way in which every note is produced, both by valve and slide instruments," declared an announcement. The first song competition was held in this year, but only one of the eight prize-winning songs achieved any degree of popularity, Alec Greig's "I am redeemed." The first band tutor, for the cornet, appeared in July 1890, and the Salvation Army bandmaster's full score of the monthly band journal was first commenced in September 1892. The early part of 1899 saw the publication of a new song-book which was pronounced "a distinct improvement," and a band-book containing many more congregational tunes than that published in 1884 was produced in November 1900.

The General decided that now Salvation Army bands were making surprising progress musically, there should be some further development in instrumental music, and Slater was commissioned to produce a selection and some original marches. The first, which might be described as a *true*, selection, "Old Song Memories," appeared in January 1902 and was given away to bands as a novelty. Four months later the first properly-constructed march, "The Morning Hymn," was published.

The "musical department"[1] as it was first named, was established on 22 October 1883, at the Clapton training home, under the personal supervision of Commandant Herbert Booth, but when he moved his residence to New Barnet the department was also moved there in order to be near him. Then came a change to 98-102 Clerkenwell

[1] *The History of The Salvation Army*, vol. ii, p. 123

Road in the City itself, where the trade department was situated. Slater by this time had long been in full control. A further change took the department to Queen Victoria Street.

V ORGANIZING THE FIGHTING FORCES

Chapter One

CORPS OFFICERS AND THEIR CORPS

BETWEEN the years 1886 and 1904 and often despite bitter persecution—or, perhaps, because of it—corps sprang up like mushrooms in the cities, towns and villages of the United Kingdom. To change the metaphor, some of these corps, particularly the smaller ones, were like oysters. They opened up to emit a pearl, in the shape of a convert who was destined to become an outstanding officer, and then closed up again soon after, sometimes never to re-open.

The Annual Report for 1887, published in the first issue of the 1888 *War Cry*, gives the statistical position of the Army at the end of the preceding year, with the advances made in corps and officers throughout the world. An increase of 476 brought the world total of corps to 2,262, and an increase of 1,492 brought the world total of officers to 5,684. The Army itself was a third larger than it was at the beginning of the year, and its forward steps were much more striking and important than those of any previous year in its history. During 1886 no fewer than 148,000 persons confessed conversion at the penitent-form in the United Kingdom alone. The Bishop of London, in summing up the results of the Church of England's efforts in the Metropolis, had mentioned, among other facts, that it had assembled in its London churches 11,000 persons on weeknights; thereupon the Army made a survey to discover that on one ordinary weeknight in November 16,746 persons had gathered in its London barracks, with no other attraction than the Gospel of Christ.

* * *

Regularly inaugurated battles against ignorance, apathy, sin and the devil as they shape themselves in the (roughly) 18,000 rural villages of England dates back only to 1885 [wrote "S. F. S." in the *War Cry*, dated 5 November 1887]. But tonight, along the deep, red-banked lanes of Devon, through the already frost-touched Suffolk valleys, up and down streets where so much noise never was heard in the old days unless some man were going home to his miserable wife and bairns, "rare drunk," in hundreds of villages the tramp of soldierly feet will sound tonight, and the rude clogs and heavy boots made for wearing in snowdrifts and plough-field, will be "beautiful" indeed, for their very ring on the hard, frosty ground will mean "good tidings"!

This was made possible by the Camp System, which followed the Outpost System: a village worked from a corps by a corps and for a corps. This system was given up when it was realized that it ignored a vital principle—it was centrifugal instead of centripetal. The outpost depended upon its parent more than upon itself. The Camp System gathered into groups from two to five tiny hamlets, no one of which alone could support an officer, and gave them a man *or* woman, or perhaps two men or women who, though living at the camp centre, yet *belonged to* the whole camp.

"Egyptian darkness is not an exaggerated figure of speech to apply to the religious life of villagedom," says the *War Cry* for 29 July 1893, announcing the General's determination to launch a universal village campaign which was to include the circle system. A circle corps consisted of two or more societies grouped together under the command of one or more officers. Some circle corps were under the command of an Agent-Captain, actually an officer on probation. His duties involved a three-fold plan: salvation work, assurance work,[1] and Salvation Army trade. Each society had its sergeant-major, who acted as Captain in the absence of the officers. For instance, High Barnet, in Hertfordshire, operated seven societies, a coach-house serving as a place of worship at Potters Bar and a cottage at South Mimms, London Colney, Radlett, Shenley, Hadley and Northaw. By the end of the year more than 20,000 villages with their total population estimated at 15,000,000 were being catered for spiritually by circle corps. Brother Dick Moses, of Falmouth, had the distinction of being the first of several envoys appointed under the circle system, at the beginning of 1896. He was in charge of Flushing, an out-post of Falmouth corps.

Another outcome of the attention which the General and the Chief of the Staff continued to give to the village war was the appointing in April 1898 of six provincial circle officers, all of them field officers running large corps: Ensigns Warman, McDuff, H. Johnson, Hudson and H. W. Ward and Captain Hughes, who were made responsible for the prosperity of existing circles and the opening up of new ground. The provincial circle officers were to work under Brigadier (later Colonel) Otway, secretary for village war to the British Commissioner. Also under their charge were the field batteries; a field battery was a light one-horse van, with platform attached for outside meetings, provided with two berths, and with accommodation for two men.

The General was constantly concerned about the welfare

[1] p. 226

of his officers, and among other considerations decreed that the offerings at the holiness meeting held at all British corps on Friday, 17 June 1887, should be devoted to the Sick and Wounded Fund, from which officers who were sick, injured or weakened by overwork should be temporally supported. More than 2,000 officers were then serving in the United Kingdom. In the issue of the *War Cry* for 14 January 1888, an appeal was made by the Field-Secretary for bags of potatoes or vegetables, fish or other eatables, to be sent to the Officers' Homes of Rest at Maindie Hall, Pentre, at 5 Arlington Villas, Brighton and at 15 Gore Road, London, E. In January 1889 a minute was issued making it compulsory for every field officer to take a furlough of at least twelve days once in twelve months. In May 1890 it was announced that all officers were *compelled* to take a fortnight's rest every year, when their corps would be officered by "specials" set apart for temporarily filling a gap.

* * *

Although extraordinary methods were commonly employed by officers in the early days in order to attract people to their hall, Bramwell Booth described a method that was quite new even to him when writing on 18 March, 1893, to his father:

> At Hackney Wick, where there has been the most awful struggle, the two girls a fortnight ago decided to put in practice one of your off-handed suggestions at the recent Council in London. And having one evening put their night-dresses on over the uniform went out, to the immense sensation of the whole population. Result: place crammed with men every night since, 30 souls in the fortnight, 20 of them, men. Whole neighbourhood stirred.

A five weeks' siege announced in the *War Cry* to commence on Sunday, 19 November 1893, was to be "a desperate attack on the Works and Fortifications of the Powers of Darkness." In his letter to his officers and soldiers the General wrote :

Let there be Sieges of Public-Houses, Music Halls, Markets, Sieges at various times, weekdays as well as Sundays. Sieges of Factories, Mills, Foundries, at Dinner hours and other hours.

The siege was concluded " with a Great Christmas Triumphant Rejoicing over the Prisoners Captured and the Spoil Taken."

* * *

When the General visited Nottingham in March 1886 the *War Cry* reports that he met " the Bonded Officers," presumably the financial local officers—treasurers and secretaries—who had had to sign a bond prior to their appointment. " The General enlarged upon the important duties of Bond Officers." Later in the year it was stated that " it was always intended that local officers should change frequently." A definite period was fixed, at the expiration of which the commission lapsed ; a General Order issued by Bramwell Booth on 10 July stated that " all the Treasurers' and Secretaries' Commissions should lapse on the 9th of August," and be sent by treasurers and secretaries to 101 Queen Victoria Street. The transference of the cartridge book to the care of the corps secretary resulted in the more regular and systematic distribution and collection of cartridges and, says the *War Cry* of 1 February 1890, resulted in a steady rise in the United Kingdom of £500 per year. At a staff council held in the early part of 1890 the General decided that every corps in the United Kingdom should, after 12 April, hold a soldiers' assembly on the Tuesday night of each week. An open-air meeting was also to be held, but no procession. Cartridges were to be brought to this meeting, and the divisional officer was to decide whether it was expedient to call over the names in the cartridge book when receiving them.

In August 1900 the Chief of the Staff invited 250 local officers, both men and women, from the London province to spend a weekend camp with him and Mrs Booth at the Hadleigh Farm Colony. One of the party described the occasion as "the happiest, holiest, liveliest holiday of my life." Included in the number were "Dan the Dustman," "Pat the Police Terrier," "Diamond Eye" from Peckham, "Whisky Hot" from Marylebone, and "The Man in Three Uniforms" from Lambeth. The Chief spoke for seven hours during this "holiday" weekend of spiritual counsel.

* * *

A regulation uniform for both men and women was decided upon in May 1887. A good serviceable man's Norfolk jacket for summer wear could be bought for 14s, with trousers at 7s. A woman's Norfolk jacket, trimmed with three rows of Hercules braid, cost from 9s. 6d, and a skirt from 8s. Regulation caps were obtainable from 3s 6d. Bandsmen were at liberty to select a red-topped cap in place of the navy blue.

* * *

On 19 November 1887, a General Order was issued by William Booth stating that

> No barracks are upon any consideration to be let or used for Political Meetings of any kind, as The Army exists for the salvation of men of all parties, and the use of the barracks by speakers on either side tends to create ill-feeling and to prevent men from coming to the services who might otherwise do so. In every case where from some special considerations of friendship to The Army exceptions have been made, the above results have followed, so confirming us in this determination.

The question of a Salvationist's perfect freedom so far as politics is concerned was clearly stated in the *War Cry* of 13 October 1900, in reply to an erroneous statement made by Dr John Clifford, an outstanding London minister, to the Baptist Union. The doctor declared that the General had issued an order forbidding his soldiers to exercise the vote at the General Election; but on the actual day that Dr Clifford made his charge the following statement appeared in the Army's official organ:

Our Officers and Soldiers are well aware that, while each Soldier is free to vote for the candidate whom he thinks is likely to best promote the good of the State, The Army, as such, is neutral. Politics is not its work, and, therefore, no barracks, banners, musical instruments, or other property belonging to The Army must, in any way, be employed to further the interests of any political candidate or party.

* * *

An historical survey of Salvation Army bands at the beginning of 1903 stated that the drum was used for the first time in March 1880 in a council of war, as the staff gatherings were then called, conducted in Wales. "It was borrowed from a worldly band for the occasion." The Fry family band assisted at this council. Chatham, in August 1880, had a band of eight players marching in two ranks—a big thing in those days—although the instrumentation was made up, oddly enough, of fifes, flutes, violins and concertinas.[1] Middlesbrough I had a band of four violins which led the march. The same was the case at Leamington, while Gloucester could boast of a properly-formed drum-and-fife band. Carlisle had a large and efficient band. At Sheffield II the band consisted of a cornet, a violin, a concertina, several flutes and two triangles. The triangle and the cymbals were very popular. The

[1] *The History of The Salvation Army*, vol. ii, p. 118

band at Mexborough, in January 1881, possessed an astounding combination of a violin, a flute, a bell and a huntsman's horn! Old Basford[1] in the same year employed two violins, a banjo and a brass whistle. A concertina band was "in full swing" at Battersea in 1882.

It was a natural consequence that, having decided upon preparing, printing and publishing its own band music, the Army should undertake the making of the instruments, and so an instrument-making factory was established, in a small way at first, with only a man and a boy, in May 1887.

Alfred M. Philpot, an early-day apprentice, states that in 1896 a full set of silver-plated instruments, at a cost of £400, was ordered and made for the band at Oldham II. This was to have been put on show at the exhibition in the Royal Agricultural Hall, but William Booth saw the instruments during his inspection of the stands prior to the official opening and was greatly displeased. "Is this the way the bands waste their money while I am going around the world begging for the Darkest England Scheme?" he demanded of Philpot, who was in charge of the stand. Philpot says that the instruments had to be put out of sight, and that it was quite a number of years before Bramwell Booth, realizing the economy involved in the long run, gave instructions for silver-plated instruments to be made at the Army's factory, although Regent Hall had a "silver band"—the instruments were nickel-plated—in August 1882.

A radical advance in connection with the Army's musical forces was made by the Chief of the Staff when on Sunday, 10 December 1899, he conducted a day's councils with 300 bandsmen at Clapton. At that time more than 10,000 of the Army's 15,000 bandsmen were serving in the United Kingdom. The councils were preceded by a

[1] *The History of The Salvation Army*, vol. ii, p. 117

musical festival, the first to be held; 500 bandsmen participated, including the International Staff Band under Brigadier (later Commissioner) George Mitchell, and a string band conducted by Major Slater. Councils for bandmasters and songster-leaders were held at Clapton for the first time at the beginning of 1903. The Chief of the Staff conducted them; 350 bandmasters were present, representing 800 bands and 12,000 bandsmen in the British Territory.

Answering the question: "Should not The Salvation Army have well-trained choirs as well as bands?" the editor of the *War Cry* replied in the issue of 26 November 1892:

We certainly cannot see any objection in principle to a certain number of soldiers associating together, with the sanction of the Captain, for the purpose of taking a prominent part occasionally in salvation singing. Of course, the songs and music must be provided by The Salvation Army. But the whole drift of choirs, in our judgment, is to confine the singing to the few, instead of making it the servant of many, and until the danger is less we advise all corps to be guided by their leaders.

On the last Sunday in September 1898 twenty-four soldiers of Penge, who had been formed into a singing brigade by Commissioner Carleton, a bandsmen of the corps, commenced conducting their own afternoon and evening open-air meetings with the Commissioner as their sergeant, and working on the ordinary brigade system. On this occasion they sang an original song composed by Adjutant Ruth Tracy to "Annie of the Vale," "a ringing Christy Minstrel piece of music," and an old song to a new tune, "Isle of Beauty." While it is claimed that Penge was the first *commissioned* singing, or songster, brigade, a similar brigade had been in operation for some years previously at Kilmarnock 1 corps in Scotland.

* * *

A terrific gale of wind blew down the two-storied barracks at Derby I, Nun Street, during the night prayer-meeting of Sunday, 3 February 1889, and resulted in the death of two young people, and injuries to some twenty others. The roof crashed, the side walls tottered and fell and the floor in the least crowded part of the upper room in which the meeting was being held gave way in the centre, precipitating a considerable number of people into the ground floor below. The Rt Hon. Sir William Harcourt, M.P., headed the list of gentlemen appointed to institute a relief fund. Only a year previously the corps had suffered the loss of its barracks by fire. Bristol Circus was destroyed by fire on a Sunday in August 1895.

Chapter Two

SUPERVISING THE FIELD

An important extension of Army operations in Great Britain was announced during April 1893 when the General decided upon further developments of staff oversight in such a way as to bring the Home Office[1] and International Headquarters into close touch with local affairs, and at the same time establish stronger bonds between the larger and smaller corps operating in the same section of the country. This entailed the country being divided into provinces, the boundaries being so arranged as to include three or four of the existing divisions. Each province had its headquarters situated in a city or town within itself. A new position was created, that of Provincial Officer,

[1] p. 201

whose chief assistant was to be known as the chancellor of the province. Eleven provinces were instituted, with headquarters at Clapton, Cambridge, Bristol, Liverpool, Manchester, Newcastle, Sheffield, Birmingham, Glasgow, Edinburgh, and in Ireland. Major (later Commissioner) William J. Richards, who was appointed to Manchester, was the first Provincial Officer. The duties of the Provincial Officer included those of the former chief divisional officer, but were essentially wider and more representative. He was to represent the Home and Territorial Headquarters on the Field. "It would not be far out," says the *War Cry*, "to call him a sub-territorial officer, with a sub-commissioner's responsibilities and duties," although "he is not quite that."

Writing to the General in his own hand on 16 August 1892, Bramwell Booth had expressed his strong disapproval of the Divisional Officer's position which his father had instituted in 1880.[1]

If the Provincial is a live man who *works* [he wrote] and has not too much geography to cover if he lives on the ground, why do we want a D.O. at all ? . . . Is it possible to retrace our steps ? Should we be seriously worse off without them if we had 6 efficient Provincials with, say, 4 Travelling Inspectors each ? What does a Corps want after all with a D.O. once a fortnight ! *It is too often.* Are we not overdone with Staff—Field Staff included—which in its turn makes other Staff ? "The big fleas must themselves have little fleas to bite 'em !" . . . The money saved would pay for many things, including a living and permanent staff of specials to raise hard places—that is a rank of officer who went in and *officered* a poor go till he raised it and was *supported* while doing so by London. To spend £50 in salary while raising a poor thing enough to go of its own weight *would pay us a hundred-fold !* . . . I believe I am right in suggesting that we have *one* chance of *permanence* next to the Holy Ghost—viz. in the FIELD OFFICER.

[1] *The History of the Salvation Army*, vol. ii, p. 50

Evidently William disapproved of Bramwell's disapproval for while Provincial Officers disappeared from the British territory more than fifty years ago, Divisional Commanders remain.

England's first woman Divisional Officer[1] was Staff-Captain Polly Ashton, who was appointed on 24 February, 1890, to the command of the Herts. and Beds. division with headquarters at Luton. A year later she farewelled for Canada. The next woman Divisional Officer was Staff-Captain Rebecca Chatterton, who was appointed to the Brighton division a few weeks later. So successful and welcomed were these appointments that within a few more weeks Staff-Captain Annie Bell was appointed to the command of the Northampton division.

The rank of Ensign was introduced in 1888, Captains McKernon, Storey, W. E. Rosie and Smith being gazetted in the *War Cry* on 10 March. In November staff officers began to wear silver stars on their shoulder-straps to denote their rank. One star on each shoulder indicated an Adjutant, two stars a Staff-Captain, three stars a Major, four stars a Colonel and five stars a Commissioner. An Ensign wore shoulder-straps, but no stars. Officers of lower rank were not allowed to wear either stars or shoulder-straps.

On 2 August 1890, Major George A. Mackenzie, Field-Secretary for the United Kingdom, was promoted to the rank of Brigadier after seven years' service. This was announced officially in the *War Cry* gazette and commented upon in the Chief Secretary's Notes of the following week: "This is a new rank, coming betwixt a Major and Colonel. The crest and S's are worked in blue"; but in the gazette dated 5 October 1889 it had been announced that Major (later Commissioner) George Kilbey, of the Sydney and Western Division, Australasia, had been promoted to be

[1] *The History of The Salvation Army*, vol. ii, p. 19

Brigadier and to have the oversight of all operations in the colony of New South Wales.

Commandant Herbert Booth decided in November 1891 to appoint two under-secretaries to assist the Field-Secretary, and the United Kingdom was divided into two portions by a line running, roughly, from the southern part of Lincolnshire across to the Dee and taking in North Wales. Major Hodder was appointed as the South British under-secretary and Major Eadie as the North British under-secretary. They were responsible for the prosperity of every division in their territory.

In January 1897 an essentially *British* staff council was held for the first time at Clapton. Hitherto the distinction between International Headquarters staff and the Home Office staff had not been strictly adhered to in such councils held under the presidency of the General. The special correspondent of the *War Cry* reported that "startling changes and developments" were discussed, including better employment for soldiers, improved systems of giving and collecting money, pedlars and vans for the villages, and more work in connection with the junior war.

Chapter Three

THE INTERNATIONAL COMMAND

"A Day in the Chief's Office" is graphically described in the issue of the *War Cry* for 8 January 1887, and is a revelation of the amazing indefatigability of this twenty-nine-year-old second-in-command of an already world-wide organization. Bramwell Booth is heavily bearded, has a shock of thick black hair, freely sprinkled with grey, and his brow is deeply-lined; evidences of the mighty responsibility so early thrust upon him in controlling the Army's vast ramifications. From the early morning of this day he studies the multifarious letters and documents that flow unceasingly to his large writing-table, handing over certain important items for the attention of Commissioner Railton, and immediately dispatching reply telegrams, or a messenger for an officer he wishes to see. A cable arrives telling of the General's tremendous meetings in the United States. A Continental letter unfolds a story of rough fighting and endurance by hardy salvation soldiery, of scanty mid-day meals for five people eaten from the same plate, the only one in the quarters. A staff-officer enters and is given his orders; a diminutive messenger-boy is asked to get the Chief into telephonic communication with Commissioner Carleton of the trade department; the officer-in-charge of the work in London and a rescue home officer seek the Chief's help—a man has been arrested and free legal aid is hoped for; a horrible case, a young girl being involved. Bramwell Booth solves the immediate problem.

A French count is shown in; he wants to know something about "L'Armée du Salut." The arrangements for the welcome home reception to the General—who had been campaigning in America—are discussed with Colonel Nicol. More visitors, more letters, more arrangements. Five staff-officers are allowed five minutes each for their particular perplexing problems and requests. The Field-Secretary, a messenger from the property department, a clerk from the legal department, the cashier, the foreign correspondent, a Divisional Officer, and a score of others with an endless panorama of business file in and out. Then the tireless Chief gets down to his personal dictation until lunch-time, when a few slices of brown bread constitute his meal. Commissioner Railton returns with the latest news from South Africa—the Army has commenced in the diamond fields. The legal clerk is back with a number of lease agreements for signature. A provincial Major is ushered in with a number of matters that only the Chief can settle. The secretary of the National Vigilance Society has called concerning a court case. He is followed by the cashier, who brings cheques for signature. Passages to India and America for forty or fifty officers must be settled at once with the shipping company. A rebellious officer is gently but firmly dealt with. A woman in distress is brought in. She used to clean the old Christian Mission offices, so that she is personally known to the Chief, who sees that her case is thoroughly investigated. Now Dr Washington Ranger, the Army's blind lawyer, is announced, and a long and tedious conference follows with representatives of the company interested in the Building Association.[1] It is four o'clock and a dense fog hangs over London, but the Chief is still pouring over his papers. A Swedish visitor is shown in and the war on the Continent is discussed. Between seven and eight o'clock the Chief leaves for home for rest and refreshment prior to more hard labour until the midnight hour. "Little does the outside world guess the mental toil, harassment and care that this great movement costs its leaders," concludes "Mahlah," the interviewer.

* * *

International Headquarters had a very narrow escape from total destruction by fire on Saturday, 16 April 1887, when at about three o'clock an alarm was raised. The staff had just time to vacate the building. Dense volumes of smoke and flames issued from a large quantity of paper stored in the lower portion of the premises at 101 Queen

[1] p. 233

Victoria Street, where the book department was situated, and the stock was seriously damaged. It was dark before the fire was completely mastered.

Another alarming fire broke out in the small hours of the morning of Tuesday, 2 December 1889, at International Headquarters. The cause was unknown, but the fire, which started on the top stories—there were seven—extended no further down than the third storey, thanks to the energy of the firemen, but every floor was literally flooded with water. The Chief of the Staff was on the spot soon after, " calm and collected as usual, giving clear, concise directions to the officers around him, for the salvage of papers, books, &c., as well as the preservation of important documents." When the headquarters staff, numbering about three hundred, came off duty, the Chief issued instructions for the main portion of them to go to the junior soldiers' war offices at 36 Upper Thames Street. It so happened that the fire occurred at the time when those concerned were working out arrangements for the big farewell of officers and change of corps throughout the country. Ali the farewell sheets were destroyed. The General himself arrived on the scene as soon as he reached London. When asked how the catastrophe affected him he answered : " None of these things move me ! " " Amid all the desolation the headquarters boys cleaned themselves, put on their dainty white helmets, and with highly-polished instruments, assembled outside. They were soon surrounded by the crowd. . . . They sang—and sang so sweetly that we shall never forget—Oh, what a Redeemer is Jesus, my Saviour ! "

* * *

Colonel Alex M. Nicol, in command of the London division, was appointed the first permanent Secretary for Foreign Affairs on 25 February 1888.

In June 1900 Commissioner Cadman was appointed the first Travelling Officer, with authority to move rapidly about the world as occasion required, attend and conduct councils, preside at public demonstrations, make known the principles and methods of the Army, and advise and help leading officers ; in fact, to act as the General's representative both at home and abroad.

Another new and important position was created in May 1903 when Commissioner Pollard was appointed by the General to act as Chief Secretary to the Chief of the Staff. In the latter part of 1904 the direction of officers in the United Kingdom, which hitherto had been the responsibility of Commissioner Coombs, came more directly under the Chief of the Staff, with Colonel (later Commissioner) Hay continuing as Chief Secretary and Colonel (later Commissioner) William Eadie as Field Secretary.

* * *

In February 1889 Commandant Booth commenced a new department which planned the work of the spiritual specials and other headquarters specials, and the arrangements for Commissioner Eva Booth's meetings. Adjutant Cox was in charge. Today this is known as the special efforts department.

* * *

Another extension was made to International Headquarters in April 1889 when three floors of the adjoining premises at No 99 Queen Victoria Street were annexed. These contained twelve rooms with staircases. Behind and adjoining No 101 was a fine four-storey building with the ground floor fronting Upper Thames Street. It was the same width as " 101 " and was added to it on lease for £450 per annum.

The Oriental Club, situated in New Bridge Street, above the Blackfriars Station of the District Railway, was acquired by purchase in January 1890 for a new branch of International Headquarters, the Home Office, as it was called, which is the National Headquarters of today, and which was under the control of Commandant Booth. Each of the three floors was capable of accommodating a staff of nearly 800 persons, and a temporary hall built on the roof could hold a congregation of some 200 persons. It was in this hall in May that the Chief of the Staff officially conducted the opening of the Home Office, the staff—known as "Home-lot"—of which had been temporarily housed in Clerkenwell Road following the fire at "101." It is interesting to note that the first prayer was uttered by *Captain-Sister* Clarkson. Bramwell Booth was in a reminiscent mood. He spoke of the one room which had served as a headquarters in 1870, when two officers directed affairs generally. A house was then taken in Victoria Street, Hackney, one room of which was used as an office. This headquarters was succeeded by a two-roomed establishment over a second-hand furniture shop. Then came transfer to the Market in Whitechapel.[1] The vestry became the headquarters, but the work increased so rapidly that the long room used for night meetings was taken over as an office. A small house was acquired in a neighbouring street for the accountants and later another was secured for the uniform department. "Now," said the Chief, "there are 506 people employed in the offices of the combined headquarters, and 570 in the headquarters of the various countries outside of the United Kingdom." A paragraph in the *War Cry* for 15 April 1893, headed "Flitted!" announced that the business of the Home Office would in future be carried on at 101 Queen Victoria Street. "No-one liked the place," said Com-

[1] *The History of The Salvation Army*, vol. i, p. 137

missioner George J. Jolliffe, who was then the Commandant's secretary, "nor did visitors enjoy the climb to the top, where H. H. B. had his own office—there was no elevator."

* * *

In the Christmas Number of the *War Cry* for 1890 Mrs Bramwell Booth announced the foundation of a Women's League, "especially of young women, who desire to be used for the salvation of souls, and for the general extension of the war." There was to be a subscription of 6d per quarter, and a small badge and ticket of membership provided. The *Deliverer* was to be the organ of the league, the objects of which were five-fold :

1. To promote the entire consecration of all its members to God and His service in The Salvation Army.
2. To promote the salvation of souls, especially of young women, by individual effort and personal dealing.
3. To promote the rescue and restoration of fallen women and the protection and warning of those in moral danger.
4. To promote the training of children for the war, upon the principles of love and obedience laid down by the General and Mrs Booth.
5. To promote the encouragement and consolation of each other at all times, especially in seasons of sorrow, sickness or trial.

* * *

A travelling combination known as the Household Troops Band was formed on 12 April 1887 for the dual purpose of conducting evangelistic campaigns throughout the British Isles and setting up a standard for corps bands, its first appointment being at Hounslow on 14 and 15 May. Although provided with food and clothing, its thirty members received no salary, and usually slept in halls, chapels or barns. Their uniform consisted of a second-hand military tunic of a greenish shade, blue serge trousers, an old military white helmet, military gaiters and an overcoat. They carried a knapsack and a pair of military blankets on their shoulders. Except on very rare occasions the bandsmen walked from place to place, often enduring ignominious opposition. Their first tour was undertaken in the Midlands. In October 1888 the Household Troops Band became the first Salvation Army musical combination to visit an overseas country when it commenced a most successful five months' tour of Canada, which was followed by a month's campaign in the United States of America. Staff-Captain Harry Appleby, a cornetist of unusual ability, was the first bandmaster, and he was succeeded by Caleb Burgess. One of its members, Frederick G. Hawkes, became Slater's assistant in the music editorial department in 1892, and next to his chief played the largest part in helping to build up the international reputation of Salvation Army music and to increase its repertoire. Arthur Robert Goldsmith, who was to become an outstanding composer of both vocal and instrumental music and joint head of the music editorial department with Hawkes, had his first composition, "Why Jesus came," published in the December 1895 number of the *Musical Salvationist*.[1]

* * *

The Juniors' Staff Brass Band was formed in the early part of 1889 by the boys employed at International Headquarters. In December 1891 Staff-Captain Fred W. Fry was appointed bandmaster of the International Staff Band, but the beginnings of the Army's premier brass combination were inauspicious, for no report of its activities appear in the *War Cry* until August of the following year, when "a brass band, twenty-six strong, with Staff-Captain Fry

[1] p. 182

at its head, composed of 'crack lips' from the International, Home Office[1] and the Trade Headquarters," participated in the General's salvation campaign in Holland. The International Staff Band as such is first mentioned in the list of participants in the funeral procession of Colonel Pearson, which marched from the Great Assembly Hall, Whitechapel Road, to Bow Cemetery on 22 October 1892. When the Household Troops Band was disbanded in the following year, Bandmaster Caleb Burgess took charge of the Staff Band. Re-organized officially by a minute issued by the Chief of the Staff on 23 September 1893, the International Headquarters Brass Band, as it was called, comprised "twenty-five in number, who will special every third weekend and one night per week as well as taking part in extraordinary demonstrations." Its first appointment was to the Hoxton Slums on 3 October, and its first weekend at Hackney on 8 and 9 October. Adjutant Marshall was appointed leader and Brother Jabez Lyne, bandmaster. In order to secure the advantage of the cheaper rate on the railways for parties of fifteen, beyond which number the rest of the party paid full fare, the International Staff Band, with Lieut.-Colonel Mitchell as bandmaster, became the International Staff *Bands*, and travelled 1,000 miles during 1903 with the British Commissioner (Coombs). The International Trade Band, comprising members of the staff and employees of the various departments at Trade Headquarters in Clerkenwell Road, was formed by Ensign (later Colonel) Fred G. Hawkes in April 1895, and quickly rose to a front rank place among Army bands, but its existence came to a speedy end when it became necessary to have separate buildings for the printing and instrumental departments.

[1] Formed during Herbert's Booth command of the work in Great Britain, it lasted for only eighteen months. Sir David Morgan, a wealthy Welsh industrialist, was a member of this band during his youth

Music and song flooded the Exeter Hall in January 1891 in a festival, the first of its kind, conducted by Commandant and Mrs Booth, and in which the cadets, the dossers' brigade and the Household Troops Band participated. New songs and choruses were introduced, some of which have maintained their popularity to the present time.

* * *

In May 1898 it was decided that the boys and girls who worked at International Headquarters, and who had until then been commissioned as Lieutenants without any field training, must henceforth enter a training home, under the same conditions as applied to candidates in general, before being allowed to wear the yellow braid of an officer. At a meeting conducted by Commissioner Pollard the first batch of eight youths accepted for this new arrangement included Alex Mitchell, who was to become a Lieut.-Commissioner; Cecil Rees, who became a Lieut.-Colonel; and William Richards who, when a Brigadier, died on missionary service in Korea. Four months later the boys returned to headquarters to resume their former position, but with the rank of Lieutenant.

* * *

International Headquarters, with its labyrinth of departments in Queen Victoria Street, was financially supported (1) by the generosity of the Army's friends, (2) by Auxiliary contributions,[1] (3) by the Publishing and Trade Departments, and (4) by a portion of the money raised by Self-Denial Week.[2]

[1] *The History of The Salvation Army*, vol. ii, p. 84
[2] p. 215

Chapter Four

OFFICERS—THEIR SUPPLY AND DEMAND

The amazing expansion of The Salvation Army during the early eighties, particularly so far as the opening of corps on the British Field was concerned, created a corresponding demand for men and women to take charge of them. Prior to the International Congress of 1886 a great deal had been achieved in devising and putting into effect measures for obtaining and training officers.[1] The ever-increasing need for leaders, however, and the urgent desirability that, as the general standard of education improved, cadets should receive instruction that would keep them at least as equally informed as the people they were to lead, had been a problem not easy of solution, and had resulted in a period of general experimentation, during which the training of officers passed through various phases.

At first the urgency for reinforcements had led to the curtailment of training to an extent that had robbed it of much of its effect. Happily, some of the cadets whose training had been cut short, and who had been sent on to the field within a very few weeks, were of sufficient spiritual and mental calibre to enable them to rise to the demands placed upon them, they later being appointed to positions of great responsibility; but there were others upon whose capacity the strain was too great. It was soon realized that something more was needed and strenuous efforts were made to meet the necessities of the case as they became evident. Mrs Booth early described the aim and character of the Army's training.[2]

[1] *The History of The Salvation Army*, vol. ii, chap. 12

[2] Appendix B, p. 384

It was announced in the *War Cry* for 9 October 1886, by the Chief of the Staff, that a further revision of the plans for receiving and training cadets had become necessary and that the General had decided that action should be taken forthwith and the following system be put into effect:

1. Cadets to be grouped together in Brigades of from twelve to twenty—Lads or Lasses, as the case may be—under the immediate control and care of an efficient officer attached to the Training Home Staff. They will then be sent to various positions in the field, the preference always being given to Corps struggling against great odds and needing extraordinary effort. Where necessary houses will be taken for certain periods at such places, these serving as little branches of the one great Training Home, where the same rules and regulations will be strictly observed, the same teaching and instruction given, and operations conducted in a similar manner.

2. Miss Booth (the Training Home Mother), Miss Eva Booth, Commandant Herbert Booth, and Major McKie will pay frequent visits to all the Depots, holding special meetings with the Cadets, and also using their influence in helping spiritually and financially the various corps at which they are placed.

3. In order that the Training Home may have an opportunity of more justly testing the qualities of Cadets, and in order that these may, in their turn, have a better chance of being actively engaged under the eye of their Training Home leaders, a Division comprising the counties of Northampton, Rutland, Hertford, Bedford, and Buckingham, has been granted to the Training Home, and will be worked under the direction of Commandant Booth. Major Oliphant, of the Headquarters Staff, has been appointed to Northampton to take charge of the Division.

4. After a period of service at a Depot Cadets will be drafted into the division attached to the Training Home, where they

will serve for a time as Officers, under the eye and immediate care of the Training Home.

5. At certain times the Homes in London will be filled for a course of deep spiritual instruction and blessing, when every Cadet will have the opportunity of coming into personal contact with the General, Mrs Booth, and other leaders of the movement.

A year later another special announcement was made by the Chief:

From every part of the world comes still the cry, send us men and women with love, with courage, with backbone, with the daring, reckless Calvary spirit. The need is greater than ever.

The General had given orders that so soon as the necessary arrangements could be completed, the number of cadets in training should be increased to 1,000. In his *War Cry* Notes for 19 January 1889 the Field-Secretary was pleading desperately for

Men! Men! Men! Oh, my God, send us men! Never mind, if you *do* stammer, or if you have a wooden leg, or a weak chest, or if you have only one eye, or have no platform ability. If you are a Salvation Army soldier, and have got brains, energy, tact, and business ability, don't let this appeal haunt you till you die, write the Field-Secretary straight away.

Later, he cools down a little:

We want the best intellects, the clearest brains, the warmest hearts and most successful men.

Evidently in those days it was a case of "Whosoever will, may come"!

In *A History of the Training Homes* published in *All the World* for August 1890, Major Oliphant, surveying and confirming the development of the work as already set out, added the information that at the time thirty-two training garrisions were established in London. By 1894 the training system had reached, under Field Commissioner Eva Booth, a commendably efficient and regular routine. First, as the main plank in a new system, there were " eight solid weeks of training at Clapton at the outset of the cadethood." Into this period was compressed a skeleton of Scripture knowledge, to be built upon systematically for seventeen months afterward ; instruction in reading, writing and arithmetic for those who needed it ; and such teaching in the doctrines, discipline, organization and methods of The Salvation Army as would meet the cadet's most pressing wants in the next four months, which he was to spend in practising what had been preached to him. The cadet then went to a corps in the London divisions which had an outpost that he would work under the direction of his training leaders. Then followed another short period at Clapton.

It was further intended that when commissioned the new officers should remain on probation for another twelve months during which they would follow a course of Bible reading and the study of selected books, meeting every three months for instruction by Commissioner T. Henry Howard, or the Field Commissioner. By this time the " Garrison " system had been abandoned because, for one reason, it was found that when so many cadets were available to do the work of the corps, the soldiers tended to leave it to them, with obvious results.

From time to time various alterations of the system were made until by 1903 the period of training at Clapton had reached six months. In June of that year the General announced that the period of training was to be extended to ten months, and the training home buildings were altered so that the number accommodated was raised from 200 to 500.

The General also stated that he believed some of the best of the Army's young people would feel that the longer term of training would give them a much better opportunity for qualifying themselves for their life-work. He also expected that some of his soldiers would see in this arrangement a stronger promise than ever that their children would "be wisely trained for the glorious work to which I urge them." New lecture-rooms, new dormitories, new class-rooms, new dining-rooms would have to be provided. Larger premises would have to be allotted for cooking, washing and bathing. Additional officers' quarters would have to be found for the larger staff. The Congress Hall required additional accommodation, especially for its young people and children, its local officers and bandsmen, and the cost was estimated at about £15,000. He hoped to have the new buildings ready by the following November when 500 men and women would be needed for training.

At an Exeter Hall gathering on 11 January 1904, 570 cadets—including 60 in the Women's Social Work[1] Training Home—were received by the General who, in the course of his address, gave a concise description of what they were going to be taught:

In the first place [he said] they are going to be taught sound doctrine. . . . They are going to be taught the evil of sin, the verity of the Great White Throne, the certainty of everlasting Heaven and hell. . . . They are going to be taught the Cross of Calvary and the meaning thereof. They are going to be taught facts. They are going to be taught the Bible. They will be taught history, secular and religious, how to rescue their fallen brothers and sisters, how to get sinners saved, how to get people to the penitent-form, how to resist temptation themselves, how to maintain their faith in God, and how to fight their way to Heaven. . . .

Then, turning to the standing cadets, he told them:

[1] *The History of The Salvation Army*, vol. iii, p. 192

You are not coming into Salvation Army Officership to get a living, to win the favour of men, or even to save your soul. But because you believe that position gives you the opportunity of bestowing the largest measure of benefit on the poor world, and saving the largest number of its inhabitants from sin and misery here and hereafter.

Commissioner David M. Rees was the training principal and Lieut.-Colonel Harriet Lawrance head of the women's side. The actual re-opening of the training homes took place on Thursday, 28 January, the occasion being marked by a public meeting in the adjoining Temple. Thus was closed the period of experimentation in regard to this most important aspect of Salvation Army procedure. The main framework of its provision for the supply and training of its officers was now set for many years to come, although, as would be expected, there has been development in curriculum, in manner of teaching and in giving cadets practice in actual work on the field.

* * *

An interview with the Field-Secretary, Brigadier James Hay, in 1896, reveals interesting statistics regarding field officers in the British Territory; there were then 2,600, 100 of whom had completed ten years' service, 200 held staff rank, and 500 were married. In those days all local officers' commissions went out from the Field-Secretary's office.

* * *

Throughout August, September and October 1886, the "Life Guards," as the 200 men-cadets of the training homes were dubbed, carried out an extensive campaign, marching the 300 miles, under Commandant Herbert Booth and Major McKie, back to London from Newcastle-upon-Tyne, to which city they had travelled from London by steamship. Three three-wheeled tandems used for "flying attacks" were known as the "Royal Iron Horse Artillery." The women-cadets, divided into three "flying squadrons" under the command of Staff-Captains McDouall, "Forward" (Kirkby) and Lawrance, respectively, visited no fewer than 109 cities and towns in the South, Midlands, and Eastern counties.

* * *

It has now been discovered that Annie Rees, of Merthyr Tydvil, was the first cadet to enter the Gore Road training home in April 1880,[1] and before she was seventeen years of age. She eventually married and, as Mrs Adjutant Harry Whitchurch, was promoted to Glory from Hamilton, Scotland, in September 1895. An extract from the personal diary of F. W. Fry reveals that his wife was the first cadet to be commissioned :

> We sold off and came to London on May 14th, 1880, Agnes C. Peck [later Mrs Fry] and other Salisbury Soldiers coming up to these meetings [Whitsuntide]. After these meetings Miss Peck was received into the Training Home, and was the first Cadet to leave the T.H. In June she went to open Newtownards, Ireland.

Chapter Five

THE SINEWS OF WAR

The Salvation Army has always approached the subject of finance with the same care and thoroughness that have characterized every other part of its organization, and the

[1] *The History of The Salvation Army*, vol. ii, p. 67

system it employs has earned the unqualified commendation of financial experts and authorities who have had cause to study its workings.

Among other things the annual balance sheet for 1887 stated that the cost of training the 848 officers at Clapton had been £12,366, which was more than £900 less than for 1886, when the officers had numbered but 609. The saving had been made "in consequence of improvement in our plans." 89,319 had been added to "our sitting accommodation [in corps buildings] at a cost of over £30,000." Most of the London newspapers published articles concerning this balance sheet. The *St James's Gazette* through misapprehension no doubt, spoke as though the General had paid £250 for a yacht for his own use.

But this [comments the Field-Secretary in his *War Cry* Notes] is so modest a thing by the side of the £60,000 house tale that it is scarcely worth correcting. *The Times* had a leading article, nearly two columns long, about our advance, written with sails set to catch both sides of the wind. It was, however, a strange oversight of that usually well-informed paper to say that this was the first balance sheet we had published, more especially seeing that they themselves devoted a column to the consideration of our 1885 balance sheet.[1] The General has written to them reminding them of this, and enclosing balance sheets for ten years. Surely that old tale about our issuing no balance sheets is not going to start again!

The Army was running no fewer than eight different funds in February 1888, viz: the General Spiritual Fund for the maintenance and general oversight of the work in all parts of the world; the National Fund; the National Training Home Fund, to meet the cost of training and equipment of officers; the Sick and Wounded Fund, to provide homes of rest and necessary treatment for officers who broke down through disease or overwork; the

[1] *The History of The Salvation Army*, vol. ii, p. 333

Foreign Service Fund, to meet the expense connected with the sending out of officers to all countries, and the opening up of fresh fields of battle; the Rescue Fund, for the salvation of fallen girls and women—twelve homes were maintained in Great Britain alone[1]; the Slum Fund, to meet the expenses connected with the establishment and maintenance of the various slum posts in the lowest and poorest neighbourhoods of London—fourteen slum posts were in full operation; the Cellar, Gutter and Garret Fund, another branch of slum work[2]; and the Property League.[3]

In 1887 the father of an officer left her £5,000 in his will on condition that she resigned from the Army within six months of his passing. She carried on, however, and the trustees distributed the money to hospitals and other charities, but the daughter declared that the Lord had distributed to her a hundred-fold in spiritual blessing. One of the Army's largest bequests in these early years was between £60,000 and £70,000 left by Mrs Bell, of Harviestoun Castle, Clackmannan, Scotland, who only a few weeks before her passing had provided hospitality to the General and the Chief of the Staff in her home.

THE SELF-DENIAL EFFORT

An all-out effort to relieve the financial strain of the Army, and to carry forward and extend its work, was announced by the General in a letter to "Beloved Comrades and Friends of the Salvation War," published in the *War Cry* for 14 August 1886. The unprecedented trade depression of the previous two or three years was telling upon the Army's finances, for in many parts of the country its soldiers,

[1] *The History of The Salvation Army*, vol. iii, chapter 2
[2] *The History of The Salvation Army*, vol. iii, p. 20
[3] p. 232

belonging almost exclusively to the working classes, had been reduced to the deepest poverty, and this had resulted in the emigration of large numbers to Canada, the United States and Australia. Many regular contributors, owners of land or of manufacturing businesses, had suffered from the depression and had not been able to give of their money as formerly.

Despite the desperate position the General was opposed to retrenchment. The duty of the hour, he said, was "Forward!" Enumerating the six different purposes for which he particularly required money William Booth wrote:

> We propose that a week be set apart in which every Soldier and friend should deny himself of some article of food or clothing, or some indulgence which can be done without, and that the price gained by this self-denial shall be sent to help us in this emergency.

By this paragraph was inaugurated the great annual Self-Denial Appeal which has been an established fact in every country in which the Army is working and which has provided the main source of its income down the years. William Booth asked for at least £5,000. The first Week of Self-Denial began on Saturday, 4 September. 50,000 persons were wanted to join the Self-Denying League and were asked to fill in a form containing their names and addresses and send it to headquarters. The issue of the *War Cry* for 4 September contained a long letter, prominently displayed, from Mr J. E. Billups,[1] writing as a fellow-soldier. His one urging reason for making the Self-Denial effort a big success was that it would send "our dear General" to America with the joyful assurance that he would be free from financial care. "Let us all give our

[1] *The History of The Salvation Army*, vol. i, p. 252; vol. ii, p. 282

littles," he pleaded, "for the War Chest." In this same *War Cry* the editorial launches into prophecy :

There is another consideration which adds importance to the coming week. The Army will probably on that occasion take another step in the direction of making history. The example cannot fail to be followed up in the future, for the enormous probability is that on this first week of September a new method of maintaining and extending the Kingdom of God will be inaugurated. Through the long years of the world's future, thousands and hundreds of thousands in public and in private will in this particular week give themselves up to special labour and Self-Denial for the Salvation of mankind.

A secular newspaper declared, in making reference to the Self-Denial League, that the Army was evidently on its last legs, or it would not be compelled to have recourse to such an expedient.

If the Army is on its last legs [replies the *War Cry*] our critics must confess that they are rather remarkable ones, seeing that on them during this very year The Army had marched for the first time into hundreds of towns and villages delivering thousands of drunkards and harlots and thieves, and other poor slaves of sin and the devil, and is hoping to enter before the year closes four or five new nations ; nay, on these legs it has just sent forth a shipload of missionaries to India, making a grand total of a hundred sent to foreign countries in six weeks.

The secular press, from *The Times* to the provincial papers, reprinted the appeals in some instances with quite favourable comments. The religious newspapers described the effort and seconded the appeal. "Surely," wrote the *Methodist Times*, "such work as this ought not to be crippled for want of a few thousand pounds in the richest country in the world." A whole column of small type relates how enthusiastically the leaguers entered into the new idea :

The General [he always set the pace in any new move] started ten days ago by giving up meat.

A very prominent officer CUTS THE HAIR of a still more prominent Officer (not before it was wanted) and this saves sixpence.
A gentleman gives up going to Scotland to see a great friend married.
A Captain gives " what salary comes to me for that week."
Another Officer sends the money he has been saving up for a new tunic and will patch up the old one. His wife will send 5s out of her market money and three of his children will send 6d each from their money boxes.
An old friend knocks off his pipe and promises £1 as the result.
A gentleman and lady drunk hot and cold water instead of tea, cocoa, coffee and milk.

According to Bramwell Booth [1] the Self-Denial Appeal came out of a remark of Major Carleton on the platform of the old Exeter Hall, to the effect that he proposed to " give up his pudding " for a certain period in aid of the Funds. " Why not have an annual effort," said the Founder, " in which everyone shall be invited to perform some act of self-denial ? "

Despite all the propaganda and the appeals the £5,000 was not forthcoming, the total amount raised being some £180 short of the target. This was a national appeal and was not made in 1887, but in 1888 a universal appeal was launched and a Week of Self-Denial instituted from 6 to 13 October for the extension of the Army throughout the world. A whole page of the *War Cry* of 1 September was devoted to a letter from the General. He says : " Missionaries invite us to Algeria. Then there is Egypt. . . . In Alexandria a band of Christians cry to us to come and help them, saying that they wait to be Salvationists." He suggests that " the Self-Denial Effort originated in Great Britain two years ago become an annual institution, and to let it embrace the whole world." Again £5,000 was the target for Great Britain, and this time the effort was a fine success. The General's most sanguine expectations were surpassed, for

[1] *Echoes and Memories* (Hodder & Stoughton, 1925)

the total reached £8,293. Friends outside the ranks added £4,606, and the estimated amount contributed by overseas countries was £2,100, thus making a grand total of £15,000.

It was now definitely decided that a Self-Denial Week should be held every year, "sheer necessity" demanding that the effort be made. Success again attended the 1889 effort, and the total sum contributed from all sources amounted to £20,041, Australia's share being £2,100, the highest of all the countries outside Britain.

The front page of the *War Cry* for 4 October 1890 contained Mrs Booth's last message, for she passed away on that very day.[1] It was a letter concerning the Self-Denial Effort, and one sentence in it has lived through seventy years: "Self-Denial will prove your love to Christ." The total was £30,577, an increase of £10,000 on that of the previous year. Sweden's contribution rose from £322 to £2,333—a magnificent result "considering the poverty of her people." Australia and New Zealand combined contributed £6,500, an increase of £4,190 on the previous year's total and nearly £480 more than Great Britain. These figures give an idea of the overseas countries' appreciation of the work of the Army in their midst.

In his letter of 26 September 1891 the General reiterates the advice he had given in previous letters regarding the Self-Denial Effort. "Do thyself no harm," he writes, "do not injure yourself in any practice of devotion or service unless some great and valuable end is to be gained thereby." That year the result was described as "brilliant," there being yet another increase of £10,000. France, Switzerland, Norway and Belgium each doubled its total. 1892 saw another increase of nearly £8,000, but 1893 dropped a little, to a £300 decrease, and again in 1894 to a decrease of £3,577; but this was on account of the American Self-

[1] p. 303

Denial Fund being entirely devoted to the New Memorial Headquarters in New York. The *War Cry* for 28 September, 1895 contained some striking panels declaring that

ROMAN CATHOLICS will rally to the help of our Self-Denial Week because, among other things, The Salvation Army is truly catholic in spirit and practice.

NONCONFORMISTS will help us because we have maintained, at great cost and sacrifice, the right of British citizens to worship according to the dictates of their conscience.

METHODISTS of all shades will loyally support because in essence The Salvation Army is the work of John Wesley brought up to date.

UNITARIANS will support us because, strong as their objections are to our teaching, they recognize that our Movement makes for the brotherhood of man.

The PLYMOUTH BRETHREN as one man should help us because at almost every service the Scriptures are read and expounded.

The SOCIETY OF FRIENDS will join us because we place woman on the same platform as man in the service of God.

An interview with Major (later Commissioner) Wilfred L. Simpson, the international cashier, revealed that £20,000 of the total amount of £43,000 reached in the 1895 appeal was counted in his office at "101," and many of the collecting envelopes contained only a few pence each.

Self-Denial Week had been brought on earlier in the year in 1897, and by 1904 had reached what was described as the "magnificent total" of £56,000—a substantial advance on all previous years—as every former effort, declared the General, had been confronted with difficulties. Political strife, governmental uncertainties, the threatened depression in trade, the Lancashire cotton famine and the weather had all combined to make comrades nervous about achieving the 1903 total of £55,000, let alone smashing it.

When the British and Foreign Bible Society celebrated its 100th anniversary on Sunday, 6 March 1904, the Army donated £1,000 from its Self-Denial Fund. The Society had approached the General with a view to the Army co-operating in its effort to raise £250,000 in order to clear itself of debt and put it in a first-class financial condition. The date, however, happened to correspond with Self-Denial Sunday, and the General thought that to make two appeals at the same time would be to court failure for both.

THE RELIANCE BANK

Yet another fresh adventure connected with finance was the establishment of The Salvation Army Deposit Bank, of which Major Ernest A. Bremner was appointed secretary in the summer of 1890. By the end of the year no fewer than 64 branches had been opened in England, Scotland, Wales and Jersey. The following advertisement appeared in the *War Cry*:

A good and competent local manager, having a suitable central address in a main thoroughfare, is wanted in every town where The Salvation Army Bank is not yet established.

One-third of all deposits was invested in securities authorized by the government and realizable any day; the balance was lent on mortgage on real estate, and a large reserve fund accruing from the profits, it was announced, would be used for consolidation and extension. Interest was paid at the rate of 2½ per cent per annum.

In a *War Cry* interview in August 1893 Major Bremner, now styled the manager, stated that within the first eighteen months the bank, which was then being worked on the same principle as any other ordinary bank, had a turnover of nearly £400,000, with some 2,000 accounts, representing investors in the U.S.A., France, Holland, Gibraltar, Egypt, and India, as well as in the United Kingdom. Interest was now allowed at the rate of 3 per cent, or 4½ per cent on loans for ten years. In 1900 the business was transferred to the Reliance Bank Limited, a legally-constituted body registered under the Companies Acts. No fees have ever been paid to the directors, of which the General for the time being is president, and profits, after adequate provision for reserves has been made, have always been paid over to The Salvation Army. The capital in 1962 was £60,000; the reserve funds, £276,993; and deposits, £2,941,627 (31 March 1962).

THE DARKEST ENGLAND SCHEME

Following the absorption of the first £100,000 which inaugurated the Darkest England Scheme, the General was forced to launch an appeal for another £65,000 two years later because the public failed to contribute the £30,000 per year which he had emphasized would be needed to carry out the Scheme,[1] and by January 1893 £15,000 had been received in money and promises. Among the well-known contributors were Lord Brassey, the Earl of Aberdeen, Messrs Cory of Cardiff, Messrs Crossley of Manchester, and the Marchioness of Ripon. Meanwhile provision for the present expenditure was of the first importance and to meet it the General introduced a plan to assure a permanent annual income. He suggested two methods: First, to push the Social League, which had been founded a few weeks previously, and which had already about 500 members; and second, the formation of the Darkest England Light Brigade, which he hoped would have a membership at

[1] *The History of The Salvation Army*, vol. iii, p. 96

least 100,000 strong. The Social League consisted of three orders: 1. Those willing to undertake to collect five guineas per annum; 2. Those who would engage to give a guinea per annum; and 3. Young People who would promise to give or collect a guinea annually. Those who joined the Light Brigade would simply engage to place at least one half-penny per week in a box which would be provided for that purpose and which would be collected by agents regularly every quarter.

I propose [wrote the General] to initiate a new method of emphasizing what is known as "grace before meat" [the idea being that the box should stand upon the dinner-table], so that when you and your friends sit down to the comfortable repast which Providence sets before you, you may be reminded of those not thus favoured, and have the opportunity to send a mite to alleviate—nay, to assist in saving them from further destitution. . . . Let us . . . send a crumb from our tables to some poor Lazarus, who, if not at our door, lies somewhere in the dark places of our great cities.

"Grace before meat" boxes are still in use in the British Territory.

The Financial Secretary's department at International Headquarters was merged in the office of the Chancellor of the Exchequer (Commissioner Pollard) in August 1896, thus uniting all the money-getting departments with the spending departments under one authority. Colonel Barker was appointed to assist the Commissioner generally with these newly-added responsibilities, and was specially charged with the oversight of the subscribers' and press departments. Major (later Commissioner) George J. Jolliffe was made responsible to the Commissioner for the management of the Light Brigade as a distinct department. The *War Cry* of 11 November 1893 makes reference to Financial-Special and Mrs Turner, who were attached to the Financial Secretary's department. Their work was to collect funds for special purposes. Later such officers were known as special collectors and are today attached to the public relations department. The collector's branch of the subscribers' department was opened in 1898, Adjutant Alfred G. Hamilton and Captain J. C. B. Ellis being appointed as the first official collectors, and having the whole of the British Territory for their ground.

THE TRADE DEPARTMENT

By the end of 1886 divisional trade depots had been opened at 4 Lambeth Hill, London, E.C., Bristol, Cardiff, Plymouth, Birmingham, Nottingham, Leeds, Glasgow, Newcastle, Manchester and Belfast. On Monday, 30 January 1893, a new sale-room was opened at No 94 Clerkenwell Road for the sale of publications, uniform, musical instruments, tea, kaffy—a substitute for coffee—and social wing productions. The trade department was already operating at Nos 98, 100 and 102.

In July 1895 the Army in England began to manufacture its own "hallelujah" bonnets in Nelson Street, Luton, noted for its straw-plaiting. Bandsman Biggs, of the Temple corps, was the manager. He had previously been in the hat-making business for himself, but had volunteered to engage in Army bonnet-making. About this same year a shop was opened at Blyth in connection with the trade department and a van visited the villages in the area. This venture, however, was not a financial success.

In order to facilitate the extension and development of the international trade headquarters, the wholesale warehouses had been transferred in October 1896 to new and enlarged premises at 77-81 Fortess Road, Kentish Town, in north-west London. The retail trade was carried on through local shopkeepers, a list of whom was published from time to time in the *War Cry*. London retail orders were executed at 98 Clerkenwell Road, where Mr William Harriss, who had had a life-long business experience, was in charge.

The *War Cry* for 19 April 1902 gave a clear and concise explanation as to why The Salvation Army traded :

Briefly, because we cannot help it. When the Army commenced its operations, and adopted a distinctive uniform for its officers and soldiers, it was found very difficult to induce business people to supply us with the kind of thing we required. Hence, it was necessary to provide our own uniform.

Then, in order to reach a greater number of people than we could ever have done by talking, we were compelled to institute the *War Cry*, which was quickly followed by other periodicals ; and, so that we might get the greatest number out at the least possible cost, it was necessary for us to have our own printing machines. The result has been that millions of people have been provided with good, sound literature, and great numbers have been saved and sanctified.

Another reason for our trading operations is that our people may procure the best possible goods at a reasonable price ; that they may know where to purchase clothing consistent with their profession, as well as books and literature calculated to bless them and teach them how to be better soldiers of Jesus Christ.

Again, our Trading Departments have become a valuable financial auxiliary to the international friends of the Army. These friends benefit by the balance of profit remaining, which in the past has amounted to many thousands of pounds, with which to help carry on our world-wide Missionary Work.

For instance : By simply drinking tea supplied from the Trade Department our comrades and friends have largely enabled the General to maintain and extend our Foreign Work. For these reasons, everyone interested in the Army's many crusades should avail themselves of the Army's Trading Departments, and do their best to influence other people in the same direction, knowing that they will thus be doing both themselves and their friends a service, and at the same time be assisting to promote the work of salvation throughout a sin-cursed world.

TITHING AND TEA

The need for a consistent and regular supply of money to maintain and extend the Army's multifarious activities was a continual source of anxiety to William Booth who, in the early part of 1897, held a council, composed of the leading staff officers of Great Britain, at which he proposed changes in the existing financial plans. The time of holding the Self-Denial Effort was altered from October to the end of March in order to leave the field clear for the harvest festivals; and, to leave the corps free to help themselves financially at other times in the year, the quarterly collections[1] were to be discontinued entirely, the loss of £8,000 per year being made up by setting apart 50 per cent of the harvest festivals income for the sick and wounded, the general maintenance, the training and the missionary funds, which would suffer so seriously from the discontinuance of the quarterly collections. It was anticipated that the harvest festivals, being now separated by a longer period from the Self-Denial Effort, would in future produce double the usual amount. Each officer, soldier and friend was asked to lay aside a tenth of his income for the purpose of assisting the work of God, and this every officer in the council had promised faithfully to do as an example; and it must be remembered that in those days every officer lived very precariously, his or her life being one of continual self-sacrifice, especially among corps officers. In his letter, published in the *War Cry* and written from Stockholm, to explain these changes, the General also took the opportunity to commend the Tea League, which had 43,344 consumers of Salvation Army tea, and brought in a trifle on every pound sold. The Lord's Corner was another idea

[1] *The History of The Salvation Army*, vol. ii, p. 82

upon which he commented—"a beautiful method for raising funds to spread salvation." This consisted of setting apart a corner of one's garden for God, giving Him a tree, fixing up a bee-hive, planting some potatoes, letting Him have a chicken, or a corner of the window, or making something for which one had ability, selling it and giving Him the profits. The General assured his readers that he was "giving the dear Lord at least a tenth of my own income. I have joined the Tea League, and fixed Him up a corner of my garden."

Chapter Six

ASSURANCE AND INSURANCE

A small concern, The Methodist and General Assurance Society, Ltd., established in 1867 as The Free Methodist and General Benefit Society, Ltd., the business of which had had almost faded out, approached William Booth in 1891 through one of its directors, James Field, a Salvationist, with an offer of the Charter and Title of the Society to be used in association with The Salvation Army. The General consulted his leading officers and decided to accept the offer and to begin operations as soon as possible. "The lack of thrift and care—the recklessness of the people of this country is appalling," he declared. "I am not sure whether, if you can get a man to assure his wife or children, you might not count it the first step toward getting him to make sure about his soul." Only the Charter was taken over; the working machinery, in addition to the few remaining policies, were distributed among other societies. The transactions for the transfer of the Charter were carried out in his quarters at Kenmure Road, Hackney, by Major (later Commissioner) David C. Lamb, who was then the right-hand man to the Property Secretary. At first the office transacted annuity business only, but in 1893 arrangements for the transaction of life assurance business were made, and in January 1894 the first policy was issued. Ten years later, on 18 April 1904, the Board of Trade issued a certificate of a change of name whereby the Society, dropping the words "Methodist and General," became "The Salvation Army Assurance Society, Ltd."

Toward the end of 1894 it was decided to decentralize the Society so that it became a self-formed, self-sustained organization with an administrative staff. Commissioner Carleton was appointed its first Managing Director.

The first batch of industrial branch proposals to reach the Chief office was but a handful, "and getting the latest Salvation Army infant on to its feet was a matter of no little moment," for the staff was small—two men on full time, one man on half-time and a youth. At the end of the first year's work the premium income was but £421, the funds amounted to £14,220 and 2,474 policies were in force. In 1895 the Society held 38,465 policies, with a premium income of £6,992, the assurance funds totalling £14,039. In 1904 the premium income was £123,517 in the industrial branch and £33,394 in the ordinary branch, the funds amounted to £197,790 and the policies in force numbered 342,046. In 1962 the position was: premiun income £2,123,007 in the industrial branch and £773,417 in the ordinary branch. The total funds amounted to £23,640,548 and the policies in force numbered 1,825,973.

Soon after the Society was formed opposition—fierce, bitter and strong—became apparent, as was anticipated. The press generally and certain of the financial and commercial organs in particular attacked the Society and pro-

No 3596 C.

Certificate of Change of Name

OF THE

Methodist and General Assurance Society Limited

I hereby Certify, That the

Methodist and General Assurance Society Limited

having, with the sanction of a **Special Resolution** of the said Company, and with the approval of the BOARD OF TRADE, changed its name, is now called the

Salvation Army Assurance Society, Limited

and I have entered such new name on the Register accordingly

Given under my hand at London, this Eighteenth day of April One Thousand Nine Hundred and four

H. B. Bartlett

Registrar of Joint Stock Companies.

A facsimile of the Certificate which changed the name of The Methodist and General Assurance Society into The Salvation Army Assurance Society, Limited, in 1904.

phesied terrible crises and dire misfortune. In those days the view was commonly held that children were often neglected and their deaths accelerated for the sake of the assurance money, and the Army's Assurance Society, to meet effectively any charge of this kind, issued a special notice in its prospectus to the effect that :

In order to protect the interests of children, the Society reserved to itself the right to pay the funeral and medical expenses direct to the undertaker and doctor, instead of handing the sum assured to the parents in such cases as, in the opinion of the Society, were open to suspicion.

This desire to do good was, as might have been expected, misrepresented by competitive assurance societies as an unwarranted interference with the liberty and rights of the policy-holders ; but in 1898 an influential assurance journal referred to the matter in these terms :

After four years The Salvation Army puts it on record that only in one solitary case was there ever enough suspicion to warrant putting their special precautionary clause into operation. The insurance world is under a very substantial debt to The Salvation Army for carrying out such a brave and useful experiment. The amount of money collected during those first days seemed hardly commensurate with the expenditure of time, energy and worry involved.

Assurance, the official magazine of the Society, was issued first in May 1898, under the editorship of Staff-Captain George Clutterbuck, who until then had been editor of the *Young Soldier*. The Chief of the Staff, in contributing an article to its pages, coined a phrase that was to become a tradition : "Holiness unto the Lord—that is our trade mark. Anything that cannot be done in harmony with it must not, shall not, be done by us or ours." In June 1904 the matter and composition of the magazine became more insular and it was for some years published under the title, *Head Office Review*.

A general order published on 12 February 1898 stated that:

The positions of Superintendent and Assistant-Superintendent of the Salvation Army Life Assurance Departments will be recognized as ranks of officership in The Army. Comrades holding these positions are to be addressed as "Superintendent" and "Assistant-Superintendent" and these ranks are, at the present time, equivalent to the rank of Adjutant and Captain respectively. The uniform will be the same as worn by an Adjutant and Captain with the addition of "Life Assurance" on the shoulder straps.

At the first Life Assurance councils held at Clapton in 1900 the General, in the course of what he styled his "ordination blessing," made the following statement regarding the why and wherefore of the Army's embarkation upon the business of life assurance. There were then 103 officers and employees at the headquarters of the Society; 3 Inspectors, 42 Superintendents, 157 Assistant-Superintendents and 1,155 Agents comprised the field staff.

There has never been anyone else who has adopted such a thing. Assurance agencies and companies have made a great deal of money, but nobody has gone with the simple motive of saving the souls of the people, and using the profit that is made to the shaking of the foundations of the Wicked One.

Look at the extraordinary opportunities that you possess in your present position for saving the souls of men. To begin with, look at the access you get to the homes and hearts of the multitude by means of this Society. The Assurance agent goes in and out—threading his way down the slums and alleys, up the stairs—edging into the homes of the masses.

The agents of this Assurance Society must be God's agents. Now, if you are to be God's men you know very well you must be united to Him—drawing life from Him like the branch in the vine drawing its sap out of the vine, taking away the stem that dies which is only fit to be burnt. Are you united?—that is the point. Are you in possession of spiritual life? Have you the Spirit of God within you? Can you say, "I am united to God; I belong to God?" It's no use trying to do God's work

without God's power. You must have God's nature. No matter how long you polish glass, it will only be glass when you have done ; you cannot make it a diamond.
I don't want any business founded on falsehood—God forbid ! Any buttresses and foundations that are built upon falsehood will totter and fall. We want men and women who are true—who would not tell a lie to save their souls. The agents of this Society should look God Almighty in the face and say, " I never tell a lie in my reckonings. I am true and honest—true in everything through and through ! "

These were the ideals of the Society and these ideals—of business principles being allied to religious practice—have been maintained throughout the Society's long and prosperous history. The influence of the agents and those over them among the many thousands of policy-holders has been such that their advice has been sought in almost every phase of domestic life—in tracing a relative, maybe a prodigal son or daughter, in persuading couples living together irregularly to marry, and so forth. Many definite cases of conversion have also been registered as a direct result of the personal dealing of the agents.

A libellous and ridiculous statement appeared in *The Commercial World* in July 1903. For some years this bi-monthly periodical had shown a foolish and unreasoning hostility to the progress of the Society, but this latest charge was so utterly false and reckless that Commissioner Carleton was compelled to take action against the editor, F. W. Buckle, who, however, sought to justify his magazine's mis-statements. Upon the representations of the Society's solicitors the editor eventually published an apology in the issue dated 1 February 1904. The magazine had published an article which stated that a Salvation Army Assurance Society agent had " prayerfully " persuaded a poor widow to transfer her policy from " a first-class office " to the Army's society, which persuasions " were accompanied by most disreputable insinuations against the *bona fides* and fair dealings of thoroughly respectable companies, together with hints at punishment in the hereafter for supporting such concerns"! The *Commercial World* regretted that it had been entirely misled as to the facts, and also deeply regretted its unjustifiable comments.

Often the agents of other societies sneeringly told the Army Assurance agents that when a claim was made the Salvationists had to take the drum to the street-corner in order to collect enough to meet it.

In October 1891 a department was established at International Headquarters to attend, not only to the insurance of Salvation Army properties, but also to the properties of soldiers and friends, the insurance being effected in the Liverpool and London and Globe Insurance Company, the Midland Counties Insurance Company and other leading offices of good standing. The profits accruing from the business were, of course, to "strengthen our hands, and enable us the better to push the war both at home and abroad." The insurance was in connection with loss from fire, and plate glass and boiler damage, the rate being from one shilling and sixpence per £100 per annum on buildings and two shillings per £100 per annum on their contents. In 1900 the department became associated with the Assurance Society.

CHAPTER SEVEN

THE ACQUISITION OF PROPERTY

To meet the considerable difficulties encountered in obtaining or erecting suitable corps buildings a new scheme was devised by the General and announced in the *War Cry* for

2 October 1886. It was to be known as The Salvation Army Property League. Its plan of operations was to purchase or erect barracks, enlarge those already existing, or acquire suitable property of any description and hold it in the name and on the behalf of the Army, standing in the relation of landlord to the corps. A corps wanting to purchase or build a barracks had to raise one-sixth of the entire cost, the League furnishing the remainder, building the hall and the corps paying a reasonable rent. The League was to enrol no fewer than 20,000 members paying a minimum contribution of a shilling per quarter, thereby producing £4,000 per annum. The members would be called shareholders. Gifts and legacies would, it was expected, continually add to the funds of the League, which would borrow either from building societies or private sources. The Salvation Army Building Association, which had been established two years before,[1] had not sufficient funds at its command to fulfil the demands, consequently many important building plans had fallen through. The secretary of the League was Staff-Captain Brick ![2]

During the period under review William Booth opened a number of the very many halls that had been erected in various parts of the British Isles. The citadel at Runcorn, built at a cost of £1,500 on the site occupied by the "Old Hall," the oldest building in the town, was opened on Friday, 23 July 1886. The General rode through the town at the head of the procession in an open carriage drawn by a couple of greys. On the following day he presided at the stone-laying ceremony of the Oldham citadel, which was opened in the following June. On the last day of the year he opened the Tunbridge Hall in King's Cross. The occasion was the first Army meeting to be held in the district.

[1] *The History of The Salvation Army*, vol. ii, p. 87

[2] p. 377

After first holding their meetings in cottages, then over a baker's oven, and finally in a hay-loft over a stable, the Salvationists of Penge, in South-east London, entered a new barracks of their own in Maple Road on Sunday, 5 December 1886, when it was opened by Colonel Nicol. During 1887 the Army acquired more property than in all its previous seventeen years of history, doubtless the outcome of the activities of the Property League; but the year 1889 was described as "the most remarkable in the history of The Salvation Army, and more especially in the history of the Property Department, for never before have we launched out on such large undertakings, or had such brilliant successes"; and Colonel Elijah Cadman seems to have been the man behind the scenes.

It is impossible, of course, to give a list of all the properties acquired, but a few of the outstanding ones were Croydon Central Fortress opened on Christmas Day 1887 by Colonel Nicol; the New Public Hall, Blackburn, opened on Sunday, 2 January; Bradford Barracks on 19 November 1888; and Pembroke Hall, Liverpool, both as a barracks and divisional war offices, on 19 August 1889. The stone-laying of the magnificent Aberdeen Citadel—it cost £20,000—on 17 August 1893 was attended by the Earl and Countess of Aberdeen, each of whom laid a foundation-stone. The Citadel was opened on 21 June 1896 by Commissioner Coombs. Sheffield Citadel was opened on Saturday, 27 January 1894, by Commissioner Howard. Seating 1,800, this building cost £7,500. A great trophy of grace by the name of William Booth was the divisional sergeant-major. About the year 1895 Alexander Gordon was appointed the staff architect at International Headquarters, two of his first assignments being the new citadels at Barnsley and Grantham. Carlisle Citadel was opened by Commissioner Howard on Sunday,

5 January 1895, and Limehouse Citadel by the Field Commissioner (Eva Booth) on Sunday, 21 April. The opening of Bristol Citadel took place on Saturday, 19 December 1896, by Commissioner Coombs. Hull (Icehouse) Citadel was opened by the Commissioner in the following year, on Saturday, 6 February.

In the summer of 1900 the Grecian Theatre[1] was razed to the ground after the Army had vacated it at the expiration of the lease, and a police-station built on the site.

1 *The History of The Salvation Army*, vol. ii, p. 216

VI DEMONSTRATION, EXHORTATION AND JUBILATION

CHAPTER ONE

ANNIVERSARY CELEBRATIONS

THE growing vigour of The Salvation Army found expression in a fashion characteristic of adolescence. Its recurring birthdays were made occasions, not only for mutual congratulation, but for displaying the spirits of its people and demonstrating the extent of its operations. The Alexandra Palace at Wood Green, North London, was the venue for the first three anniversaries of the period now under review—1887, 1888 and 1889. The appearance of Catherine Booth added much to the interest and helpfulness of the first of these events, but in 1888 she was unable to be present in the grounds for more than a short while.

The anniversary of twenty years' hard fighting, with such a measure of victory as the Christianity of modern times has never known, calls, we think, for some acknowledgment [said the General]. Nay ! demands it. Accordingly, we have arranged for a celebration after the fashion which seems most likely not only to express our gratitude to Almighty God for the benefits of the past years, but to stimulate the Army to mightier efforts for the achievement of still greater victories in the days to come. . . . Let us keep the main purpose of our life and work before us, and do all that lies within our power in order that the 18th of July, 1887, may mightily help forward the salvation of souls, the sanctification of believers, and the inspiration of thousands and thousands of our comrades with more of the dying love of Jesus.

The crowds who attended were far greater than the most optimistic had anticipated. The spiritual meetings, the musical festivals, the presence of Salvationists from overseas, the farewell of officers for missionary fields, each with increasing effect and in rising numbers, made such occasions memorable. In 1888 the sight of twenty Torquay Salvationists in prison garb marked the fight then being waged for the right to march the streets with bands playing.[1] The rate at which the Army was making progress was indicated in that at an interim demonstration at the St James's Hall in 1889 the 7,000th officer was commissioned.

The General's sixtieth birthday on 10 April 1889 was celebrated in the grand manner with a monster banquet and meetings in the Clapton Congress Hall which were attended by his "trusty friends," Mr T. A. Denny and Mr Frank Crossley, of Manchester. In his lengthy afternoon address the General told the story of his father's conversion on his death-bed, and related details of his own remarkable life. Immediately after the banquet Mrs Booth, extremely weak and bearing the traces of much suffering on her face, was tenderly led on to the platform for "The feasting of souls." Evidently aware that she was a dying woman, she said, "Having the prospect of the fight soon ending in my own case, I cannot help but feel deeply moved." [2]

Nearly £5,000 had either been promised or given as an "Ebenezer gift" before the meeting was brought to its conclusion. At night the General changed from an autobiographical to an historical address:

They call the government of The Salvation Army a lot of hard names—autocracy—but I reply to them that it is the government that God Himself has invented. It was the government of Eden; it is the Family government. It is the Patriarchal

[1] p. 266
[2] p. 303

government; it is the government of Mosiac economy. Moses was the General, yet his people were free. I say it is going to be the government of Heaven.

For the 25th anniversary in 1890 a move was made to the Crystal Palace, Sydenham, and Catherine Booth sent her last message[1] to the huge audience of 40,000 Salvationists crowded in the nave. Thereafter, especially for a particularly notable occasion, this large and imposing glass building, with its spacious halls and wide-spreading grounds, was frequently the chosen scene of action.[2] Next year, notwithstanding that the day of celebration was rainy, the turnstiles registered an attendance of 62,000. By this time the doings of such a festivity had become more or less patterned. In tents erected in the grounds and in many of the small halls available in the Palace building, every branch of Salvation Army activity and enterprise had its representative demonstration. Immense gatherings in the central transept commenced with the General's reception at 9.30 a.m. In the afternoon "The Biggest Band in the World—Brass, Concertina and Tambourine—10,000 instruments," provided a programme.

The effect [ran the report] was far more stupendous and magnificent than ever known before, and we see how, by the grace of God, a vast force of musicians is spreading all over the country to bear on the wings of music the message of Salvation.

The Jubilee Campaign of 1894, which commemorated the General's fifty years of Christian warfare, began with "Two Days of God" meetings in the new Queen's Hall, Regent Street.[3] This hall, one of the largest in London, and one of the most charming and convenient in Europe, was

[1] p. 303
[2] Destroyed by fire in 1936
[3] Destroyed during the Second World War

used by the Army for the first time on 9 and 10 April, the second day being the General's birthday. In the course of an interview prior to the event William Booth said :

A wave, not only of doubt, but positive unbelief—call it by its right name, Atheism—is passing over the nation, and I should think the spirituality of the country has suffered in proportion. I am not very conversant with the religious life of the Churches, and I may wrong them ; if so, it is not of intention, but I should be inclined to say that there is less secret prayer, and less striving to live in the Spirit as well as in the outer form of the life that Jesus Christ lived on the earth, than there has been for a hundred years.

"Indescribable acts of Divine power" were witnessed in the Queen's Hall. The gatherings resulted in 517 seekers and 120 applications for officership. The crowds were unprecedented, thousands sought admission in vain. Birthday greetings flowed in from all parts of the world, including messages of congratulation from Sir William V. Harcourt (Chancellor of the Exchequer), the Rev. Hugh Price Hughes, Prince N. Galitzin, and the Rev. Samuel Wright (President of the United Methodist Free Churches), who wrote :

What Methodism did for the Church of England and Nonconformity in the eighteenth century, the example of the devotion self-sacrifice and enthusiasm of The Salvation Army has done for modern Methodism.

The launching of a Jubilee Scheme for the raising of £50,000 was introduced to the public and £7,000 was secured before the night meeting. Mr John Cory and four anonymous friends contributed £1,000 each, and Mr Richard Cory and a staff officer £500 each. The *War Cry* reporter describes the platform at night :

It represented a perfect Sanhedrin of class and nationality. A Russian princess, whose name carries with it honour and virtue and benevolence, sat near to the Foreign Secretary. A Scottish baronet, and one of London's big shipowners ; M.Ps, clergymen, mission workers and philanthropists ; the merchant prince and foreign Press reporter ; the hospital nurse, Scripture reader and hardy artisan, cook and housemaid ; your typical West-end masher, all embedded, we might say, among Salvationists.

It having been decided that from 1894 onward anniversary gatherings should be held at the Crystal Palace only once in every three years, the next event took place during the year of Queen Victoria's Diamond Jubilee, 1897, when the General sent a message to Her Majesty to which came a reply from Windsor Castle addressed to *General* Booth :

The Queen wishes to express to all the members of The Salvation Army now assembled for the triennial Congress her heartfelt thanks for their touching message of loyal congratulations and earnest good wishes. Her Majesty fully recognizes the great and varied work so courageously undertaken by the Army on behalf of so many of their unhappy fellow creatures in different parts of the empire. The Queen fervently trusts that Divine guidance and blessing may accompany all future efforts of the Army.

It was noted with considerable satisfaction that Her Majesty had graciously and specifically acknowledged the General's well-won right to his title, so bringing to an end the small-minded prejudice which from time to time had denied this to him.

In view of the Church's previous antipathy[1] it was of more than passing interest that the General was invited to the great open-air Thanksgiving Service at St Paul's Cathedral in connection with the Queen's Jubilee, he being represented by Commissioner Howard, who was provided with a seat quite close to Her Majesty's carriage. Commissioner Carleton was also present officially, as were Colonel (later Commissioner) Adelaide Cox and Ensign

[1] *The History of The Salvation Army*, vol. ii, p. 136

The International Staff Band (Bandmaster Caleb Burgess) in 1893

Hallelujah !

The Great Welcome at the Crystal Palace, 16 March 1896

Rowe, of The Borough corps, the two last-named being the only women sent by any body throughout the British Commonwealth to represent the Christian Church in the dominions over which a woman had reigned for sixty years, and who was the titular head of the Church of England.

As the Army continued to grow in strength and capacity it was found advantageous to hold anniversary celebrations and the like at various provincial centres ; this was done for the first time in 1898.

William Booth reached his seventieth birthday in 1899 and the *War Cry* dated 8 April was almost exclusively given over to his life and work. A six-coloured portrait was included as a presentation plate. On his actual birthday a Thanksgiving Service was conducted by the Chief of the Staff in the Exeter Hall. Reserved seats were 1s. but the general admission fee was 1d. The General himself was campaigning in Australia. The *Daily Chronicle* came out with a finely-drawn portrait of the General on his birthday, 10 April, and an appreciation written by Bramwell Booth :

> His greatest power lies in his sympathy [he wrote]. His heart is a bottomless well of compassion. He knows no man and no nation after the flesh, and yet he has brothers in all the families of the earth who demand his sympathy and help.

Chapter Two

THE ARMY'S SHOP WINDOW

From 12 to 17 November 1887 a Universal Exhibition of Thank-offerings was held at Clapton in connection with the Anniversary of the training home. The object was :

to give every corps, officer, soldier and friend an opportunity of presenting to the Lord a portion of their *goods* (small or large) as a token of their thankfulness to Him for raising up The Salvation Army and sending forth its officers into this and other lands.

Special excursion trains were run from all parts of the country and a spacious temporary building was constructed as an extension of the Temple behind the Clapton Congress Hall to house the various departments of the exhibition. One lady provided sufficient furniture for six bedrooms, a gentleman sent a parcel of overcoats, and a manufacturer 100 yards of the best serge. Among other curious contributions were seven sheep, five sucking pigs, three goats, a heifer and a calf. Gifts came from many places overseas. Several opera shawls, handsome cushions and similar articles were returned with thanks to the donors, as they were considered " hardly necessary in a Salvationist's house " !

The exhibition was opened by Miss Emma Booth and Commandant Booth. A holiness council was conducted on the Sunday morning by the General and Mrs Booth, during which the youngest daughter, Miriam Booth, of the Chief of the Staff, was dedicated by her grandmother. At the Monday afternoon banquet, at which 800 persons were assembled, the chairman, Mr T. A. Denny, stated that 100 officers were being sent out from the training homes every month. He did not think there was anything comparable to that in the history of the Church of God in this country. £2,000 was raised from this meeting. On the Tuesday the General conducted an all-day conference on Pure Religion at the Congress Hall.

" One of the greatest, most representative, and most successful missionary meetings ever held by the Army, or indeed by any religious organization," took place in the City Temple, Holborn Viaduct, on Tuesday, 12 June 1888, under the presidency of the General, who spoke on "The Salvation Army and the Salvation of the World." It was the first occasion on which this outstanding centre of religious activity had been used by the Army and this through the generosity of its celebrated minister, Dr Joseph Parker. India, Australasia, Canada, France, Switzerland, Assyria, China and other lands were represented. The Household Troops Band occupied the choir seats in the gallery. The opening song, "Soldiers of our God, arise," to the tune of "Come, landlord, fill the flowing bowl," most probably shocked the circumspect regular members of the City Temple's congregation, who were present in large numbers.

An innovation in a Salvation Army gathering was the putting of a resolution by the General, which was seconded by Mr John Cory, of Cardiff, and supported by Mr Richard Cory, that:

This meeting has heard with shame and disgust of the conviction of ninety-nine honest men and women of God at Torquay, for marching with music through the streets on Sundays to bring the lost to the Saviour's feet, and trusts that every Metropolitan Member of Parliament will vote for the Bill just introduced by Mr H. H. Fowler, for the repeal of clause 38 of the Torquay Harbour Act, and so wipe out this shame and scandal from the country.[1]

The resolution was carried unanimously. Commissioner Coombs told of the conversion of a Trappist monk in Quebec, and of salvation victories among the sea-fishermen on the coast of Labrador. Commissioner Booth-Tucker—shortly to return to India leaving behind his bride, the General's daughter Emma—related the story of the capture of an Afghan chief, who sent in his resignation to Sir Frederick (later Field-Marshal Earl) Roberts, and became a cadet; Commissioner Howard referred to the Chinese

[1] p. 266

corps of Sydney, Australia; Pantoni, an Australian aborigine, Ching Wing, a Chinese, and Major Musa Bhai, an Indian, also participated.

The following June (1889) saw a "tremendous" ex-prisoners' demonstration in the Exeter Hall where 100 Salvationists wore prison garb decorated with broad arrows at this, "the most unique of all" occasions—the reporter's language was somewhat extravagant in those days. A procession of 1,000 Salvationists led by mounted officers, Torquay brass band coming next, and the ex-prisoners behind it, marched down Moorgate Street, past the Mansion House and St Paul's Cathedral. The City police were kind and courteous, but when the Metropolitan police were encountered at the beginning of the Strand they gave instructions for the Salvationists to march to the Thames Embankment and disperse there. Commandant Booth, who was in charge, refused to comply with what he considered to be an unreasonable demand, especially as the Strand was not so congested as were the City streets, and gave orders for the processionists to disperse on the spot and take to the footpaths for the remainder of the short distance to the Exeter Hall. The police, however, pushed the Salvationists about "in a most disgraceful manner," and ordered the one and only banner, upon which was emblazoned, "Prisoners for preaching Christ in the Streets," to be furled. This it was impossible to do under the circumstances. Within a few minutes the police and some of their supporters had torn the banner and smashed its poles.

We are not "thin-skinned" [said the General] and we are not met to whine about a trifling matter. Neither, I am sure, do we bear any grudges. If the magistrates or the policemen, or the turnkeys, who had had the handling of our comrades on the platform, were to be seen at the penitent-form, the persecuted Salvationists would be the first to put their arms around their necks and do for them the best thing that one man could do for another—help them into the liberty and joy of the Kingdom of God!

There had been 762 prosecutions in the United Kingdom and 243 abroad; 549 convictions in the United Kingdom and 112 abroad.

Cases had been instanced where health had been ruined and even life lost through the hardships our dear Comrades had had to undergo in the prison cells. I cannot understand how it is that when a man saves a fellow-creature from drowning, or from a burning house, he should be rewarded with a medal and have honours heaped upon him, whilst if a Salvationist tries to pull a man out of his sins and out of hell-fire he is sent to keep company with felons in a prison-cell.

Before embarking for his campaign in South Africa, New Zealand, Ceylon and India in the August of 1895,[1] the General was given a tremendous farewell at the Alexandra Palace on the Bank Holiday Monday, which included a wonderful picnic for 4,000 children, and a splendid march-past nearly a mile long, "altogether a remarkable Heaven-on-earth holiday." This "was *not* the triennial gatherings of the clans. It was confined to the London province," and yet it was estimated that some 30,000 people passed the turnstiles by 3 p.m. The event was described as "The capture of Bank Holiday . . . the acquired right of the world, the flesh, and the devil." An army of cadets had worked from midnight to provide the refreshments. The Field Commissioner (Eva Booth) led the singing in the "Battle of Song," but when "His Blood can make the vilest clean" was being sung, the General characteristically jumped up from his chair, seized the Commissioner's baton and himself conducted the singing of his favourite chorus. Commissioner Howard wielded the baton with all the skill of a professional conductor over the large body of 500

[1] p. 161

instrumentalists in the brass band festival. A "new departure" was the call for an encore from the International Headquarters Band (Staff-Captain Appleby) by the "Knights of the Press." This encore was provided as was an encore in the "Battle of Song." These happenings are mentioned because encores have long since been forbidden in the Army. At the end of the programme "the applause was so terrific as to bring down a few panes of glass from the roof of the spacious hall." The General also addressed the several hundreds of junior soldiers' workers assembled for tea in the gigantic dining-hall.

> In this day [he said], when everybody is shouting and shrieking "One man is as good as another" (and ever so much better !) ; shouting out that they are not going to be servants any more, but all masters, the lords of creation, and the ladies also ; teach *your* children that they are to live to do good and render service to their fellow-men in any station to which God may assign them.

The main features of 1896 and 1899 were Salvation Army exhibitions at the Royal Agriculture Hall, Islington. To many people the Army was only what they had seen or heard of one particular form of its service, possibly its street meetings, and was all too often based upon calumny. Both exhibitions, but especially the second, gave, as one newspaper noted, "a bird's eye view of the organization's work from Whitechapel to Fiji." Another said it was "a show of unique character, illustrating by living examples the work of The Salvation Army throughout the world." And yet another, "the most remarkable display that has ever been seen in connection with a religious organization." Officers representing forty-seven nationalities presented demonstrations in costume. Each exhibition and its associated Sunday campaigns—the famous Sadler's Wells Theatre was the scene of one—covered two weeks in July and August, and more than 800 seekers knelt at the penitent-forms.

Chapter Three

SPIRITUAL OFFENSIVES

Far more in number and of much greater significance alike in their effect and their revelation of the object and spirit of Salvationism, were the year-in, year-out campaigns carried on throughout the homeland field. They were also a pattern of what was going on in every country where the Army flag was flying.

Foremost were the "Two Days with God" series of meetings, which met with amazing spiritual results. The first, which the General described as a holiness convention, were held on 6 and 7 December 1887, in the Exeter Hall. An announcement stated that the meetings were to be devoted entirely to personal religion, and that it was hoped that multitudes would be enabled to give themselves up to the service of God, to do His will and to live for the salvation of the world. Whenever he was in the country the General was the leader of the "Two Days"; in his absence the Chief conducted. All-nights of prayer[1] under the Chief's direction were also frequently held in various parts of the country.

At the second of the "Two Days with God" in 1887 Mrs Booth gave her last Exeter Hall address. Her subject "How to Consecrate," was a heart-searching setting-out of what is required by God of those who profess to be His servants, and was fully characteristic of her straight-forward dealing. Two days of spiritual seeking and devotion were held in this Strand building on fourteen occasions until 1900; in addition, contemporaneously and later, scores of such gatherings were held at provincial centres, the first

[1] *The History of The Salvation Army*, vol. i, pp. 60 and 237

being conducted in the Free Trade Hall, Manchester, on 30 and 31 January 1888.

Series of central holiness meetings on Thursday afternoons for periods of three months in the seasons when London audiences could be gathered were also conducted in the Exeter Hall, with Mrs Bramwell Booth and Commissioner Howard as leaders. Similar efforts to deepen spiritual life were made in other large cities as opportunity offered.

It was about this period that the custom was established of launching campaigns to suit the season of the year. The 1898 winter campaign of the British Field, then under the command of Commissioner Coombs, had for its target, among other things, the following objectives :

40,000 prisoners. Increase of 6,000 senior and 2,000 junior soldiers. Increase of 10,000 in *War Cry* circulation. Every corps of 50 soldiers and upwards to open at least one new society (outpost) and to provide one new envoy per 50 soldiers. In every town with a population of 20,000 with only one corps a second to be opened. A soul-saving battalion to be organized in every corps of 50 soldiers and upwards. Musical demonstrations in slums and market-places of large towns and cities with the express object of getting sinners saved on the spot. Organize the Young People's Legion. A special junior and young people's week for the salvation of children and making of junior soldiers. A " Red-hot Brigade " to be raised in every division to lift hard corps and fan the soul-saving fire in every direction.

In the summer season the plan was to go where the largest number of people were to be found, mainly at the seaside. The objectives and methods were changed from time to time.

It was seldom, despite his ultra-strenuous public life and not-too-robust physique, that the General was reported as being ill, but on 2 March 1891, after having completed by far the most important campaign he had yet undertaken in

Europe he returned to London in a very exhausted state of health. He had been absent for exactly a month and in that time had visited Norway, Sweden, Denmark, Germany, France and Belgium, delivered sixty-five addresses, and travelled more than 3,681 miles.[1] Nevertheless, he met the heads of departments on the day after his return, but two days later he was unable to visit Headquarters and all his appointments were cancelled. At this time he was weighted with anxiety owing to the illness of three of his daughters—Emma, Eva and Lucy. Within a day or so of his recovery the General was again on the warpath, but his very heavy fortnight of campaigns in Huddersfield, Nottingham, Hull and Glasgow, for Easter, reduced his powers of resistance and, falling a victim to influenza, he had reluctantly to cancel his visit to Belfast and Dublin.

Apart from the great campaigns held in the principal cities of the British Isles the indefatigable Commander-in-Chief of The Salvation Army visited the smaller towns and villages, and not always were things at their highest level. In writing to Bramwell on 10 February 1893, he describes the situation at Burnley :

I fought my way through, stiff and cold as everything was, with a few parsons scattered about the place ; I poured red-hot truth like a whirlwind upon them.

This was in a chapel. On the same day he writes yet another letter to Bramwell :

St Helens was like a whirlwind ; heaps of colliers and chemical workers and all sorts of people. 17 souls in the afternoon ; 44 at night ; people wounded all over the place.

A Five Weeks' Siege, which was to be " a desperate attack on the works and fortifications of the Powers of Darkness " in the British Territory, was launched by the General in a " Two Days with God " series of meetings in

[1] p. 150

November of that year and resulted in 358 souls taking "a platform plunge." The General declared that he had "never realized that I have been so inspired by the Holy Ghost as I have been at these meetings." The theme for this vigorous soul-saving Siege was "Boundless Salvation," and it was with this thought running through his mind that he wrote what has come to be known throughout the Army as "The Founder's Song":

> O boundless salvation! deep ocean of love,
> O fulness of mercy, Christ brought from above,
> The whole world redeeming, so rich and so free,
> Now flowing for all men, come, roll over me!

This song of seven stanzas took up a whole page of the Christmas Double Number of the *War Cry* for 1893. This Siege was the first of a number of similar character to take place throughout the years.

A most disastrous gale interfered with big concentrated efforts by provincial and divisional leaders—nearly 2,000 mariners found a watery grave, scores of ships were totally wrecked, and the loss of property on land was in proportion, as the result of this great storm—nevertheless, the "Boundless Salvation" Siege continued, the General laying siege to Londonderry, Belfast and Dublin, the Chief of the Staff conducting memorable "All-nights of Prayer" in Liverpool, Bristol and Portsmouth, and 298 seekers being registered in Major Wright's four days at Norwich.

On 12 and 13 March 1895 a two days' campaign was held in Exeter Hall where 445 seekers knelt at the mercy-seat and thousands stayed to pray until 3 a.m. the next day. Of two midnight marches through Piccadilly, one was led by the General himself.

Thirty-eight years after his first battle on Mile End Waste in 1865, William Booth re-visited the spot on 18 October 1903, when he conducted a Sunday's campaign in the

Pavilion Theatre in Whitechapel. The *War Cry* reporter describes the district :

As I walked along Whitechapel Road to the General's last meeting, I stumbled over a shoeblack, declined the bronchial cry of the curbstone jeweller who offered his wares, as well as the request to buy chestnuts, hot as the cinders. Potato, fish and other stalls, as well as hundreds of open shops were doing business on a Sunday night, and this was *not* the Continent ! The saloons were full, the beer-taps busy, the wiry, skinny waifs of children, delirious with freedom, the young men and women loud and lewd.

That night the General preached one of the greatest sermons it had been the reporter's privilege to hear ; great in constructiveness and tone ; great in faith in the things whereof it dealt ; great in passion and *com*passion. The *Daily Chronicle* stated that " no verbatim report could do justice to the General's address, delivered as it was with a magnetic force which found immediate response." He had been in reminiscent mood. It was, he said,

thirty-eight years last July since I walked over here from Hammersmith. Half-way on the journey I stopped to rest—I was not very strong in those days !—so I tarried and talked with a friend about salvation. After dining with him, I came on here and, in the name of Jehovah, lifted up my voice for the first time in this vast continent of evil. What marvellous things have happened as a result ! The Salvation Army is the outcome of the consecration I then made. It was born almost on this very spot. The old tent in which so many glorious scenes were witnessed stood not many yards from here.[1] I was laughed at, mocked at, ridiculed and given the cold shoulder by all sorts of people, religious and otherwise, but I went forward.

[1] *The History of The Salvation Army*, vol. i, p. 2

CHAPTER FOUR

INTERNATIONAL CONGRESSES

A second International Congress was held in London in 1894[1] to mark the fiftieth anniversary of the General's conversion and the twenty-ninth of the commencement of The Salvation Army. It opened with a welcome to the 500 representatives who attended from all the countries in which the work had been established. Hindus, Zulus, Hottentots and Kaffirs, some resplendent in native attire, attracted the attention of wondering crowds, as did the ebony faces and star-spangled costumes of the contingent from the United States. A day at the Crystal Palace was part of the programme, 75,000 persons entering the grounds.

So wide a development of the General's Darkest England Scheme had been made by this time that an exhibition at the Palace created considerable interest. It depicted "Destruction Street" with "its multitude of infamous establishments" at one extreme, to "the institutions and departments already in working order," at the other. The young people's work had reached so excellent a standard of expansion that the juniors were "strongly and picturesquely represented . . . their general appearance, discipline and ability were the subjects of special observation."

The General, at the close of the Congress and under the heading of "What next?" published in the *War Cry* a message characteristic of his attitude on all such occasions:

Hard work has opened new countries, converted sinners, enrolled soldiers, organized corps, trained officers, raised funds, secured buildings, completed organizations and placed us in our present position of discipline and power and influence. . . . But beware,

[1] *The History of The Salvation Army*, vol. ii, p. 298

oh, my soul, beware—and let all others whom it may concern beware—of despising the day of small and feeble things! You won't get everything on a magnificent scale. Thousands will not compose your audiences on every occasion, nor hundreds flock to your penitent form every night, but let us be grateful for the bruised reed and smoking flax, and mind we do not break the one nor quench the other. Praise God for ones and twos and see to it before all else that we do the work given to us with all our might, and that we do it well.

The effect of the Congress in its impact upon the public was immeasurably increased by an "invasion of the provinces." Divided into three contingents the overseas representatives went on tour from 19 July to 31 August, visiting many of the important cities and towns of England, Scotland and Wales, and creating tremendous interest. *The Times*, in an editorial comment on the Congress, stated that it was a remarkable gathering, "an outward and visible sign of a movement which has not spent its force." The writer saw "behind the waving banners and varied uniforms sustained and disciplined enthusiasm." Putting the question, "Has it justified its existence as a separate religious organization by its achievements?" he answered in the affirmative.

THE THIRD INTERNATIONAL CONGRESS

In the *War Cry* for 26 March 1904 the General issued a Manifesto which announced the forthcoming International Congress Campaign to take place from 24 June to 8 July in the Royal Albert and Exeter Halls, at the Crystal Palace, and in the International Congress Hall to be especially erected in the Strand and capable of seating more than 5,000 people, nearly twice the number that any other available building in the Metropolis would accommodate.

Forty-nine different countries and colonies were to be represented. This mammoth undertaking, larger than two Congresses which had preceded it, was under the direct control of Bramwell Booth, whose right-hand man was his Chief Secretary and International Chancellor, Commissioner Pollard, a recognized master of detail.

The Australians—fifty-three comrades under the leadership of Commissioner Thomas McKie—were first to arrive after eight weeks at sea. They had conducted sixty meetings on board the *Afric* during the voyage. Among the party was Major Perry, an Englishman by birth, who had become the foremost cinematographist in the Southern Hemisphere. When the Prince and Princess of Wales (later King Edward VII and Queen Alexandra) were in Australia the Major was employed by the Governments of Victoria and New Zealand to take cinematograph records of the celebrations; and when the Earl of Hopetoun was installed as the first Governor of the Commonwealth, the Government of New South Wales also requisitioned the Major's services.

From the United States came 350 Salvationists, including the National Staff Band in cowboy costume, Commander Booth-Tucker having chartered the new Cunard liner R.M.S. *Carpathia* for the journey to Liverpool and back to New York. The cost for each passenger was a fraction below a halfpenny a mile, with everything found. Thousands were drawn to Euston Station for the arrival of this large party. The Japanese contingent included Staff-Captain (later Commissioner) Gunpei Yamamuro, then the editor of the Japanese *War Cry*. Three hundred came from Canada, with a Bermudan coloured band, two pioneers from Klondyke, and the Salvationist-mayor of Moncton. Taborda, a typical Gaucho (cowboy), accompanied the South American group.

The opening of the Congress on Friday, 24 June in the

capacity-filled Royal Albert Hall was described as a dazzling ceremony :

It defies a parallel [said the *War Cry*]. It closed one epoch in our history and opened another. It was the beginning of new recognition from the King on the throne, the First Magistrate in the City of London, and the Metropolitan press down to the coster with his wheel-barrow, the "whip" on his rank, the prodigal at the saloon bar, and the outcast and forlorn.

An "electrifying world procession" of Salvationist-representatives passed before the pride-filled General like a "human kaleidoscope." Said the General :

This may be looked upon as the inauguration of one of the greatest religious assemblies that the world has ever known—indeed, I am not sure quite anything of an exactly similar character has ever taken place in the history of Christianity. . . . The Salvation Army is likely to live because the foundations on which she is built are sure. Storms have beaten upon her, winds have howled around her, lightnings have flashed and thunders have crashed, and yet she stands firm today. Her foundations might be likened to various layers of hallelujah concrete—indestructible material. We might call the first layer mutual interest. We are mutually interested, interlaced and interlocked ; bound together to help one another both for this life and the life to come. But there is a layer lower down—the foundation of love to God and love to man. And lower down still you have the foundation of a rational organization ; and lower down still the rocks of Eternal Truth, of the Word of God. We are founded upon the truth of the Bible and the truth that is revealed there. And lower still—if we want to go lower—you will find the infinite wisdom, the unchanging, inexhaustible power, and the mercy of the Almighty God, the Father, Son and Holy Ghost. The foundations are good. My comrades, let us praise God that there is no danger there !

On the following afternoon the General opened the International Hall—"our spic and span leviathan temple"—erected on a spot in the Strand which a few years previously, he said, might "have been very well designated as the Devil's Home." The London County Council had acquired the site and cleared away the "rookeries and dens of iniquity," thereby rendering a service to the Metropolis. In his address the General presented some fascinating statistics: The Army was speaking 31 languages in 49 different lands; it had 7,210 corps and societies; the number of officers and cadets totalled 14,291, the local officers 45,339, the bandsmen 17,099, the junior soldiers 325,000, the Social institutions 644, and its periodicals 65, with a circulation of 1,125,000 copies per week. Every week Salvationists held 500,000 open-air and 970,000 indoor meetings, and visited on an average 11,000 drink-shops.

The Times wrote:

Looked at purely as a spectacle The Salvation Army's demonstration in the Albert Hall last night was remarkable. Those who formed and those who witnessed the spectacle were obviously moved by intense devotion to a cause and loyalty to a Leader.

The *Daily Telegraph* reported:

The severest critics have never denied the organizing ability of The Salvation Army. But the inaugural meeting of the International Congress at the Albert Hall must be described as a model of skilful and dignified management. . . . A gathering of this kind, especially in the absence of all rehearsal, might easily have meant the reconstitution of Babel. Such, however, is the directing power at the helm of this great evangelizing Organization, and such the admirable discipline of its component parts, that was what to all intents and purposes an indoor military review passed off with a distinction and a picturesqueness which would scarcely have disgraced the Horse Guards Parade.

Perhaps the outstanding feature of this International Congress was the audience granted to "the Rev. William Booth, Commander-in-Chief of The Salvation Army," as the Court Circular put it, by His Majesty King Edward VII

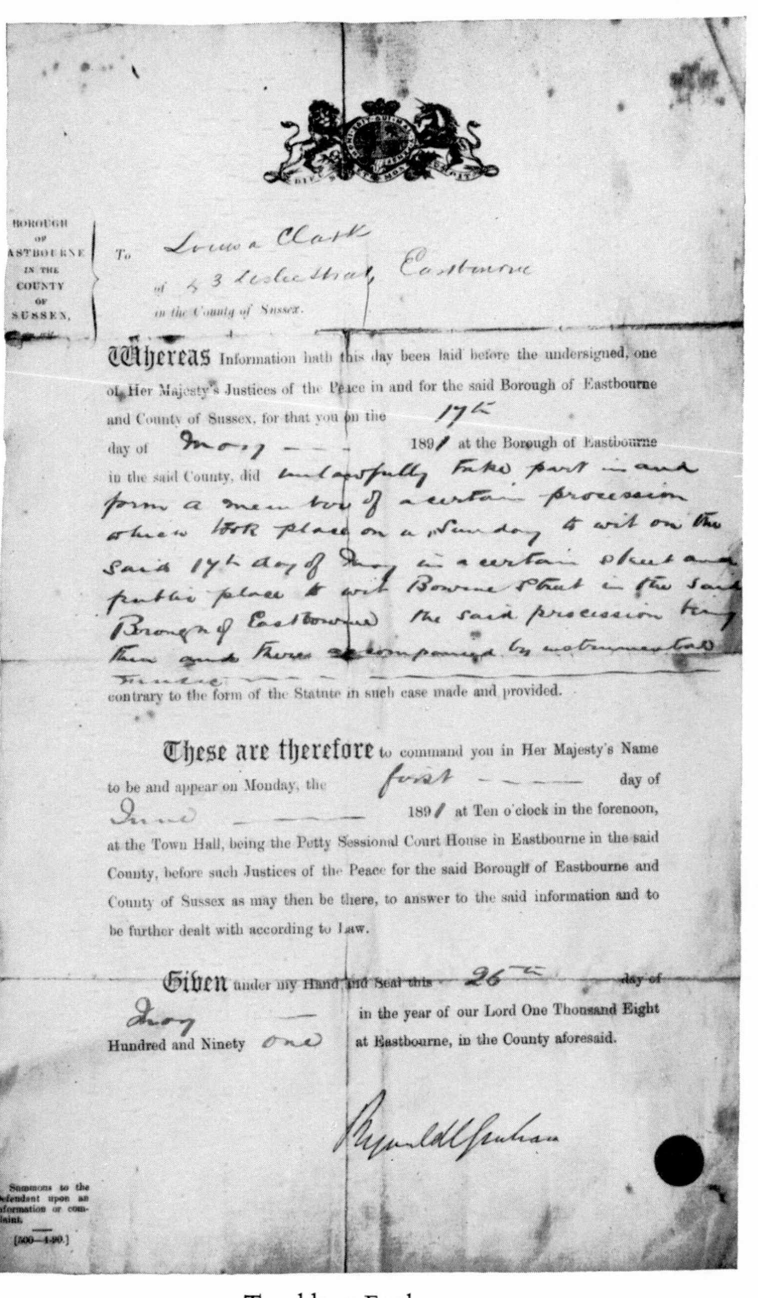
BOROUGH OF EASTBOURNE IN THE COUNTY OF SUSSEX,

To Louisa Clark of 43 Leslie Street, Eastbourne in the County of Sussex.

Whereas Information hath this day been laid before the undersigned, one of Her Majesty's Justices of the Peace in and for the said Borough of Eastbourne and County of Sussex, for that you on the 17th day of May 1891 at the Borough of Eastbourne in the said County, did unlawfully take part in and form a member of a certain procession which took place on a Sunday to wit on the said 17th day of May in a certain street and public place to wit Bourne Street in the said Borough of Eastbourne the said procession being then and there accompanied by instrumental music contrary to the form of the Statute in such case made and provided.

These are therefore to command you in Her Majesty's Name to be and appear on Monday, the first day of June 1891 at Ten o'clock in the forenoon, at the Town Hall, being the Petty Sessional Court House in Eastbourne in the said County, before such Justices of the Peace for the said Borough of Eastbourne and County of Sussex as may then be there, to answer to the said information and to be further dealt with according to Law.

Given under my Hand and Seal this 26th day of May in the year of our Lord One Thousand Eight Hundred and Ninety One at Eastbourne, in the County aforesaid.

Reginald Graham

Summons to the Defendant upon an information or complaint.

[500—4-90.]

Trouble at Eastbourne

The magisterial summons issued to Louisa Clark, who participated in a procession 'accompanied by instrumental music' during the Eastbourne trouble

The Home of Rest, Clacton

at Buckingham Palace on 22 June. The *Daily News* aptly summed up the powerful consequences of this royal audience:

By this signal mark of favour he [His Majesty] has extinguished what remained in some intolerant quarters, of the storm of hostility which The Salvation Army had at one time to encounter. Sneers at The Salvation Army can now hardly pass comment in the literature and the conversation of a certain class.

The *St James's Gazette* wrote significantly : " General Booth wears no inverted commas round his title now."

The General arrived at the Palace in an ordinary hansom cab, attended by Commissioner Pollard, and was conducted to the audience chamber by Lord Churchill.

The interview [says the official statement for publication] was of a most gracious and cordial nature, and General Booth was much impressed by the King's kindness, as well as very grateful for the opportunity of submitting to His Majesty some information with reference to the work of The Salvation Army. As General Booth was leaving the King's presence His Majesty expressed his sympathy with the objects so near to the General's heart, and his cordial good wishes for the continued prosperity and success of the work of the Army.

On the first Sunday the overseas contingents " specialled " at various centres in the London area. Everywhere enormous crowds were attracted and hundreds were turned away because of packed houses ; many seekers were recorded.

Two whole pages of the issue of the *War Cry* for 2 July were given over to an artist's impression of the opening of the Strand Hall and two to giving a list of excursion trains to the Crystal Palace on the following Tuesday, with times and fares. The return fare from Penzance—306½ miles from Paddington—was 16s.

A " Two Days with God " included " the most wonderful prayer-meetings in our history." It was estimated that 30,000 people attended the gatherings in the International

Hall. Sir George Williams, founder of the Young Men's Christian Association, and the Rev. John McNeil, Prebendary Webb-Peploe and the Rev. F. B. Meyer, all numbered among the great preachers of the day, were present at one or other of the meetings led by the General. "The singing," declared a lady-journalist of the first rank, "almost hypnotized me into a Salvation Soldier on the spot." The radiant General was superb and fearless in his utterances. "Ours is a real war," he cried. "Let him who thinks we are playing at soldiers come and try his hand on the plains of Gujerat, in the slums of London, or among the outcasts of New York or Melbourne." The representatives participated in all the gatherings. Captain Washima was introduced as one of the only three or four Japanese women ever to have spoken in public outside her own country.

The second Sunday's meetings were held in the International Hall, in which the General gave his last preachment, and resulted in 161 seekers at the mercy-seat. Day after day during the Congress people found themselves unable to gain admission to either this especially-erected hall or the Exeter Hall.

The *Morning Leader* described the seventy-five-year-old General as "this Caesar of evangelism, this Napoleon of the penitent-form"; and the *Daily News* said: "He is a theologian, argumentative in style, symmetrical and sermonic in the arrangement of his matter, and in delivery calm and decisive."

Thanksgiving Day—the Army's 39th anniversary—at the Crystal Palace drew some 70,000 people to south-east London.

Rake history as we will we can find no adequate comparison to it [says the *War Cry*]. It was a day of unparalleled joy. . . . The place was holy. The General did not travel by train to the Palace as usual, but, for the first time, drove in a motor. One of the reporters seemed to discern in this departure a touch of ostentation. Even on that day he was advocating the claims of the poor to a circle of notabilities which included Sir Robert Pullar, Lady Frances Balfour and Lord Glenesk, and everywhere the General went throughout this great Congress Campaign he was accompanied by his eldest son, the Chief of the Staff: The chief breakwater of The Salvation Army, trusted and obeyed as no other man, except one, in the world.

In one tent forty-six men and women sought the Saviour, including a woman who confessed to the crime of murder. At a "Poor Man's Feast" in the International Hall on the Monday afternoon 1,600 men and women from the London shelters were given a strawberry and cake tea.

The United States Ambassador, Mr Choate, received the entire American contingent in the drawing-room at the Embassy, they having marched "in all the glory of their Congress war-paint from Exeter Street, Strand, Commander Booth-Tucker at the head."

The International Congress of 1904 saw a triumphant finish at the Royal Albert Hall, in which the General delivered an impassioned charge to his field officers:

> Yours is the highest, noblest, grandest calling in God's universe; and if you are to discharge it in harmony with the wishes of your Lord, creditably to The Salvation Army, satisfactorily to your General, you must make haste with the message of mercy with which God has entrusted you for a dying world.

In the audience were Lord Rosebery, the Earl of Aberdeen, the Bishop of Hereford—who later in the week made reference to the work of the Army in Westminster Abbey—Earl Grey and Major-General Sir Robert (later Lord) Baden-Powell.

Three brilliant displays of the Army's musical ability, vitalized by the spirit of salvation, took place at the Crystal Palace—on the polo ground, in a festival in the great transept, in which 3,500 bandsmen participated in the afternoon, and a singing festival in the same hall at night. The review of the troops, 20,000 of them, by the General, occupied one hour and a half in passing the saluting base. During the International Staff Council, which was attended by 1,000 officers and which followed the great public gatherings, a message was received from Buckingham Palace :

W. Bramwell Booth, Salvation Army Council, Congress Hall, Clapton.

I am commanded by the King and Queen to say that they feel greatly touched by the telegram which you have sent them on behalf of the Council of The Salvation Army. It afforded His Majesty much satisfaction to receive your General and to forward a message to The Salvation Army through him. The King sincerely appreciates the allusions in your telegram to his efforts to promote international peace and good will, and he rejoices to think that they have not been entirely without effect. Their Majesties direct me in conclusion to express their warm thanks to the Staff for their good wishes, and they trust that the good work which The Salvation Army has already achieved through their faith and energy may be constantly increased—Knollys.

Chapter Five

A GREAT EVIL

The Sunday closing of public-houses occupied the attention of the General in May 1889, and in a letter published in the *War Cry* he wrote of the " special opportunity " which " presents itself for lifting up our voices unitedly against a great evil"—a Bill which was being brought before Parliament by Mr James Stevenson.

Myriads of poor children, who never enter a public-house through the week, are sent every Sunday to bring home dinner-beer, and to learn on that day of all others a short cut to Hell.

Scotland and Wales had already got their liberty from the liquor traffic on Sundays. Why should England be less free? Soldiers and friends were invited to sign the petition which was to be found at each of the Army's barracks.

This petition was taken to the House of Commons on Monday, 24 June, to be formally presented to the House on the following day. Containing no fewer than 436,000 signatures, it was three miles long, and the hefty trolley on which it rested, drawn by four horses with outriders, and preceded and followed by bands in brakes, presented a most striking spectacle on its way through the City from International Headquarters. Three staff officers, including Commandant Herbert Booth, also rode on horseback in the procession. Unfortunately the Sunday Closing Bill did not secure a majority on Second Reading and made no further progress.

The Children's Messenger (Liquor) Bill passed through Parliament in August 1901, and so became law. "Children under twelve years of age," it said, "shall not enter public-houses for the purchase of beer and other spiritous liquors." The Army, of course, gave support to this legislation.

In February 1902 the General launched a new crusade against the Drink Traffic in the Exeter Hall, where between 150 and 200 converted drunkards occupied the platform. There were in Great Britain 122,419 public-houses, in London 14,362. New measures included the enrolment of known drunkards in every town, village and parish in which the Army was at work. The already-established drunkards' brigades were to be renamed the "drunkards' friends." There were to be midnight meetings in the streets especially for the drunkards. Part of the scheme was to arrange for a guard-room in every neighbourhood to which drunkards could be taken at any hour of the day or night. Drunkards were to be visited in their homes; publicans, too, were to be especially catered for. Statistics showed that the total estimated expenditure of the United Kingdom on intoxicating liquors between and including the years from 1880 to 1902 amounted to £3,654,590,246, or an average of £159,000,000 per year.

The Army welcomed the new Licensing Act which came into force in January 1903 and which helped Salvationists considerably in their desperate task of saving the drunkard. The Act dealt with drunkenness. Any person found drunk while having the charge of a child apparently under the age of seven years could be apprehended. Husband and wives could obtain orders of judicial separation for habitual drunkenness, and a woman could, with her consent, be committed to a licensed inebriates' home. All clubs selling intoxicating drink had to be registered.

The Army continued to identify itself at all times with every effort brought before Parliament in connection with the Drink question, including the Compensation Acts, the Veto and that dealing with inebriates. The General, the Chief of the Staff and Mrs Bramwell Booth also frequently made reference to the power of the brewers and licensed victuallers both in Army meetings and sometimes in gatherings organized by temperance associations. At a temperance meeting in the Exeter Hall in May 1903, when the Bishop of London presided, Mrs Bramwell Booth was able to state that during the previous twelve months 5,000 drunkards had knelt at Salvation Army penitent-forms. She also made the courageous statement that "when the various railway companies insisted upon the drivers of their locomotives being abstainers, surely the time had come when every professed preacher of the Gospel should be under compulsion to abandon intoxicants."

A manifesto addressed to the Nation providing a basis for definite legislation on the Drink Question was issued by the friends of temperance in October 1903. Those of the General and the Chief of the Staff were among the signatures.

* * *

Gambling also was continuously and vigorously attacked and Staff-Captain (later Colonel) John Thomas Hillary, the Divisional Commander, was announced as the hero of the Doncaster Crusade of 1896 when he led his forces on to the race-course on St Leger Day—a first-time occasion to which the *War Cry* of 19 September gave nearly a full-page report in leaded type.

VII THE FIGHT FOR THE STREETS

Chapter One

TROUBLE AT TORQUAY

THE right to march in procession so far as common law is concerned was decided by the Court of the Queen's Bench Judgments on Appeals on 17 June 1882,[1] as also was the placing of responsibility for riotous opposition upon aggressors, and upon authorities to give proper protection to lawful processionists.

Special Acts of Parliament, however, forbade processions with music, other than military, in certain places on Sundays, and the first to put this prohibition into effect was Torquay, under the thirty-eighth section of the Torquay Harbour and District Act, 1886, which became known as "The smuggled clause," as the ratepayers seemed to know nothing of it.

No procession shall take place on Sunday in any street or public place in the borough, accompanied by any instrumental music, fireworks, discharging of cannon, firearms, or other disturbing noise, provided that the foregoing prohibition shall not apply to any of Her Majesty's Navy, Military or volunteer forces.

The fight opened with the appearance in court on 23 August 1886 of the corps officers and three soldiers charged with contravening the Act. A compromise proposed by the Local Board was accepted. This provided that The

[1] *The History of The Salvation Army*, vol. ii, Appendix J

Salvation Army might march on Sundays if it did so unaccompanied by instrumental music. On the following Sunday, however, four bands were allowed to play at the head of a friendly society procession, in consequence of which the Chief of the Staff informed the corps officer that if other bands were permitted to play the Army band might do so. The band played in the streets, a second prosecution was instituted and three Salvationists were fined £5 each and another £1. Four members of the friendly society were also convicted on the same day, the presiding magistrate stating that "as the justices regarded friendly societies as institutions that deserved to prosper, they would only impose a fine of ten shillings."

On 8 October 1886 the corps officers and the bandmaster were each sentenced to a month's imprisonment in default of paying the fines. In January 1887 Captain Tom Kyle having been fined £1 for playing his concertina while marching through the streets, and the justices not being prepared to state and sign a case, a *rule nisi* was obtained and an action brought before the Lord Chief Justice, who decided against them. In January 1888 the Captain was fined £2 and nine bandsmen and the standard-bearer £1 each, but they elected to go to Exeter Gaol, and were welcomed back amid great public rejoicings led by Staff-Captain Eva Booth. Captain Hopkins, a one-armed man, had his artificial arm taken from him, and although the doctor was appealed to, it was not returned until his sentence had been served. The *Pall Mall Gazette* gave a 2,000-word report of this event. In the House of Commons the Home Secretary, being questioned by Professor Stuart, expressed the opinion that the sentences were not excessive, although he admitted that the Home Office had said, at the time the Torquay Harbour and District Act was passing through the House, that the thirty-eighth clause ought to have been struck out of it.

From time to time the prosecuting authorities were given a clear view of what unprejudiced persons thought of their proceedings. When, on 15 March 1888, a Salvationist was sentenced to a month's imprisonment in default of paying a fine of £3, the senior magistrate, Mr E. Vivian—who had protested in a similar case eighteen months before—remarked that he not only declined to unite with his brother-magistrates in the finding, but strongly disapproved of the action of the Board. He believed there was a vast number of people who did not take sides with the Board, and who did not appreciate the fact that the county gaol was being filled with perfectly respectable human beings. He called attention to the wording of the clause which read "accompanied by any instrumental music . . . or *other disturbing noise*." It had been brought out in cross-examination that no one, not even the police themselves, considered the band "a disturbing noise."

The *Western Daily Mail*, commenting on the situation, wrote :

> The Salvation Army has done too much good work to deserve the vicious treatment which the Local Board has considered to be their due, and the sympathy shown them by all classes is abundant proof of the unpopularity of the persecuting spirit. The opinion very naturally prevails that the Torquay Local Board are solely prompted in their special aggressiveness by the worldly wish to maintain the reputation of the watering place as a centre of aristocratic bearing. The Salvation Army are too much convinced of the necessity of their work to be swayed from their course by such advertising aspirations.

More imprisonments followed, then Major (later Colonel) John Roberts, the Divisional Officer, and six other Salvationists, including Captain (later Brigadier) William H. Gilliard, were sentenced to various terms of imprisonment on 30 April 1888, the Major being committed for a month. Mr F. W. Crossley[1] had participated in the meetings the previous weekend. The "prisoners" were always welcomed home with a public demonstration, often in both Exeter and Torquay. At Whitsuntide Commissioner Carleton joined Staff-Captain Eva Booth who led demonstrations which included Sunday musical processions. Both were summoned and convicted, with eighteen others. The Commissioner was fined £1 or 14 days' imprisonment, and so were the others, with the exception of the Staff-Captain, upon whom the magistrates, notwithstanding her protests, would pass no sentence. Eleven Members of Parliament paid eleven of the fines. One soldier, although having served his term, had his household effects sold by public auction, "under distraint by order of magistrates' warrant."

Appeal against these sentences had been made to the High Court, but before a decision was given the matter had been taken up in Parliament. Petitions asking for a repeal of the offending clause in the 1886 Act, with more than a quarter of a million signatures, had been presented. The signatures included those of Canons Wilberforce and Holland, the President of the Wesleyan Conference, the Chairman of the Congregational Union, the Chairman of the Baptist Union, Drs Joseph Parker and McLaren, and nearly 7,000 residents of Torquay. Mr Henry H. Fowler, M.P. (later Viscount Wolverhampton), had given notice that if the Home Secretary did not bring in a bill to repeal the clause he would, and on 4 June 1888 he fulfilled his promise. Rejection of the bill was unsuccessfully moved by Mr Cavendish-Bentinck, already notorious for his opposition to the Criminal Law Amendment Act, 1885,[2] and it was duly sent to committee. The principal witness at the Parliamentary Select Committee's sitting, which met

1 *The History of The Salvation Army*, vol. iii, p. 208
2 *The History of The Salvation Army*, vol. iii, p. 32

on 12 July, was Staff-Captain Booth, who was examined with the greatest courtesy and kindness by Sir Charles Russell, Q.C., the chairman.

At the enquiry it was stated that the thirty-eighth clause had not been asked for by Torquay, and the Board had no desire to oppose its repeal, though it had felt compelled to prosecute where the law had been broken. As a matter of fact, the Board had not only previously petitioned the House against the Repeal Bill, but had continued its prosecutions up to the very day fixed for its second reading.

The Select Committee reported to the House of Commons in favour of the proposed amendment on 19 July 1888, and the bill was read a third time and sent up to the House of Lords. The General visited Torquay on 8 August to announce at a thanksgiving demonstration that the Royal Assent had been given to the bill which repealed the obnoxious clause. He also paid tribute to the steadfast courage of the forty Salvationists who had bravely stood up for their rights, and suffered imprisonment.

A proposal put before the Bath Town Council by its parliamentary committee that a byelaw similar to the thirty-eighth clause of the Torquay Act should be placed before the Committee of the House of Commons for legalization, while it was deliberating on the Repeal Bill, was rejected by the full council.

Chapter Two

THE EASTBOURNE RIOTS

Eastbourne Town Council had, by pursuing similar tactics to that of Torquay, brought about the inclusion of an identical section, No 169, in its Town Improvement Act, 1885, which Act was passed by the House of Commons, "the members," said Bramwell Booth at an Exeter Hall meeting, "not knowing that this particular clause which was aimed at The Salvation Army was in it at all. . . . It was got by a trick." As a matter of fact the clause was actually struck out by Lord Redesdale, the Chairman of the Committee, when the Act passed through the Lords at the time, but it was re-inserted without the Army's knowledge by a House of Commons Committee consisting of only five members, one of whom voted against it.

While the Torquay proceedings were oppressive and vexatious in the extreme, there was this difference: that those at Eastbourne were inspired by unreasoning, implacable animosity toward The Salvation Army, to which full expression was given by the mayor, William Epps Morrison, himself, before he took office. He thought, he said, that the town council should do all in its power to put down "The Salvation Army business which was opposed altogether to the spirit of true religion." To this he added that, if the Army defied all "polite overtures," the council must resort to the skeleton army to do the work for it. Indeed, the mayor actually asked the Home Secretary for permission to leave the Salvationists to the fury of the rabble, which permission the Home Secretary very properly declined to give. One of the first things Morrison did when he became mayor was to lead the council in getting the 169th clause inserted in the Act. Councillor Chambers, who drafted the bill, admitted in a letter to *The Times* on 14 September 1891 that the 169th clause was inserted for the express purpose of preventing The Salvation Army from conducting its usual musical processions should it extend its operations to Eastbourne. He also admitted, when questioned in the Parliamentary Committee proceedings which eventuated, that he had called the Army "an atrocious, infamous and degrading movement."[1]

Further sinister light is thrown upon the situation in that Mayor Charles C. Shoppee, of Ballarat, Australia, who was at the time conducting a similar campaign against the Army, received from Eastbourne's mayor a letter of commendation and "good wishes."

Eastbourne Corps was opened on 9 January 1890, and the first tussle between the council and the Army took place on 8 September, when Captain Emily Goss and some of her comrades, who were summoned in the August for singing in the street, appeared before the magistrates. The case was dismissed and the council thereby "ignominiously defeated," according to a report in the Brighton *Argus*. Although charged on 24 August, Staff-Captain Appleby, bandmaster of the Household Troops Band, was not brought before the court until October, when he was fined £1 in each case and 15s costs or seven days' imprisonment for being associated with a procession and a band of music. By May 1891 a corps band was ready for service. The mayor was duly and courteously informed and a compromise suggested: that the band would on Sundays play in procession only in certain specified streets. This was rejected and a hostile resolution passed by the council on 11 May.

The conflict proper started with the appearance before the local magistrates of Captain Bob Bell and four of his

[1] In his book *Eastbourne Memories*, published in 1910, Mr Chambers remained bitter toward the Army. "A long time elapsed before the Corporation of Eastbourne was again seen at Westminster," he wrote, "and the circumstances were in the highest degree discreditable to those who dragged the Corporation there. . . . There were riotous scenes in the streets, brought about by the wicked misconduct of the Booth faction in defiance of the law and of the wishes of the inhabitants at large. . . . It was well understood at the time that the votes of the M.P.s concerned would have been different, perhaps widely different, if a General Election had not been coming off in a few weeks, and many members were frightened by the threats of the Salvationists.

soldiers who were, in June 1891, fined £5 or a month's imprisonment—the maximum penalty, which they served. A week later thirty comrades, including four women and a blind man, were before the magistrates—fifteen under twenty-one years of age were let off. They would all have been discharged had they promised the chairman that they would not "break the Act" in future. Everyone refused to make any such promise, and the maximum penalty was inflicted on them.

From Thursday, 25 June to Sunday, 28 June, Field Commissioner Eva Booth visited the town, conducting three meetings on the Sunday. An accident had rendered her unable to take so prominent a part in Eastbourne as she had done in Torquay. In an effort to bring about an amicable settlement of the trouble, but without result, the Commissioner called upon the mayor and Councillor Chambers, who avers that he "had even to submit to the assaults of Miss Eva Booth's tongue delivered in my own house." Perhaps this fact gives the clue as to why no names were taken during the Sunday!

A tremendous welcome home was given to Bell and his four fellow-prisoners by 2,000 Salvationists from London and the south of England, who marched in procession through the town with Commandant H. H. Booth, Field Commissioner Eva Booth and Commissioner Howard at their head. The day ended, however, in the Salvationists being unmercifully attacked by a large crowd, the police having to charge with batons. One comrade's head was split open with a poker. Thenceforward a constant stream of Salvationists flowed to and from Lewes Prison.

Added to the bitterness of these prosecutions was the constant ill-treatment—described as brutal and indecent in the extreme—received by men *and women* Salvationists at the hands of a mob, numbering at times 7,000 and more, which had been all too ready to act on the mayor's incitement. Official approval made them feel that to them had been given the task of "putting down the Army." The police were held back from giving proper protection; indeed, on more than one occasion they had been sent to break up the Army's processions, even when without music and perfectly legal, by riding down those who were participating. Many processionists were injured, some seriously. Even when charged with assaulting Salvationists, rioters were dealt with so leniently by the magistrates that they were encouraged in their wrong-doing rather than deterred from it.

On the Sunday following Bell's welcome home nine bandsmen of the Camberwell, London, corps went to the help of their Eastbourne comrades. These nine included William and Lieutenant Henry Haines, who later became a Lieut.-Commissioner and Colonel respectively. These bandsmen were not only roughly handled by the mob of some 1,500 hooligans, but were, by the personal order of the mayor on the spot illegally, it was later admitted, arrested and detained by the police in the town-hall. They appeared on summons before the magistrates and on 23 July were committed for trial, charged with conspiracy and unlawful assembly. Mr H. H. Asquith, Q.C., M.P., who was later to become Prime Minister of England, appeared for the defendants.

A week after the arrest of the Camberwell bandsmen 101 local men were sworn in by Mayor Morrison as special constables, bound by a solemn oath to "unite for the preservation of the peace and for the borough." The local press described this innovation in terms of ridicule, for these would-be valiant defenders of the law were never called upon to leave the precincts of the town-hall.

When, on 8 August, the Camberwell bandsmen appeared

at the Sussex Assizes at Lewes before Mr Justice Hawkins, he opened the case by appealing for a compromise settlement. Mr Marshall Hall, who was to become a famous advocate, was one of the counsel for the prosecution. In a previous case he had told the court that "General Booth stood out in this country as a perfect monument of the folly of the day—a perfect masterpiece of autocratic power." The Army's solicitor undertook that there should be no band playing for two Sundays while the council considered the suggestion, but it was rejected. The case was then removed, upon the Army's application, to the Central Criminal Court for hearing on 2 December. In the meantime the authorities did nothing whatever to protect Salvationists from the continued assaults of a riotous mob for months on end. Women were actually trampled under foot, kicked and beaten. Mr Justice Hawkins, who was again the judge, whittled down the charge to two counts in place of six. The jury brought in a verdict of "Not guilty of conspiracy, but of unlawful assembly," giving as their reason for this, when the judge questioned them, that the bandsmen had taken their instruments "down there and so broken the Act." The judge at once pointed out that walking along carrying instruments was by no means unlawful, and refused to accept the verdict.

In November The Salvation Army's solicitor had informed the town council that it intended to promote a bill to repeal Section 169 of the Eastbourne Improvement Act of 1885. The council decided to oppose it, their resolution being approved in an open poll of the ratepayers, the figures being: For opposing the bill, 5,331; against, 738. The mayor sent a letter to many local boards throughout the country asking if they approved of Clause 169, but met with very little sympathy. In Edinburgh Councillor Harry Smith moved that the council refuse to entertain the request.

Eastbourne had made itself a name of infamy in England by its barbarous, intolerable oppression of a law-abiding body of citizens, The Salvation Army, and the Council should have neither let nor part with Eastbourne in the matter.

On 4 December a proclamation was posted in Eastbourne signed by the mayor and town clerk, purporting to forbid "the holding of meetings, or delivering of addresses in streets, parades or foreshores by any person or persons . . . on Sundays." For this there was no authority; indeed, legal advice was given that not only was the proclamation *ultra vires*, but that the police, and those ordering them or commanding them, should they attempt to disperse such gatherings, would render themselves liable to prosecution for assault. The proclamation was withdrawn when the Methodists announced that they, too, would fight it to the death. Nevertheless, the police most brutally dispersed Salvationists when *standing*—not marching—and playing on the Sunday. The mob, it is recorded, pelted police and Salvationists alike with *frozen* snowballs on one occasion. When proceedings were taken against the mayor and chief constable, the illegality of the action was acknowledged by the payment of damages into court.

During November a crudely-illustrated hand-written four-page leaflet called *The Eastbourne Scorpion* had commenced publication at one penny per copy. It was published by J. W. Moorton, of 84 Pevensey Road. In the April 1892 issue the following notice appeared:

Such has been the success of our little *Scorpion* that it has been decided to publish permanently as a monthly serio-comic local illustrated Review. We are grateful by the reception of our rough attempt to amuse the local public, and hope that those whom we attempt to caricature, although they may consider the effect is poor, will say "There's no malice in it."

The phrase is difficult to understand for the General and the

Army were very frequently scathingly attacked. An example of the *absence* of malice is hardly evidenced in this extract:

It is probable that every M.P. who supports the Booth Bill will be promised by Booth a free pass to Heaven. A promissory note, however, of which he is a maker, is more likely to be honoured in hell. And M.P.s need not hug themselves with the belief that by supporting this fraudulent religious organization they can wipe out as with a sponge their enormous sins and iniquities.

In the subsequent review of the case of the Camberwell bandsmen on 27 January 1892, by the High Court of the Queen's Bench Division, five judges gave it as their unanimous judgment that there was

not any evidence on which a reasonable jury could have acted in finding the defendants guilty of an unlawful assembly . . . no one had suggested that on that occasion anything was said or done by the Army or the band which in the least degree could have tended to provoke any human being to suppose they intended a breach of the peace . . . a large crowd had assembled around this peaceable body of persons engaged in prayer. . . . The crowd had assembled for the purpose of jeering and annoying the members of The Salvation Army . . . not one of the crowd ever raised hand or voice to prevent the brutal outrages perpetrated on the bandsmen while they were proceeding peacefully and lawfully along the streets. . . . They had a perfect right to walk over the streets carrying their instruments . . . there was not one aggressive act done or word uttered which proved the bandsmen had gone to Eastbourne with intent to break the peace tumultuously.

It was also pointed out that even had there been an attempt to break the law, the law provided punishment for such, and any violent action by a mob was not only unwarranted, but itself punishable. Indeed, persons who were guilty of such outrages deserved punishment even more than those who broke the law innocently, thinking they were conscientiously entitled to do so. On one occasion the Duke of Portland and two Members of Parliament were witnesses of these disorderly scenes.

Another significant omission on the part of the police was that although Staff-Captain Rebecca Chatterton (Divisional Officer), a relative of Vice-Chancellor Chatterton, of Ireland, had been sentenced to a month's imprisonment at the beginning of the trouble, she was never taken to Lewes, despite the fact that she gave every opportunity for this to be done. It is noteworthy also that—as in the case at Torquay—the Field Commissioner was able to impress the Select Committee favourably, the chairman himself remarking that she had given her evidence in a most pertinent manner.

Attempt was made by representatives of the Eastbourne Council to discredit the Army by claiming that its leaders were habitual and purposeful lawbreakers. But this was rebutted by the Chief of the Staff (Mr Bramwell Booth) when giving evidence before the Select Committee in both Houses. He then stated that when, as in the case in point, The Salvation Army was made the victim of a clause which involved so serious a deviation from the general Common and Statute Law of the country, it was felt that Salvationists were within their rights to disobey it quietly and take the consequences by way of protest. If the usual method of local government by byelaw was substituted and such was upheld, if necessary by a test case, it was and would be obeyed. The Solicitor-General, Sir Edward Clarke, wrote regarding this matter :

> I fully admit the force of what you say as to the necessity of maintaining an actual protest against the Eastbourne Act in order to have any chance of getting it repealed, and I personally shall be glad to help in securing the repeal.

On 10 March 1892 the House of Commons passed by a two to one majority—269 votes to 122—the second reading of a bill repealing the offensive clause, this being introduced, as in the case of Torquay, by Mr H. H. Fowler, and strongly opposed by the member for Eastbourne, Admiral Field. The Repeal Bill passed triumphantly through the Select Committees of both Houses, Messrs W. E. Gladstone, John Morley and Joseph Chamberlain being among the ayes.

The bill came before a House of Commons hybrid committee at the end of April and the beginning of May, when the Rt Hon. Sir Henry James, Q.C., presided. Both Mr Fowler and Admiral Field were members. The Select Committee of the House of Lords was presided over in June by Lord Wantage. Mr E. H. Pember, Q.C., in presenting the Army's case, stated that there were four grounds upon which he asked for the repeal of the 169th clause: (1) It was a most serious alteration of the common law in one locality and by such alteration was an infringement of the general freedom of the citizens; (2) It was advisedly directed against one section of Her Majesty's subjects; (3) It had been invented and since its invention had been administered with a view to repressing an unpopular form of religious propagandism; and (4) It had been productive of disastrous breaches of the peace. The Committee decided that the bill should proceed. Third readings in both Houses were agreed without further divisions, and the Act came into force on 1 September 1892.

The newspapers generally were on the side of the Salvationists in commenting upon the victory after the second reading of the bill, but *The Times* was a little unkind in seeing political expediency in the decision.[1]
The *Daily News* wrote:

The Salvationists are entitled to say that they won a great victory

[1] p. 270. See note

in the House of Commons yesterday. It was, however, a triumph not only for them, but for the cause of civil and religious freedom as well.

The *Star* stated that

Everyone must admire the heroic tenacity with which the men and women of The Salvation Army have striven quietly and peacefully to maintain their position against the forces of bigot-made law and disorder.

The General, in a letter of congratulation to the soldiers of Eastbourne corps, wrote :

Your comrades throughout the world, who have eagerly read from week to week the story of your devotion, and who have prayed God for the continuance of grace and strength to enable you to persevere, are rejoicing in the tidings of victory which are now known to all, and will for years to come make the name of your town a watch-word and a stimulus in the defence of liberty to publish Christ and His salvation to the sons of men. And now, what next ? There must be no exultation from any selfish or party feeling : on these grounds let there not be even an unfriendly reference to the past. As far as possible let the very memory of it be buried in oblivion. Let it not be forgotten for a moment that we have not been striving for the mastery, or in any spirit of self-glorification, but solely for the liberty to spread the knowledge of that religion the essence of which is love, and the manifestation of which is only by deeds of mercy, making known the life and work of the Christ who came to save. . . .

The Eastbourne corps had won a great victory indeed, but it was magnanimous in its hour of triumph. It had refrained from all Sunday open-air work from the time of the decisive second reading. A report in the *War Cry* of 23 April stated that this was in order to allow time for feelings to cool and for the police to get the upper hand over the forces of disorder. In September it was further reported that the corps had made all-round progress, and was marching with band playing, unmolested, every Sunday. By the end of November, a record covering five months showed that 80 seekers had knelt at the penitent-form, 35 recruits and 28 new soldiers had been made, *and the band was doing splendidly*.

After the repeal of Section 169 of the Eastbourne Improvement Act of 1885 the council decided to make byelaws which would practically re-enact the provisions of that section with a view to preventing the processions and demonstrations of the Army through the streets on Sundays, but the Home Secretary refused to approve them.

The storm of opposition which broke over The Salvation Army at this period was not without advantages. W. T. Stead, writing when it was at its height, shrewdly commented :

> Much as The Salvation Army has been helped by its friends it would have been at a comparative standstill but for its enemies. They have enabled it to pose as the champion of liberty of speech and liberty of procession ; they have furnished it with a noble company of officers whose university has been the jail, and who have been tempered in the furnace of tribulation before they have been called to the ministry of love for the salvation of the lost. . . . The greatest danger which menaces the Salvationists of today is the possibility of their becoming so respectable that they will no longer be exposed to the biting blasts of ridicule and denunciation, which, like Kingsley's Nor'-easter, has made them the men they are.

Chapter Three

TECHNICAL OBSTRUCTION

The five years following the first International Congress were heavily-laden with instances of " official " persecutions, mainly in connection with street obstructions, and this notwithstanding that decisions in the Army's favour were given from time to time in courts of appeal. One such appeal was made against the conviction and sentence of eight Salvationists at Ryde (Isle of Wight) in July 1886 for "singing and speaking" in the streets, under a byelaw which made it illegal to do so without a licence from the mayor. This byelaw was declared invalid by the Court of the Queen's Bench and the magistrates' decision reversed with costs.

It is difficult to understand why Salvationists were sent to prison over and over again for offences that the Home Secretary, Mr (later Judge) Atherley Jones, had declared the police were instructed not to treat as such. In reply to a question in Parliament in September 1886 he had said that the Home Office had

issued no instructions with regard to the recent prosecutions of evangelical and socialist lecturers for street obstructions. The instructions given by the Chief Commissioner were that the police were never to interfere except where there was positive obstruction to traffic. He was not aware of any admission on the part of the police that they had ever interfered except in these circumstances. In his opinion the instructions of the Chief Commissioner were quite proper and in accordance with the law and he had no intention of interfering with them.

The Army made every effort to work in harmony with local authorities, as is proved by the following Special Order issued that month from headquarters:

Everybody go on as usual. If told by the police to move on, obey courteously and promptly and appeal to us. Do your best to avoid collision. Keep away from places where you know there is ill-feeling. Leave the direction of the battle to Headquarters.

In this same month the *Methodist Times*, doubtless with shades of John Wesley in mind, sounded a note of warning in its columns:

It is impossible to exaggerate the importance of this issue. We must move Heaven and earth to prevent either the Home Secretary or the police from having power to put down open-air preaching.

During this same month also, five Salvationists, including Staff-Captain George Mackenzie, "Salvation Smith" (Clement E. Smith), a London stockbroker, and two women-officers, were charged with wilfully obstructing the highway in the village of Markyate Street, some four miles from Luton, and—with the exception of Smith, who paid his fine, otherwise his goods would have been distrained upon—sentenced to seven days' imprisonment. Three years later Mackenzie attended a Commission of the House of Lords to give evidence as to the treatment of Salvationists in prison. The chairman, Lord Aberdeen, expressed a strong opinion as to the legality of Mackenzie's hair being cropped.

The two lad-officers at Buckingham were sent to prison for fourteen days, the complainant being a publican who declared that his wife was ill and that the Salvationists disturbed her; but the meeting concluded immediately this fact was made known. The action was brought under a new byelaw, similar to the one at Ryde, which had been declared by the Court of the Queen's Bench to be illegal. Special excursion trains were run to convey those who wished to participate in the "welcome home" of the officers from Aylesbury Gaol; some 3,000 persons gathered outside Buckingham railway station. A procession through the town was headed by the officers riding on horseback, Commandant Herbert Booth and Staff-Captain (later General) Higgins also taking part.

A new plan was now adopted by the Army's opponents. Instead of bringing before the bench cases of obstruction or general annoyance, they framed the false charges of causing pain and distress to people who were conveniently ill. Two officers and four soldiers were next imprisoned at Eckington, Derbyshire, one of the officers being Lieutenant Mary Fairhurst, mother of Commissioner William F. Cooper; the Lieutenant at Southport was sent to jail for fourteen days, and Mr William Kitching, Quaker-grandfather of General Wilfred Kitching, the present International Leader of The Salvation Army, spoke at his welcome home meeting.

The over-zealous Stamford, Lincolnshire, town-clerk, a Mr Atter, and the local magistrates whose previous attempt[1] to suppress the Army had involved the Home Secretary in their ignominious failure, made a further effort to do so in June 1887 by invoking the "technical obstruction" law in the case of Captain Herbert Turner and Lieutenant William Dunn, who were sentenced to fourteen days' imprisonment in Leicester Gaol. The obstruction was supposed to have occurred at a large market-place, Red Lion Square, in which the corps held its small meetings in one corner and out of the line of traffic.

The iniquity continued until September, Salvationists being again and again handcuffed when arrested and taken to the police-station. When the matter was raised in Parliament, the Home Secretary, the Rt Hon. Henry Matthews, as on other occasions, stated that no prisoner should be handcuffed unless there was definite likelihood of attempted escape. When in August the Rt Hon. H. H. Fowler asked about the imprisonments it was freely admitted that the "obstruction" was purely technical. "It is for obstructing the passage of the highway—nothing more," the town-clerk had declared. "I do not propose to prove that any person was obstructed. The sole and simple matter is the obstruction of the highway." The Home Secretary eventually agreed to release the Salvationists then serving a twenty-one days' sentence. Such a storm of protest was

[1] *The History of The Salvation Army*, vol. ii, p. 176

aroused by the press, although some sections of it did not approve of the Army's methods, that the Stamford authorities were sensible enough to cancel further prosecutions. The fact that this little town of fewer than 9,000 inhabitants was famous for its ale breweries may have accounted for the persistent persecution. Three years later from 500 to 600 persons were attending the open-air meetings and a brass band had been started.

Throughout the country this " official " persecution was more or less taken as not merely an excuse for, but an incentive to, violent assaults upon Salvationists by mobs. The disgraceful scenes that marked an earlier visit were repeated when the General, accompanied by Bramwell Booth, again arrived in Northampton for a week-end campaign in January 1887, commenting on which the *Northampton Daily Reporter* said :

Stone-throwing became most general and great missiles rained upon the little band . . . the standard bearers were attacked . . . in the most dastardly manner possible men struck right and left at the heads of the soldiers with sticks and stones . . . the mob with a brutality only equalled by its cowardice, attacked the Salvation girls. Some of their bonnets were torn off, some were struck across the head with heavy sticks . . . some, fainting with the ill-usage were with difficulty rescued and placed in comparative safety on the footpath. The General's carriage was a special target. His bodyguard kept the roughs away from him, but he was struck in the face by a rotten egg !

The mayor, Mr K. Cleaver, presided over the General's " gigantic meeting " in the Corn Exchange on the Monday evening and as a Christian regretted, as did his fellow-magistrates, the deplorable happenings of the Saturday afternoon torchlight procession.

When Captain Mary Billing and two soldiers of Warwick corps appeared before the magistrates in August 1887 for wilfully causing an obstruction in the Corn Market, a petition was signed by the townsfolk protesting against the base injustice of prosecution. Outside friends paid the one guinea fine. Captain Thompson, of Kingston-on-Thames, was sentenced to three days' imprisonment for singing and preaching in a street to the annoyance of one of the residents. He was welcomed back by Commissioner Railton. The vicar was the principal but very reluctant witness for the prosecution at Street, Somerset, where Salvationists were accused of obstructing the free passage to the church. The Captain was fined 6d, with 11s costs.

Scotland was not immune from prosecutions which, during 1887, veered round from Forfar in the east to Baillieston and Cowcaddens in the west. Although an adverse decision on an appeal in 1882[1] had left Scottish magistrates with power to prohibit singing or playing instruments in the streets, one instance only is recorded within the period under review, in which prosecution was attempted: at Alloa in 1888 when fourteen Salvationists were sentenced for defying such a proclamation. The cases were all dismissed. At the beginning of 1888 the winds blew from the north—Inverness—where Captain Evans was arrested, tried and imprisoned for twenty-four hours for obstruction. The Dean of Guild himself offered to pay the fine of 5s after deciding the case.

It was now Ireland's turn; six Household Troopers were sentenced in Belfast to a fine of 1s or twenty-four hours' imprisonment. They went to gaol. Some years before, another band was prosecuted for alleged indecency, the indecency being its playing in the streets. In Derry proceedings were taken against Salvationists for illegal assembly and obstruction, and the magistrates ordered them to enter into sureties to "keep the peace" for twelve months or in default be imprisoned for one calendar month.

[1] *The History of The Salvation Army*, vol. ii, p. 190

Against this the Army appealed, and in the Queen's Bench Division, Dublin, the court unanimously held that the decision of the magistrates was wrong and should be quashed.

Dastardly assaults night after night by "skeletons" and an organized system of terrorism and aggravation against Salvationists took place in Dorking, Surrey. The "skeletons" were fined and bound over to keep the peace after having seized a Salvationist by the throat and blackened his eyes; the fines were paid by public collections.

From time to time cases of a novel character arose. At Hartlepool in 1888 a Salvationist was unsuccessfully proceeded against under an Act of King Charles II for selling *War Crys* on a Sunday!

Alleged obstruction at Willenhall resulted in the Captain and two of his soldiers serving fourteen days with hard labour in Stafford Gaol, they being chained and handcuffed to convicted criminals *en route* from the police court. At the same court the publican, who had prosecuted, was himself fined five shillings and costs for assaulting the Captain with his whip and obstructing the Army. At Needham Market, where the justices were a clergyman and a military colonel, Salvationists were also handcuffed and marched through the streets *en route* to Ipswich Gaol. When five Dorking Salvationists were taken handcuffed through the streets to Wandworth Gaol, the matter was raised in Parliament by Sir H. Roscoe. At Sevenoaks twelve Salvationists were given seven days' hard labour—working the treadwheel—for obstructing a village roadway. Major (later Commissioner) John Lawley, in command of the Eastern division, was sent to Ipswich Prison for fourteen days for obstruction at Bungay. In the majority of cases the local press was highly condemnatory of the magistrates who were responsible for such harsh and inhuman treatment.

On 26 March 1888 Mr W. S. Caine asked the Home

Secretary in the House of Commons if his attention had been called to the organized attacks upon The Salvation Army at Chipping Norton by a gang of roughs styling themselves "The Skeleton Army," which formed processions behind a coffin and attacked the Salvationists; if he was aware that on several occasions women had been knocked down and indecently assaulted; and if he was aware that the Army had repeatedly appealed to the police for protection and had been refused. Mr Matthews replied that he had received word from the Chief Constable of Oxfordshire that the facts alleged by Mr Caine were greatly exaggerated, and that the superintendent of police at Chipping Norton had stated that it was not possible for him to provide a police guard for the processionists. The *War Cry's* special correspondent visited Chipping Norton and wrote a vivid account of his personal investigations, which proved that the chief constable had been culpably neglectful of his duties and clearly guilty of the serious offence of attempting to mislead the Home Secretary.

Instead of the state of affairs having been exaggerated, the correspondent declared, as had been stated in the public press, they had been under-rated. Evidently one of the causes for opposition was that a certain publican's takings were a pound a week less since the Army had emptied his premises. Another cause for opposition was a sermon preached against the Army by the curate of the parish church. The mayor had written the corps officer stating that he would have to put up with the consequences if trouble broke out in the town as the result of the Army declining to participate in a public dinner which had taken place on Jubilee Day the previous year. This letter was read in the council meeting and then published. The roughs, seeing the feeling of the authorities, had taken their cue and acted accordingly. Soldiers had been chased through the streets, knocked about, kicked, and even bitten, women were indecently assaulted and punched. Lieutenant (later Colonel) William Bettridge had been dashed against a wall and punched in the ribs. Some of the leading men in the town had been seen behind the scenes urging on the mob. Several constables verified the evidence given by the Salvationists, one stating that his " blood boiled " when he saw what was happening, but he could do nothing, having received orders not to interfere. Summonses against the offenders were in nearly all cases dismissed.

It was recorded in the *War Cry* that a case that no doubt had considerable influence in other quarters was that of a bandsman of Bungay, Suffolk. He was sentenced on 20 June 1889 for obstruction and in default of paying a fine of 10s and costs, to fourteen day's imprisonment *with hard labour*. An appeal was lodged, but he was not released until three or four days later, after his treatment had given rise to questions in the House of Commons. Acting upon the decisions obtained in the High Courts of the Queen's Bench and the confirmation of these in the House of Lords seven years previously,[1] the chairman of the Suffolk Quarter Sessions held at Ipswich on 18 October declared the conviction quashed.

When the crippled Staff-Captain Eliza Drabble was arrested at Notting Hill in 1889 for " disorderly conduct " and causing a crowd to assemble, she was pushed to the police-station in a bath-chair.

The Chief Constable of Nottinghamshire charged a local corps with processioning on the wrong side of the road and seizing his horse's head, although the Salvationists were actually on the right side and he, driving a dog-cart, on the wrong side ; the Captain was sent to jail for seven days. Eight Salvationists imprisoned by Chelsea magistrates

[1] *The History of The Salvation Army*, vol. ii, pp. 177 and 327

included three cadets. They were given a most enthusiastic welcome home in the Baptist chapel, the use of which was offered by the minister, the meeting being led by Commandant Booth. The Church Army frequently joined in the welcome meetings to discharged Salvationist-prisoners. Chelsea was again in the news in September 1893 when a woman-cadet was charged with singing to the annoyance of a resident, and sent to prison for five days. In point of fact she did not sing.

At East Grinstead the officer was sentenced to seven days' imprisonment for obstruction, and widespread indignation resulted, a local minister hired the public hall for a welcome home and protest meeting and himself presided. The chairman said that he had never heard of a more frivolous case. The police stated in evidence that a cart was obstructed, but the man in the cart said he would never have thought of complaining. A farmer presented a two-headed calf, a rare freak of nature, to the Assistant Field-Secretary to be sold to help defray the expenses of the action. At this time many German bands were in existence throughout the country and evidence was given time and again that while they often caused obstruction no charge was made against them. A crowd of 5,000 waited at the gates of Carlisle Prison to welcome home three lads who had been sentenced from Workington. Marshal Ballington Booth presided over the gathering in the Army hall which, once a match-making factory, was then known as "The Match Box." At Congleton in November 1889, the Captain was sentenced to seven days' imprisonment for assaulting—placing his hand upon the shoulder of—a young rough who had knocked down a lassie and then had tried to break through the ranks. The rough was not even prosecuted.

Another *cause célèbre* of the period was the ridiculous prosecution of Salvationists at Whitchurch, a Hampshire village with a population of fewer than 2,000. The action was brought by the magistrates, of whom Melville Portal was chairman, in combination with the police. Several of the Salvationists were in the employ of the magistrates, who dismissed them when they came out of prison. In a sympathetic letter to headquarters Lord Lymington, who lived at Whitchurch, concluded: "the situation of affairs has relapsed into a position which is calculated to excite public scandal and disorder." The mayor was also sympathetic to the Army. Dr Joseph Parker, of the City Temple, described the action taken by the authorities at Whitchurch as infamous. "Whitchurch handcuffs are heaven's bracelets," said the Rev. Archibald Brown. Dr John Clifford, Canon Farrar, T. P. O'Connor, Canon Wilberforce, the Rev. F. B. Meyer, the Earl of Aberdeen and Sir William Harcourt were also among the distinguished sympathizers.

Eventually, after nearly a year of persecution—during which convictions had totalled ninety (on the word of three witnesses throughout) and scores of Salvationists, including a boy of fifteen, had been taken handcuffed to prison—a great demonstration was staged. Some two or three thousand Salvationists, including a dozen bands, took part and sympathizers went down to Whitchurch by train from London and assembled outside the Portal mansion at Micheldever. The demonstration resulted in Commandant Herbert Booth, Major Alfred Barritt (Field-Secretary), and Mr Richardson, the Army's solicitor, being indicted for obstruction, riot, rout, etc. The Army having secured a change of venue from Winchester to London, the case came before Lord Chief Justice Coleridge on 1 July 1890 in the Queen's Bench Division. The result was that the jury, as *The Times* recorded, "in two minutes, merely turning round in the box, returned a verdict of 'Not guilty'." The Lord Chief Justice's summing-up was a clear statement of the Army's legal rights regarding its open-air work that did much to bring to an end the persecuting prosecutions to which it was at that time being subjected.[1]

The Eastbourne fight[2] was still to come, but from this time forward a marked decline was noticeable in the number of instances in which charges of obstruction were made, and even more significant, an increase of instances in which magistrates dismissed cases, occasionally with costs, against the prosecution. This was a very much welcomed relief, for between 1886 and 1895 prosecutions had been recorded in more than 100 places, mainly brought about by those engaged in the liquor trade.

The Chief of the Staff was charged in 1890 at Dalston police court with "aiding and abetting seven Upper Holloway bandsmen in an alleged breach of the Highway Act," but the magistrate would have none of it and the case was dismissed. He could see no distinction, he said, between Salvation Army bands and bands which played in other lawful processions.

Extraordinary action was taken by the Metropolitan police when they arrested Commissioner Frank Smith, Ensign Beddall and two other Salvationists who took part in a procession through the City of London on the occasion of the Exeter Hall meeting on 18 September 1890, the evening of the wedding day of Commandant Herbert Booth and Captain Cornelie Schoch in the Congress Hall.[3] The defendants were brought before the Bow Street magistrate. Smith was accused of ignoring a police-sergeant's instructions to disband the procession and of striking him in the chest. Beddall was alleged to have gone to Smith's rescue and to have kicked his captor's leg. They were fined 40s each; the others were discharged. Friends paid the fines.

At the instance of a publican, the officer of Poplar corps

[1] Appendix C p. 386 [2] p. 268 [3] p. 363

was sentenced to thirty-one days' imprisonment in August 1893 for holding an open-air meeting. This stirred up so much local feeling that a protest meeting was held outside the dock gates. When a resolution then adopted was brought by Mr Sidney Buxton, M.P., before the Home Secretary, Mr H. H. Asquith (later Earl of Oxford and Asquith), he ordered the officer's release. There was no more interference with the holding of open-air meetings in that district. The Lieutenant at Longton, Staffs., was sent to prison for fourteen days instead of paying a fine of 5s, which was paid a day or so later by a dissenting magistrate. Three other sympathizers offered to pay the fine, including a publican.

It is significant of what was happening in many places that socialist lecturers were mentioned. Political opponents desirous of silencing them lumped together *all* street meetings; in more than one instance this fact was stated in court, notably at Halifax in July 1900. Rowdyism remained a constant menace to The Salvation Army and it says a great deal for early-day Salvationists that not only were they prepared, as Paul wrote to Timothy, to "endure hardness, as a good soldier of Jesus Christ," but their heroic stand attracted others to the flag. An amazing thing is that in many cases persons imprisoned never considered it worthy of mention to headquarters.

In the end, however, opposition which was based on lack of knowledge of the Army's aims and the love of its officers and soldiers for the lost and its manifest purpose to save and bless even the worst of its persecutors, and which was often the result of gross misrepresentation by interested opponents, gave way. By the opening of 1889 the *War Cry* was able to write of "Our Roughs":

For the young fellows—and for that matter, girls, too—who march with us, stand at our open-airs, attend our meetings as regularly as the most regular of our soldiers, give to our collections, patronize our tea fights, do many little kindnesses for our officers and corps, and stand up manfully for us in time of opposition, we have the most sincere regard. . . . In fact, love—deep, sincere, and of the strongest character, is the true feeling of every real, sterling Salvationist . . . while the majority are apparently happy-go-lucky, don't-care-a-button-for-anybody-or-anything sort of fellows, in their hearts they regard our organization as their only hope of ever finding salvation here, and heaven hereafter. . . . "Our Roughs" *should* be His, and it behoves every Salvationist to see to this. Our responsibility is greater than has been anyone's since the day of the first "rough." . . . We must get them over the line somehow.

While it is necessary as a matter of history that these and other similar difficulties should be placed on record, and while also it is due to the memory of the courageous Salvationists who faced mob violence and prison to secure for themselves and posterity the right to witness for God in the streets in an effective manner, it is equally the case that these early-day persecutions have long since ceased and that the places concerned have made full and honourable amends. The change of attitude was emphasized when in 1927 Commander Evangeline Booth visited England from the United States of America. Met and warmly welcomed at only two hour's notice in Torquay town-hall by the mayor and other members of the corporation, she was escorted to the old court-room which had been the scene of the prosecutions. The plea that she had made therein many years before, that the magistrates should have in mind that at least some of the men they were sending to prison for witnessing to salvation had been before them, prior to conversion, charged with very different offences, had long been recognized to be valid.

Perhaps of greater importance than any other consideration is that Salvationists of the present and future should be made aware of how heavy a price was paid for the liberties that are theirs, and have full sense of the obligation laid upon them to maintain and use to the full the facilities so hardly won. And perhaps others who use the streets in which to proclaim their message, and who are unmolested in their preaching, be it religious or political, may have a kindly thought for those who, as despised Salvationists, won for them also the Fight for the Streets.

VIII CATHERINE BOOTH— THE ARMY MOTHER

Chapter One

"A GREAT ENGLISHWOMAN"

NO-ONE who held position in the first twenty-five years of the history of The Salvation Army was more loved and revered by her contemporaries than was Catherine Booth. None had a higher place in the estimation of those who, though not having known her personally, became acquainted with her character and work through the records of her doings and the virile Christianity of her addresses and books. Mrs Booth was truly the Mother of The Salvation Army and its co-Founder with her General-husband.[1] Every phase of the Army's early beginnings bears testimony to her influence as the inspirer and sharer of his labours and leadership. During the time of her last illness—indeed, on her very death-bed and up to her last hour—her influence was, and still is, an ever-increasing factor in the Army's progress and usefulness. Her teachings and her example are as potent for good today, seventy years later, as ever they were.

The intensity of Catherine Booth's concern for the success of the Purity Movement and the part she took in stirring both public and Parliament to action[2] sapped her

[1] *The History of The Salvation Army*, vol. i, p. 145 ; vol. ii, ch. 5

[2] *The History of The Salvation Army*, vol. iii, p. 33

strength, and the reaction which followed confined her to her home for several months. By the time of the International Congress of 1886, however, she had so far recovered as to be able to take a prominent part in the proceedings, and thenceforward to resume public work. Before the year had closed she had visited places as far apart as Castleford (Yorkshire) and Portsmouth. Said her husband:

She would go from the mending of her children's things, or superintending the cooking of a dinner, to the greatest assembly, and would have gone, if needs be, just as simply and fearlessly to the House of Lords.

Her public activities in 1887 were interrupted by the serious illness of her daughters Emma and Eva, but nevertheless, in addition to numerous London appointments, she campaigned from Scarborough to Eastbourne and laid the corner-stone of the new barracks at Kettering. She was continually at the General's side, closely supporting his efforts with a devotion which would seem, when regarded in the light of the separation which was so soon to come, as in the nature of a realization of its imminence.

While still laid aside Mrs Booth began contributing to the *War Cry* a series of letters on a variety of subjects which embodied her answers to the world-wide correspondents who sought her counsel. One of the last and most incisive dealt with Spiritualism:

There is but one Spirit [she wrote] allowed us wherewith to commune, and from whom to seek light and help, namely, the blessed Spirit of God, and I should advise you as you value your happiness, your usefulness, and your soul, not to seek to know any other, or to have fellowship with those who do (see Isaiah viii, 19). Remember it is not the character of the communication with familiar spirits which constitutes the sin, but the seeking of them at all. This is strictly forbidden throughout the Word of God, and the most disastrous consequences are always attributed to it. I have known of one or two sad instances of entire spiritual shipwreck through adopting a contrary course ; in fact, I have never known anything but evil come of it. Therefore I warn everybody with whom I have any influence against it.

Mrs Booth, wrote her biographer, Commissioner F. de L. Booth-Tucker.[1]

was at this time [1886–1887] in the very zenith of her success and popularity as a preacher. The prophetic severity of her denunciations of evil in no way diminished the crowds who everywhere flocked to her meetings. Realizing increasingly as life advanced the necessity of speaking plainly in regard to sin, and the conditions of salvation, she allowed no false sentiment to induce her to . . . earn the " curse " of " keeping back her sword from blood."

In November 1887 a series of lectures she had delivered in Prince's Hall, Piccadilly, was published in book form and entitled *Popular Christianity*. A pamphlet on Holiness was published in December. The last " Two Days with God " conventions at which she was present were held in the Free Trade Hall, Manchester, on 30 and 31 January 1888, and in the Colston Hall, Bristol, on 14 and 15 February, and on each occasion she gave three addresses.

Chapter Two

STRICKEN IN THE FIGHT

The *War Cry* of 3 March 1888 contained a brief announcement of Mrs Booth's serious illness, Sir James Paget having pronounced her to be suffering from cancer. She had gone across London to see him and returned home, alone. " She

[1] *The Life of Mrs Booth*, Salvationist Publishing & Supplies, Ltd.

had gone out full of life and hopes and plans," said the General; "she came back stricken, the houses changed, the streets changed, all changed." And her first thought was that she would not be able to nurse him in his last illness as she had hoped to do. Thereafter her strength failed rapidly and the progress of the disease brought about the termination of her public labours. An operation was suggested, but the fact that Mrs Booth's heart was affected helped to a decision against immediate surgical relief, although later she underwent two operations each followed by periods of intense suffering. Then a new treatment of cancer by the application of electrical needles was tried, but had to be abandoned because of her weak condition. On 10 April she spoke briefly, but with astonishing power and vigour, at the wedding of her daughter Emma, in the Congress Hall, Clapton; and on the morning of Thursday, 21 June, in the City Temple, at the invitation of Dr Joseph Parker, she addressed the congregation for more than an hour on behalf of the non-Christian nations of the world, the International Conference on Missionary Operations, attended by delegates from almost every missionary society in existence, then being held at the Exeter Hall. At the end of her address, the final exhortation of which was characteristic of her forthright manner, Mrs Booth was so completely prostrated that it was nearly an hour before she could be removed from the pulpit.

A few weeks later she was able to speak at the commissioning of London rescue officers at the Women's Social Work Headquarters, and referred to the work in which they were engaged as being "the deepest love of my heart."

Commissioner Booth-Tucker states that "To Dr Parker, of the City Temple, was reserved the privilege of affording Mrs Booth the opportunity of delivering her last message in the great metropolis," and this statement has been frequently repeated down the years, but the *War Cry* of 6 April 1889 printed a large announcement of the celebration of the General's sixtieth birthday in the Congress Hall on the 10th: "Mrs Booth will be present if at all possible. Great Birthday Banquet! Tables laid for over 2,000." Mrs Booth was not present at the monster birthday banquet, but she did address this great assembly, although she appeared to be very feeble.

With the aid of the General, and at the expense of great personal exertion, she managed to reach the temporary reading stand [says the reporter]. For a minute or two she appeared so deeply moved that she was unable to utter a word.

Her address was not without its flashes of humour:

As my dear husband was speaking [she said], I thought of his beloved mother, whom I loved as much as my own, and admired more than almost any woman I ever knew. When he was speaking of her, and making you laugh over his likening himself to her in his meekness and self-depreciation, I said to my friend there: "It is quite true, though you would not think it," for no one knows the bolstering-up, and almost dragging-up, I was going to say, that sometimes I had to do for him in those early days. You would think now that he had always been the bold and self-sufficient—as some people think—man he is, but I can assure you he went forth ofttimes with so great trembling and fear for himself that he never would have gone if I had not been behind him!

Here was homely revelation! And these were actually her last words to be uttered in a public gathering:

Look at the world, as my dear husband said, in rebellion against God. Do not forget that the well-to-do people are as much in rebellion against God as the poor. Do not forget that your neighbours and friends—everybody round about you, are in rebellion against God, and, therefore, whatever hell does mean, whatever your own notions of retribution may be, that retribution is sure to them while they continue in that state of rebellion.

Look round on them, then buckle to ; be encouraged by what you have heard of what God has done by such humble and feeble instruments, to set yourself to work, to make up your mind, as the General did, when he was eighteen, that he would spend every bit of his strength, every nerve of his body, and all he had, in preaching salvation to men. Do that, and then, whether we ever should fight again together or not, we shall meet in the morning.

Mrs Booth's address stood out as *the* event of the afternoon. She was no worse for the effort of speaking, and was able to return to her home in Clacton-on-Sea the next day.

"Oceanville," the home of rest for staff officers at this "quiet little watering place"—for which Mrs Booth left London for the last time in August 1889, and where she spent her last days—was eventually rented by the General from the Army. It had ample room for offices and secretaries, as well as for members of the family. During the first month or two Mrs Booth was able to go out for a daily drive, but the motion of the carriage compelled her to resort to slow walks along the top of the cliff, where she might be seen leaning upon the arm of the General, and sometimes actually dictating to the secretary, Fred W. Fry, as she walked with him, for her brain and her pen were continually employed, as the periodicals of those days go to prove.

The period during which Mrs Booth was laid aside was made the more distressing because it was marked by the particularly vindictive opposition to Salvationists fighting for the liberty of the streets.[1]

For the Christmas 1889 issue of the *War Cry* Mrs Booth sent a message that was to become memorable :

December 19th. 1.18 p.m. The waters are rising, but so am I. I am not going under, but over. Don't be concerned about your dying ; only go on living well, and the dying will be all right

[1] Section VII

And the General wrote " From the banks of the River " :

> She discusses her departure for the heavenly country as calmly as though it were simply a change of residence from one part of this world to another, and was much disappointed that she did not cross on Sunday. Her thoughts are continuously about the War.

But, although every manifestation of immediate death was apparent during the last days of December, it was to be nearly ten months before she crossed the River. A leading article in the *War Cry* states that

> The forty-eight hours' struggle with death occasioned scenes perhaps as remarkable for supernatural manifestation as any the world has witnessed, while the utterances of the dying mother to her family circle constituted by far the most powerful sermon she has ever preached.

William Booth, writing in the *War Cry* for 4 January 1890 said that

> watching the agony, feeling the fluttering heart, expecting every moment for it to cease to beat, hearing her commit herself to the arms of a faithful, promise-keeping God, joining herself in spirit as again and again she definitely laid herself down in the underlying, all-embracing arms of everlasting love, and then beholding her come back to life with all its realities and anguish, it has been an experience terrible to endure.

In those days of excruciating suffering messages of sympathy came continuously from all parts of the world, one from a council of 200 Wesleyan ministers held in the City Road Chapel, London ; the heartless critics also sent their messages. One trusted that in the seclusion of her sick-room, and on the verge of the eternal world, she would consider the unwisdom of a movement that trained its young converts by beating big drums and playing tambourines.

During the last months of her life Mrs Booth was visited

by various deputations of officers, one of the most outstanding being a delegation of some twenty officers representing the staff council meeting in London in November 1889. Commissioner T. Henry Howard and Colonel James Dowdle were the spokesmen as all knelt throughout at the bedside. Through Colonel James Barker Mrs Booth sent a message to Australia :

Give the Australian soldiers my love [she said], and tell them I look on and care for them just as for my English children, and expect them to gather in many and many a prodigal child who has wandered away from his Father's house.

The Household Troops Band, representing the musicians of the Army all over the world, visited her on 30 January 1890. To the Bandsmen she said :

I did not expect to see your faces any more. It is very kind of you to come and play to me. I only wish I were stronger that I might say more of what is in my heart, but I rejoice in one or two points expressed in your letter very much ; in one especially, and that is that you see the importance of keeping your music *spiritual*, and of using it only for the one great end. . . . It is the same with everything else. Meetings, testifying, singing, marching or praying. It is the human and the divine, And, when you separate the human from the divine, it ceases to have any power over souls. Don't forget that. I have often boasted that, so far as we knew, every bandsman plays his instrument with sanctified breath, and I hope it will continue to be so. I never expected to hear any more earthly music. A fortnight ago I thought I was almost within hearing of the heavenly harpers ; but here I am, shunted, for what purpose I don't know ; but one purpose may have been to see your faces. I think you have formed far too high an estimate of me and my work ; but any blessing that I can be to you, such as it is, I give it to you with all my heart![1]

The last of the gatherings in the chamber of suffering was perhaps the most significant of all, for it included

[1] *The History of The Salvation Army*, vol. ii, p. 119

representatives from France, Germany, Switzerland, Canada, Denmark, Australia, Sweden, Norway, South Africa, India and Ceylon.

Mrs Booth lived to send yet another anniversary message to her children in the Lord. This was on the occasion of the 1890 celebrations at the Crystal Palace, where her message was written in large letters on a sheet of calico coiled on a roller. As this was unwound—to be wound on another roller on the other side of the platform—the audience could read it, sentence by sentence, from the farthest corner :

My Dear Children and Friends, My place is empty, but my heart is with you. You are my joy and my crown. Your battles, sufferings, and victories have been the chief interest of my life these past twenty-five years. They are so still. Go forward ! Live holy lives. Be true to the Army. God is your strength. Love and seek the lost ; bring them to the Blood. Make the people good ; inspire them with the Spirit of Jesus Christ. Love one another ; help your comrades in dark hours. I am dying under the Army Flag ; it is yours to live and fight under. God is my Salvation and Refuge in the storm. I send you my love and blessing—Catherine Booth.

W. T. Stead visited Mrs Booth several times at Clacton, where he helped the General "as a kind of voluntary secretary and amanuensis in getting the manuscript of *In Darkest England and the Way Out* into shape." His last call was paid in the September of 1890, only a few days before she died, and Stead writes movingly in his sketch of her life-work :

The Army could no more have come into existence without Mrs Booth, than could the family of sons and daughters who are now carrying on the movement. It was Mrs Booth who made the Army the great instrument that it has been of revealing to the world the capacities and resources of her own sex, and it was Mrs Booth who, by the warmth of her love and the wealth of her prudence, supplemented the genius of her husband in such a way as to enable him, with her, to do a work for which there is no parallel in our times. . . . She was a great Englishwomen—one of the greatest Englishwomen of our era . . . " Oh, Mr Stead ! " she exclaimed, as I was leaving her for the last time, " try to raise up mothers ! Mothers are the want of the world."

Chapter Three

TRIUMPHANT IN DEATH

Catherine Booth's sixty-one years of life came to an end at half-past three on the afternoon of Saturday, 4 October 1890, the last day of the Self-Denial Week for that year, and after a night of thunder, lightning, and torrential rain. Her message for the effort had been :

My dear Children and Friends, I have loved you so much, and in God's strength have helped you a little. Now, at His call, I am going away from you. The War must go on. Self-Denial will prove your love to Christ. All must do something. I send you my blessing. Fight on, and God be with you. Victory comes at last. I will meet you in Heaven—Catherine Booth.

Bramwell Booth, describing the last scene wrote[1] :

Soon after noon, I felt the deepening darkness of the long valley of the shadows was closing around my dear mother, and a little later I took my last farewell. Her lips moved, and she gave me one look of inexpressible tenderness and trust, which will live with me for ever. Again we sang :

My mistakes His free grace doth cover,
My sins He doth wash away ;
These feet which shrink and falter
Shall enter the Gates of Day.

[1] *On the Banks of the River*, by Bramwell Booth, 1894. Salvationist Publishing and Supplies, Ltd.

Holding her hand, the General gave her up to God. It was a solemn and wondrous scene . . . the dear General bowing over his beloved wife and companion in life's long stress and storm, and giving her, his most precious of earthly joy and treasure, to the eternal keeping of the Eternal Father. . . . Their eyes met—the last kiss of love upon earth—the last word till the Morning, and without a movement the breathing gently ceased, and a Warrior laid down her sword to receive her crown.

Writing in *William Booth, Founder of The Salvation Army*. Harold Begbie says :

So passed away one of the most remarkable women of the nineteenth century, whose beautiful spirit impressed itself alike upon the most exacting of her intellectual contemporaries and upon vast masses of the poor. The development of her personality in conjunction with that of her husband is a most interesting study in psychology, and the growth of her spiritual power seems to me like one of the miracles of religious history.

With prophetic insistence Mrs Booth had frequently called upon all around her death-bed to be true to God and let nothing come between them. " Love one another, oh, love one another. Stand fast together and the devil can do his worst ! " To her family she had said :

Remember, divisions and schisms and distrust are of the devil. I know him. He comes to me. He says, " Ah, you are leaving all your children and the world and the devil will be too much for them." But they won't, will they ?

All present had replied " No ! "

On Monday, 6 October, Mrs Booth's remains were privately removed from Clacton to Clapton Congress Hall where, in response to the earnest request of the many who desired to have the opportunity to see once more her beloved features, the coffin with its glassed-in lid remained until the funeral on the following Monday. More than 50,000 persons from all walks of life processioned past the bier.

Mrs General Booth

From a photograph taken at Clacton-on-Sea,
December 1889

Mrs Booth Lying in State
The scene at the Congress Hall, Clapton, October 1890
(From *The Penny Illustrated Paper*, 18 October 1890)

Commissioner Railton, summoned back from the Continent, was given charge of the funeral arrangements, the first phase of which was a combined public memorial and funeral service in the Olympia, the largest building in London, on Monday, the 13th. The congregation began to assemble as early as three o'clock in the morning. By six o'clock in the evening 36,000 had passed through the turnstiles. Fog made the huge building seem even more vast. The daughters of the General wore in the folds of their bonnets a white ribbon on which were the words "Thy will be done" embroidered in red. The service was conducted by means of signs exhibited from the platform and corresponding with instructions given in the pamphlet-programme. Passages from Mrs Booth's writings, incidents in her life-story, verses of her favourite songs, extracts from her messages, all found a place in the service; but, as one writer put it: "Everything was cheerful, even to a kind of solemn merriment."

The funeral procession on the day after revealed a tremendous exhibition of popular feeling. Business, in the busiest hour of the day in the City, was at a standstill. The veteran Superintendent Foster, of the City of London Police, declared that he had not seen anything like it since the funeral of the Duke of Wellington, nearly half a century earlier. The bare-headed General stood alone in an open carriage acknowledging the sympathy of the immense crowds that thronged the streets, but the Chief of the Staff and Commandant Herbert Booth were on horseback, as were Commissioners Booth-Clibborn and Booth-Tucker. Four thousand officers formed an escort. On the way from the Victoria Embankment to Abney Park Cemetery, Stoke Newington, bands played the specially composed funeral march, *Promoted to Glory*.

In a leading article in the *War Cry* Commissioner

Railton deplored the fact that "not a single individual, so far as I am aware, holding a high official position of any description, secular or spiritual, attempted to take part in the funeral ceremonies." A gallery with seats, tier upon tier, had been erected at the graveside, around which were gathered some 10,000 persons; the cemetery authorities had set this number as the most who could be admitted. In an announcement of his beloved partner's passing, and at the funeral service in the Olympia, the General had already paid his unstinted tribute. At this service, conducted by Commissioner Railton, he again "did his duty like a saint and a soldier, holding the crowd before him easily and strongly, as was his wont, holding his own grief under sway to the very end."

At an officers' meeting held in the Memorial Hall, Farringdon Street, on the night after the funeral the General spoke again of his comrade-in-arms:

She called me up at four one morning in the week she died [he said], to give me a solemn message. It was that she feared the women of The Salvation Army were not going to rise up to take the place she wished for them. . . . She could never read fiction, because she wanted facts. The world to her was full of great, big black *facts*. She said to me once, "People don't really believe! I ask them what messages I shall take to their friends in heaven, and they hardly seem to believe I shall see them."

And then he referred to the Darkest England Scheme, in the preparation of which she had taken so large a part:

This is a new development [she had said] not a new departure. . . . But mind, it is all one Army! We haven't a Social Army and a Salvation Army.

Memorial meetings were held at every corps in the United Kingdom on the Sunday following Mrs Booth's funeral.

Foremost in the enterprises set on foot to commemorate her life was the immediate call for fifty officers to volunteer for service in India. How ready was the response is indicated by the fact that a contingent of fifty-five made up from the United States of America, Sweden, Canada and the United Kingdom were given a send-off from Exeter Hall on 13 November, within six weeks after the call was made.

Nearly 10,000 people braved the inclement weather of Monday, 19 October 1891, to attend a memorial service at the Crystal Palace. A choir of 3,000 voices supplied the singing, and messages, meditations, prayers and songs were "precipitated" by a special limelight apparatus on to a huge screen, forty feet square, no fewer than 280 slides being used. Bramwell Booth conducted the service, as his father was in New Zealand.

Chapter Four

TRIBUTE

Moving tributes to Mrs Booth's life and work were paid by the newspaper press in their reports of the funeral and memorial services. The *Daily News* had this to say:

> Mrs Booth was not only the devoted helpmate of the General, she was his co-worker; and many of the most fruitful ideas in Army organization originated in her mind.

The *Church Times* was gracious:

> Gifted with the power of extraordinary speech, and possessed of a winning manner, Mrs Booth was the attractive power in the Army, and by her capable earnestness and devotion of

character infused into all who came into contact with her the enthusiasm which marks the operations of this remarkable body.

The *Newcastle Leader* provided an eloquent description of her physical beauty, which is in the nature of a revelation, and in striking contrast to the wholly unjustifiable, if not cruel, statement made by Hesketh Pearson in his *Bernard Shaw* :

She [Krupskaya, the widow of Lenin] shared with Mrs William Booth of The Salvation Army the distinction of being photographically the ugliest woman in Europe. And just as General Booth spoke of Mrs William passionately as " my beautiful wife," and their daughter Evangeline also described her mother as extraordinarily beautiful, Shaw found Krupskaya irresistibly lovable.

In our opinion [said the *Newcastle Leader*], none of the portraits hitherto published do justice to the kindly graciousness and spiritual beauty of Mrs Booth's face. It was a face which had a strong fascination even for those who did not sympathize with The Salvation Army. It had none of that hard look which most of the portraits seem to have caught, but had a soft, pleading expression, with much self-possession and resolution showing through.

The *Home News* said :

Her husband was the brains of the organization, but she was the heart.

The *Penny Illustrated Paper* wrote:

There was a certain personal magnetism about her, a thrill in her beautiful voice, a note of interest and passionate sympathy in her accents, which infected you, however strongly prejudiced you might be against her creed or her method of expressing it.

And the *City Leader* somewhat facetiously stated that

Though we may suspect that many a Salvation warrior wears the uniform of the Army as a cloak for evil deeds, yet we must admit that there are also a goodly number who are sincere in their somewhat extravagant and *bizarre* faith; and it is these enthusiasts who have lost the one person who was above the breath of suspicion, and whose death is mourned by every sect, section, and denomination.

Of Mrs Booth's passing Dr Joseph Parker said in the City Temple:

She was a valiant soldier of the Cross, eloquent, clear-sighted, firm to soldierliness, yet gentle to motherliness. . . . She won all hearts. She has left us the legacy and the responsibility of a great example.

And the Rev. Hugh Price Hughes had this to say during his memorial sermon in the crowded St James Hall:

The achievement which will immortalize her memory is the fact that she more than any other of her sex has vindicated the right and duty of women to preach. Her book upon the subject is the most masterly and successful argument I have ever read. . . . Catherine Booth came to crown the social evolution of our time by accomplishing the religious emancipation of woman.

Among the thousands of messages received from all parts of the world was one from the National Plate Glass Bevellers' Trade Union.

Mrs Booth's biographer, Commissioner Booth-Tucker, adequately sums up her life-work:

We might say that one half of her mission consisted in resurrecting the buried talents of her sex, the other half in humanizing, so to speak, the spiritual; in bringing religion out of the atmosphere of the vague, the chimerical and impossible into the area of practical politics. She would not admit for a moment the monopoly of intellect in the region of salvation. Its leadership she valued, its exclusiveness she denounced. . . . She could not pause to theorize over doctrines, or to sentimentalize over the sins and sorrows of the world. Her whole attention was fixed upon dealing forth the remedy.

To *Reflections* in the *War Cry* of 8 October 1898 the General added this touching postscript :

On Tuesday, October 4th, eight years ago, my beloved wife was taken from earth to Heaven. She would have liked to have stayed with me ten years longer, not only for my sake, but for the guidance of the children and the helping of the War. I could have wished the same ; indeed, had the ordering of things been left with me, I would have kept her by my side so long as my place was on the battlefield ; I would have ordained that we should have laid down the sword together, died in the same room, been buried in the same grave, and passed together through the Gates of Gold into the presence of our Lord. It was ordered otherwise. It was settled right. While my heart has never ceased to mourn my loss, Grace has kept it from a murmuring thought. I do not know how men and women who have truly loved each other, and who have been really one in that mysterious Heaven-ordained union, but whom death has separated, can manage to satisfactorily comfort themselves without the hope of meeting again. . . . The sense of the loss I suffered eight years ago grows keener and keener as the days and the months go by ; but all the time there is the unspeakable consolation arising from the feeling that, although not with me, she is only gone on before. I cannot see her fair form, not hear her precious voice, nor have the luxury of her guiding spirit, nor listen to that spoken love which was the human Heaven of all those long years ; but I have the consciousness that she is somewhere not far away, in safe keeping, waiting till I join her again.

IX VIEWS AND INTERVIEWS

Chapter One

PRINCES AND PRESIDENTS

BECOMING increasingly well known and respected as a religious leader and also recognized as an authority on social questions, William Booth found the doors of palaces and presidential residences opening wide and their distinguished occupants eager to receive him. Also on sea voyages and long train journeys he was frequently sought after by eminent people who wished to talk with him and sometimes to seek his counsel and advice, or to express their personal appreciation of the work he was doing for the good of humanity.

The General's first interview with the ruler of a nation took place when he was received by the President of the Swiss Confederation at the Palace in Bern during May 1891. Only a few days previously he had been hemmed about by all manner of pettifogging restrictions in connection with his campaign in Geneva. The President, who was accompanied by the Minister of Justice, was most friendly, and the interview lasted for more than an hour.[1]

When in South Africa in 1895 the General was invited by President Paul Kruger to visit him on 31 August, and the *War Cry* reporter describes this historic occasion :

The President received them in a kindly, unaffected manner. . . . It was touching to witness the way in which the aged President

[1] p. 152

saw to the seating of his visitors (the General was accompanied by Commissioner George A. Pollard and Major Joseph S. P. Rauch), shaking hands with each. The General spoke to him through his interpreter. The subject of their conversation was purely on matters of religion, mostly personal in its character. . . . " Oom Paul " began to talk slowly and quietly at first, but with great simplicity, earnestness and intelligence. The General spoke of the fascination of the gold mines in the State in attracting men who only sought wealth to satisfy their own selfish desires, and the consequent necessity there was for good men in the Transvaal, and of being united to help to counteract the evil influences which attended the influx. The President listened earnestly, concurred in what the General said, and then quietly followed up these remarks by giving his own personal testimony, which he spoke of with great assurance and simplicity. He told how daily he sought the voice of God to guide him in his daily life, and in God's strength he humbly endeavoured to obey that Voice. The President also spoke of the mission church which he carried on at Pretoria.

During the following year Commissioner Ridsdel, the Territorial Commander, while a guest of Mr Beshoff, Treasurer-General of the Transvaal Government, met President Kruger, who was deeply interested in his proposal to open a shelter in Pretoria.

En route to Christiania (Oslo) in 1896 the General met on board the steamer travelling from Kiel to Kovsor, H.R.H. the Crown Prince of Denmark, father of the Prince Charles who was later to become King Haakon of Norway. The Crown Prince approached the General in the saloon and expressed his sympathy with the Army's aims and his hopes for their fulfilment.

President William McKinley, who had some seven or eight months previously received Commander Booth-Tucker at the White House, Washington, thereby giving considerable impetus to the Army's activities in the United States of America was the General's host on 10 February

1898. The General illustrated by incidents and results the principles upon which the Army is built and the progress it was making in reclaiming and setting to work the degraded and outcast classes, and the President endorsed the doctrine that without the peace of God in the heart there was little hope of permanent reformation. In a letter to Bramwell on that same day William Booth wrote :

I talked to him about Salvation, which I could do, as he is a Methodist, and either is, or was, a local preacher—anyway, he knows what religion is, and he believes in us.

Three years later President McKinley was assassinated and the General paid a tribute to him in the *War Cry* for 21 September 1901 :

The world has been plunged into mourning, not only because the President was the first citizen of a great nation, but because he adorned the office with the qualities which most commend themselves to the sentiments and admiration of the people. He was a good man, a safe and unostentatious ruler, a tender and affectionate husband, a believer in God, a respecter of religion, a true American, and a lover of humanity. He manifested a real interest in our work.

During his visit to the United States in 1903 the General was again invited to the White House, this time—on 12 February—to lunch with President Theodore Roosevelt. Also present were the Secretary of State (John Hay), the Secretary of War (Elihu Root) and the Secretary of the Interior (Ethan A. Hitchcock). The President expressed his warm approval of The Salvation Army, especially commending its colonization, women's rescue and prisoners' aid branches for, he said, while Police Commissioner in New York City, he had become convinced of the valuable work the Army was doing for the poor and criminal classes, and had ever since shown his appreciation and given it his co-operation. Mrs Roosevelt invited the Consul to a reception at the White House on this occasion when her husband, Commander Booth-Tucker, accompanied the General. Some fifty leading ladies of the country, including the wives of Cabinet ministers and other prominent statesmen, were present. The Consul also met the President and Miss Roosevelt. Before the General left New York President Roosevelt sent him a letter in which he wrote :

Let me say how glad I was to have the chance of meeting you and of having you break bread in the White House.

A communication from the Earl Marshal of England, the Duke of Norfolk, announced that H.M. King Edward VII had given command that a representative of The Salvation Army be invited to attend the Coronation in Westminster Abbey on 26 June 1902, and the General appointed his eldest son, Bramwell, the Chief of the Staff, for this duty. The subsequent admission card stated that he was to wear court dress. The Chief thereupon wrote the Earl Marshal to the effect that if he were to be present it must be as an officer of The Salvation Army and wearing its uniform. The answer was that Court dress was *de rigueur*. Then the world was shocked to learn that owing to the King's illness the Coronation must be postponed. Upon His Majesty's recovery the Chief wrote him direct on the matter of uniform and received a telegram which read :

I am commanded by the King to say that he has much pleasure in giving you permission to attend the Coronation in the uniform of your rank as a Salvation Army Officer. . . . Knollys.

The Coronation eventually took place on 9 August, and Bramwell Booth was present. Thus for the first time in history admission was found for the at-one-time greatly-ridiculed uniform of The Salvation Army on an important State occasion. At the Abbey the Chief was shown every mark of respect and consideration by officials and guests alike. This act of His Majesty commanded attention throughout the Empire, and even in other countries. Consequently The Salvation Army has never again been faced with this particular kind of difficulty. Two years later King Edward VII was to grant the General audience at Buckingham Palace.[1]

In an interview with William E. Curtis, special correspondent of the *Chicago Record-Herald*, during his American campaign of 1903, the General revealed the interest taken in The Salvation Army at that time by royalty in all parts of the world. When asked if he was still receiving encouragement he replied:

Yes, encouragement from every class; the warmest sympathy and approval of the Mikado of Japan. The King of Denmark takes as much interest in our work as Queen Victoria did. [After hearing that the Rt Hon. Cecil Rhodes had bought a large consignment of white wyandottes from the Hadleigh Land Colony, and had shipped them to South Africa for breeding purposes, Her Majesty also purchased a stock of this breed of chickens from Hadleigh.] The King of Sweden is one of our best friends, and his son, Prince Bernadotte, and the Princess, are deeply interested in The Salvation Army in Stockholm. They visit our Headquarters, and speak at our meetings. The Queen of Holland also sympathizes with our work and subscribes to it.... Not long ago one of our Captains was wandering about in a museum at Copenhagen, when a gentleman, who proved to be the Crown Prince of Denmark, approached him and said: "I see by your uniform that you belong to The Salvation Army. The Princess of Wales [later Queen Alexandra] is here and would like to speak with you." Our Captain followed the Prince to where a group of ladies and gentlemen were standing, and was there presented to the Princess and her sister, the Empress of Russia. The Princess spoke very kindly of the interest which Queen Victoria and the Prince of Wales had always taken in the work of The Salvation Army, and expressed her sympathy in the most gracious way. While she was talking, up came the venerable King Christian, eighty-four years old, who shook

[1] p. 256

hands cordially with our officer. "Young man," he said, "I like The Salvation Army; I like your social work and your Gospel work; and I like the way you keep God to the front."

The *Weekly Dispatch*, in a May 1890 issue, reported that Prince George of Wales (afterwards King George V) during his last night in London prior to joining his ship, H.M.S. *Thrush*

was a devout listener to a contingent of The Salvation Army at Islington Green. He bought a *War Cry*, and contributed liberally to the collection. Whilst the meeting was in progress a rude fellow, sitting on the adjacent fountain, amused himself by spitting on the ladies' dresses. The Prince went up to him, took him firmly by the arm, and pulled him from his perch. The fellow slunk shamefacedly away, and the hallelujah lasses smiled sweetly upon their royal deliverer.

Retired Bandmaster William Thomas, Mayor of Maidenhead in 1935, related that when he was a Captain and commanding officer of Windsor corps, after a rough Sunday evening open-air gathering, H.R.H. Princess May (later H.M. Queen Mary) and two of her sons (later H.R.H. the Duke of Windsor and H.M. King George VI) attended the indoor meeting which he conducted. At the close the Princess and the Princes greeted him with a handshake and presented him with a donation.

Chapter Two

LEGISLATORS AND LADIES

Although by the year 1892 The Salvation Army was making friends among the powerful classes, it was of considerable interest and with a sequel of unexampled importance to the organization when the General was invited to meet the Rt Hon. William Ewart Gladstone by his own fireside at Hawarden Castle four days before the Christmas of 1896. The General had ridden over from Keighley, where he had conducted a campaign on the previous day. The conversation covered almost the whole ground of the Army's history, government, aims and the question of the General's successor. Indeed, Mr Gladstone

seemed to wander over the whole World, looking in upon every work—Religious, Philanthropic and Secular—at present in existence, and turning back upon the centuries past in order that he might find an instance similar to, or illustrative of, the method adopted for arranging the successorship, as he termed it.

Among suggestions made by the "Grand Old Man" of British politics in regard to the leadership of the Army was the desirability of provision being made for failure of the "system of personal nomination by the person occupying the post of authority." Commenting on this subject, the General wrote[1] :

He appeared to sympathize with me closely when I described the anxiety with which I had regarded the question, and how, for years it had been considered steadily ; and he was still further interested when I mentioned a scheme, now being completed, for providing against the possible contingency of a General passing away who had neglected the appointment of his successor, or who, for some calamitous reason, had been proved incapable for, or unworthy of, his position, and for selecting a new General in an assembly of all our Commissioners throughout the world. I named one or two of the possibilities that might occur, and he added, "Yes, and the possibility of heresy would come under the category."

Describing afterwards to his then private secretary (Commissioner Frank Barrett) what had happened at this inter-

[1] *A Talk with Mr Gladstone*, by General Booth. London 1897.

view, the General told him that the 1904 Deed[1] had resulted from Mr Gladstone's questionings and urgings. The General's earlier attitude to the matter was indicated in an interview he gave to the *Methodist Times* (5 February 1885). When questioned as to what provision had been made in case a General should become apostate, or abuse his authority, he had replied :

> The Army is a constant and increasing check upon the General. Next week, for example, I have a meeting of all the Majors. They would soon let me know if I did anything contrary to the interests of the Army. I can do anything *with* the Army, but am powerless *against* it.

Mr Gladstone had started the conversation by remarking that in addressing his visitor as General he was, he supposed, using the title to which he was accustomed and which harmonized with his own feelings. This gave the General opportunity to explain again how its use had come about. He has recorded that in reply he said :

> Yes, that was the appellation ordinarily given to me, that I thought it duly signified my position and that I accepted it for that reason. I explained that I had not sought it, and was at the beginning strongly opposed to its use [2] ; but, that having come to the head of what was known as an army, there seemed to be no alternative but to accept the title which denoted my position. This led to some observations on both sides as to the use of titles, Mr Gladstone fully recognizing their value. I remarked that our nomenclature had been of great service to us, inasmuch as the significance of our titles was understood by the people without explanation. No matter how poor, untrained, or undisci-

[1] Messrs H. H. Asquith (afterward Lord Oxford and Asquith), R. B. Haldane (afterward Lord Haldane of Cloan) and Charles Sargant (afterward Lord Chief Justice) advised the General in the settlement of a deed of trust which was adopted in 1904 and which supplemented the deed of origin. Its main purpose was to provide machinery for removing a General who, on account of any one of certain definite causes, had forfeited his claim to the position, and for appointing a new General in a certain contingency.

[2] *The History of The Salvation Army*, vol. i, p. 234

plined a man might be, he knew the meaning of "Captain" when he joined a corps, and that it implied authority and obedience. "Yes," remarked Mr Gladstone, "everybody knows the significance of 'Captain.'"

Among the many other subjects of interest and importance referred to by Mr Gladstone was the maintenance of the central authority of the Army in distant parts of the world while allowing that free and energetic local action so necessary to vigorous growth. In regard to the extent to which the Army in the United Kingdom sent officers overseas Mr Gladstone ventured a guess that they might number twenty a year; when the General stated that from 200 to 250 were sent every year, Mr Gladstone said that it was a very remarkable evidence of the strength as well as the vitality of the movement. That the great bulk of the money required for financing corps was made up of the voluntary contributions of the people themselves was also extraordinary, he said, and a fact of essential importance from the standpoint of permanence. Mr Herbert (later Lord) Gladstone had met the General at the entrance to Hawarden Castle, and travelled with him to London after the interview.

Many years later, in the course of an article on *The Founder and His Contemporaries* Commissioner W. Elwin Oliphant wrote:

As a conversationalist he regarded Gladstone, if somewhat dogmatic, as unrivalled; as a talker he thought him far ahead of his compeers, if somewhat too much given to assuming the ignorance of his hearers. As a law-giver he considered his historical sense was only equalled by his legal knowledge, which was only second in forensic, technical, and clear statement to that of Lord Haldane, and in choice of concise language to that of Lord Oxford and Asquith. Both of these statemen he consulted as lawyers after his interview with Mr Gladstone at Hawarden, following that statesman's pungent remark that the

Army, as then constituted, was without parallel in the whole world, Christian or secular, in some constitutional respects.

At the time of their meeting Mr Gladstone was some twenty years older than the General. Within eighteen months, on 19 May 1898, the great erstwhile Prime Minister of England died. In connection with his passing it has of recent years come to light that the words of a song written by Sarah Graham, a Canadian Salvationist, was of special comfort to him. It appears that a friend of the family had heard the Lieutenant of the Lerwick (Shetland Isles) corps sing in an open-air meeting :

When the voice of Jesus calls me
  And the angels whisper low,
I will lean upon my Saviour,
  Through the valley as I go ;
I will claim His precious promise,
  Worth to me the world of gold,
" Fear no evil, I'll be with thee
When the Pearly Gates unfold."

with the chorus

Life's morn will soon be waning
  And the evening bells will toll,
But my heart will know no sadness
  When the Pearly Gates unfold.

The friend had asked that the words and music be sent to Hawarden Castle and these, stated Lord Gladstone in a postcard to this gentleman, were read to his father when on his death-bed, and at his request the chorus was sung by the family.

Another distinguished statesman who made a deep impression upon William Booth was the Rt Hon. Cecil Rhodes whom he had first met during a visit to South Africa in 1891, when Rhodes was Premier of Cape Colony, and again at Cape Town in 1895. When Rhodes visited

Friends True and Tried

1 H.R.H. The Duke of York (later H.M. King George V) 2 President Theodore Roosevelt 3 H.R.H. The Prince of Wales (later H.M. King Edward VII) 4 President William McKinley 5 Senator Marcus Hanna 6 Rudyard Kipling 7 The Rt. Hon. William E. Gladstone, M.P. 8 Frank Crossley 9 Sir Walter Besant

They Gave Warm Support

1 Dr John Clifford 2 Dr Joseph Parker 3 Sir Henry Irving (as Becket) 4 Adolf Beck 5 Mrs Bell 6 General Lord Wolseley 7 Sir Hubert von Herkomer 8 Dr J. H. Jowett 9 Lord Aberdeen

England in 1898 he made a point of going with the General to see the Hadleigh Farm Colony.[1] On the way to the colony the talk was of social redemption and land reclamation. On the return journey to London the General put his hand upon Rhodes' arm saying to him: "I want to speak to you about yourself. You're a man with much depending upon you now [a reference to the disturbed state of things, politically, in South Africa]. Tell me, how is it with your soul?" Rhodes replied: "It is not quite as well with my soul as I could wish." "Do you pray?" enquired the General. "Sometimes, but not quite so often as I should." "Will you let me pray with you now?" They knelt together in the railway carriage and the General prayed. When they stood to their feet again Rhodes held out his hand in silence, eloquent of thoughts too deep for words. Parting at Liverpool Street Station, Rhodes said to Bramwell Booth: "Ah! You and the General are right; you have the best of me after all. I am trying to make new countries; you are making new men." Rhodes died unexpectedly in the spring of 1902, his last words having become memorable: "So little done, so much to do!"

Among the many parliamentarians who stood by William Booth was Mr W. S. Caine who, writing to the General in 1894, said:

I have seen the Army at work in France, Switzerland, Canada, the States, and India, as well as at home, and every fresh experience enhances the deep respect, nay, reverence, I feel for the heroic men and women who, as its officers and soldiers, willingly sacrifice comfort, health, family life, everything indeed that makes ordinary life in this world pleasant and profitable, for the trying, arduous work of saving souls under your Generalship.

Mr Caine died suddenly at Westminster on 17 March 1903.

When Lord Russell of Killowen, Lord Chief Justice of

[1] *The History of The Salvation Army*, vol. iii, p. 136

England, died in August 1900 the Chief of the Staff paid tribute to his memory in the *War Cry*. As Mr Charles Russell he had been leading counsel for the defence in the Eliza Armstrong case.[1]

"I said a word or two quietly about the importance of the case to some of our dear officers, who had risked their very lives in order to get at these horrible truths," Bramwell said to Mr Russell, after a long conference. He was all attention in a moment, and seemed touched, and said in an undertone, "I will do my best; *will you ask them to pray for me?*" . . . He was a man of *heart*, as well as head. . . . Lord Russell's speech at the close of the case I referred to above was a wonderful illustration of what I mean. He held the court breathless while he argued and pleaded for that poor friendless woman. It was one of the most lofty and inspiring utterances of the kind I ever listened to. His whole being was moved, and he moved us all.

William Booth fearlessly tackled men and women about their souls during his journeyings, one of the most memorable occasions being his encounter with Margot Tennant (afterward Lady Oxford and Asquith), daughter of a Scottish baronet. They met in a railway compartment in 1892, and twenty-five years later the then Mrs Asquith contributed a piquant description of the conversation to the *Cornhill Magazine* for August 1917.

The following story told by Mrs Josephine Butler of her reading of the first copy of the *War Cry*, which was published in December 1879, when her husband was principal of a Liverpool college, has its special significance:

As he seated himself by my side in the carriage, he laid upon my knees a poor little shabby newspaper, saying, "There, that will interest you. I am sure you will rejoice to see it." . . . My husband, a scholar, a literary man and critical, had read this paper himself, and rejoiced in what it recorded, overlooking its many and obvious defects and its peculiar style. He was right in thinking that I should rejoice in it. I took it to my room, and

[1] *The History of The Salvation Army*, vol. iii, p. 38

read every word of it, and thanked God. . . . Some years later, I heard that a few members of the Army had come to Liverpool. I sought them out, and attended their odd little Meetings.

Josephine E. Butler wrote *The Salvation Army in Switzerland* in 1883.

In the biography of his wife, Margaret Ethel MacDonald, the Rt Hon. J. Ramsay MacDonald, first Labour Prime Minister of England, had this to say :

She went to worship with them [at Hove], and she wrote : " The meetings are very interesting, and give one an insight into a different aspect of love and worship of God to one's own ; there is, of course, a good deal of repetition and sameness, but, judging the tree by its fruits, the Army has done an immense amount of good, and its soldiers, as far as I have seen them, are full of holy zeal and steadfastness."

Miss Frances E. Willard, the American author and philanthropist, wrote in 1894 :

In the humility of the Salvation Army spirit, the warmth of its zeal, the helpfulness of its devotion, and, to my mind, above all in the wisdom that has placed woman side by side with man as a teacher, worker and administrator, The Salvation Army has proved itself to be the nearest approach to primitive Christianity of which we have knowledge in these days, when pomp and circumstance characterize the worship of God, and hierarchies hold humanity back from that liberty of the Gospel which is its crowning attraction and brightest hope.

Another generous supporter, Lady Henry Somerset, wrote in the same year :

I have often said that no engine-power in our day seems to me to be pointed with more directness and effect against the batteries of evil than The Salvation Army, led by its intrepid and devoted General.

Lady Henry wanted to become an officer and her spirit faltered only when the General made it clear that her attendance at Holy Communion would prove awkward in such a capacity.

Chapter Three

AUTHORS, ACTORS AND ARTISTS

Those who use the pen have found in The Salvation Army a rich and never-ceasing source of inspiration for either commendation or criticism in poetry, song, article, novel, play, caricature or cartoon.

Rudyard Kipling, after having formed a wrong impression of William Booth at his first encounter, lived long enough to express his admiration for the Army's leader. In his reminiscences of this occasion, 6 November 1891, Kipling wrote[1] :

We cleared the last Lamp Post in the World—Invercargill [New Zealand]—on a boisterous dark evening when General Booth came on board. I saw him walking backward in the dusk over the uneven wharf, his cloak blown upwards, tulip fashion, over his grey head, while he beat a tambourine in the face of the singing, weeping and praying crowd who had come to see him off. . . . I saw no more of him till I had picked up my P. & O., which also happened to be his for Colombo, at Adelaide. Here all the world came out in paddle boats and small craft to speed him on his road to India. . . . I talked much with him during that voyage. Like the young ass I was, I expressed my distaste at his appearance on Invercargill wharf. " Young feller," he replied, bending great brows at me, " if I thought I could win *one* more soul to the Lord by walking on my head and playing the tambourine with my toes, I'd—I'd learn how." He had the right of it (" if by any means I can save some ") and I had decency enough to apologize. . . .

A writer in the *Penny Illustrated Paper* on 20 February 1892 had this to say :

[1] *Something of Myself*, by Rudyard Kipling. London 1937

I was surprised the other day to be told that Mr Rudyard Kipling, who had met him [William Booth], had come to the conclusion that there was very little in him. Mr Kipling and " General " Booth, there is no doubt, are very different people, but I do not think, on a second view of the " General," any of the men who he has formed into one of the most remarkable organizations in the world's history would confirm this conclusion. A man does not get power for nothing.

But Rudyard Kipling had had second thoughts by the time he wrote *Something of Myself* for therein he said :

I conceived great respect and admiration for this man with the head of Isaiah and the fire of the Prophet. The next time I met him was at Oxford when degrees were being conferred [1907]. He strode across to me in his Doctor's robes, which magnificently became him, and, " Young feller," said he, " how's your soul ? "

The author of *Coral Island* and other equally famous books for boys, R. M. Ballantyne, anonymously visited the Army's shelter for men at Clerkenwell at 10 o'clock on a November morning in 1891—and immediately wrote to the *Evening News*, which had been persistently and bitterly attacking the Social Scheme—and

inspected it from cellar to upper floor, and the cleanliness of it in all respects—the well-scrubbed floors, the methodical arrangement of the frame beds and bedding, etc.—impressed me greatly.

Bramwell Booth had a " brush " with Herbert Spencer, the philosopher, in 1896, when his *The Principles of Sociology* was published. *The Times*, in a leading article on the subject, claimed for Spencer that from the inception of his system of philosophy up to that present time—50 odd years—his work had been marked by consistency. Bramwell wrote a letter to *The Times* on Spencer's inconsistency in one subject, at least. Between 1850 and 1870 he had written in *The Right to the Use of the Land* that equity did not permit property in land, but, in 1891, he admitted that he had not clearly seen in 1850 what would be implied by the giving of compensation for all the value which the labour of ages had given to the land. "If he could make a contradiction in such a matter, is it not probable that on questions of religious faith and Divine authority, he is equally unreliable?" asked Bramwell. Eventually Spencer climbed down. "It would be strange if a writer on evolution contended that his own ideas were the only things that had undergone no evolution," he replied.

Arnold White, after attending the General's meeting in Glasgow in September 1892, said that he never was in such a gathering in his life. "It would be wonderful if the poor Salvation Army was made the means of leading me into the faith of Jesus Christ." And Olive Schreiner, author of *A South African Farm*, averred that "The only form of Christianity which is a living force today is The Salvation Army." Sir Walter Besant, author of *All Sorts and Conditions of Men*, and a "thoroughly convinced believer in The Salvation Army," died in June 1901. Three years before, at the Mansion House, London, he had spoken at a meeting held in connection with the Army's social work. The Rt. Hon. Herbert J. Gladstone, the Home Secretary, had presided. "The more closely I have examined, the more stable have I found its foundations and the more remarkable its success," declared Sir Walter. George R. Sims, writing in the *Referee*, said:

The fact remains that he [General Booth] is engaged in a great work of social reform, and that, misguided or not as to some of his methods, he is doing an amount of good, which, before his coming, was left undone.

The *War Cry* of 12 May 1888 reported that "Count Tolstoi, the great Russian novelist and non-combative Socialist, has a *War Cry* every week."

Staff-Captain Agnes McDouall, daughter of a Church of Scotland minister, and author of the songs, "Jesus came with peace to me" and "I'll follow Thee, of life the Giver," was standing with another officer outside the Lyceum Theatre, London, distributing to folk arriving by carriage for the play invitations for a drawing-room meeting to be held at the house of the Hon. Mrs Burrows. An officious official asked to see the handbill, and took it in high dudgeon to Mr (later Sir) Henry Irving, who gave instructions that the officers were to be allowed to continue with their distribution. Almost the last thing he did before his sudden death after playing Thomas à Becket at Bradford was to make out a cheque for the Army's funds. And William Booth mentions in his journal, obviously with a sense of appreciation, that in the spring of 1903 "Wilson Barret, the tragedian," was present at one of his meetings, with "other rather important personages."

During the autumn of 1897 William Booth sat for his portrait to Professor (later Sir) Hubert von Herkomer, using the enforced idleness of so unusual a situation to get at the soul of the artist, as was his custom with all and sundry who crossed his path:

I have been three times to Professor Herkomer; he is an interesting man so far as his talking goes, however his painting may turn out. I hope to get at him some way or other. God must help me. He is full of worldly ambition, and yet I should think with a beautiful nature. Oh, what might he not do for God and mankind if his magnificent genius was sanctified! God will help me to say something that will be of service.

The General was as dissatisfied as ever with his performance [wrote his secretary]. Herkomer seems to think the portrait is a very good one, and that either the General is a bad judge or else the picture will prove a great disappointment. . . .

Professor and Mrs von Herkomer each laid a foundation-stone of the new hall at Watford in February 1898. So far as it is known the General did not sit for any other artist during this period, apart from one who used a very different medium—wax; in 1903 he had an interview with Mr Tussaud, the result of which is still to be seen in the world-famous wax-work exhibition in London.

Chapter Four

PRELATES AND PREACHERS

Among those who saw and appreciated the effectiveness of The Salvation Army in its days of misunderstanding and persecution, even by members of his own Church, was the Bishop of Rochester, who said at a meeting of the Church Congress in October 1886:

> If ever the masses are to be converted, it must be by an organized lay body. Let no one be unjust to The Salvation Army. They have set the Church an example of magnificent and dauntless courage.

And the Dean of Manchester, presiding at a largely-attended meeting in the Memorial Hall, Manchester, in 1887, in furtherance of the objects of the Church Army, made the following references to The Salvation Army:

> It was impossible not to give a glance at the predecessor of the Church Army in the field of evangelism, the now thoroughly well-known and popular Salvation Army. . . . To a certain extent, in the methods and organization of the Church Army, they would by no means disown the fact of having imitated and copied the earlier example. What he was most anxious to do was to avoid, while he spoke with all Christian frankness and

sincerity, even the slightest appearance of disparagement of the work of The Salvation Army. He had had very considerable conversation, and at one time rather close intercourse for a few days, with the excellent man who was called General Booth. The General had visited him in his home at Carlisle, from which he (the Dean) went with him into the Market-place and stood beside him, a great deal of ignorant and discreditable hostility and opposition being shown.

In January 1889 the General wrote Dr Benson, the Archbishop of Canterbury, for "some expression of his views with regard to the Salvation Army" and received this reply from his chaplain :

The Archbishop does not doubt the good your wide organization has done and is doing. He has no doubt of the zeal and devotion which are the secret springs of its outward growth. In this he has not changed the views which he expressed in 1882 and from which you quote. But on the other hand there are considerations—partly new and partly existing at that time—which qualify his Grace's estimation of The Salvation Army. The want of teaching, the disproportionate value attached to emotion as compared with knowledge, the unintelligent presentation of Truth as the result of this lack of instruction, the consequent tendency to awaken doubts and secularist objections, the lack of reverence; above all, the increasing tendency to Separatism and the disregard for the injunctions of our Lord with regard to the Sacraments—these are objections which form a serious counterpoise to the good which The Salvation Army is doing. Some of these, and especially the last, have become much more manifest since the date of the interview which the Archbishop—then Bishop of Truro—had with you in 1882. . . .[1]

. . . the Archbishop does not desire to enter, in detail, into a discussion of the problems of political economy which it [the letter] raises. He is convinced, however, that your plan, whatever its merits and advantages, is undeniably at variance with the conclusions of those who have, with the highest wisdom and the fullest knowledge, set themselves to grapple with the social difficulties of our great cities. . . .

[1] *The History of The Salvation Army*, vol. ii, p. 146

Evidently the General had suggested that the State should endow the Army in order that it might carry out the schemes which he was about to incorporate in *In Darkest England and the Way Out*. To this the Archbishop had strong objections :

These are objections which are based on no want of sympathy with The Salvation Army and its generous impulses to do something towards the alleviation of misery, but on most certain Laws of Political Economy which show how unsafe a guide is sentiment unenlightened by sober and far-seeing wisdom, and how great are the mistakes economically into which unthinking charity has betrayed philanthropists.

Then the Archbishop betrays what actually lay beneath his objections :

The fact that throughout you have aimed at a change of life, based upon the Love of Christ, and that this aim has had, as he is glad to believe, success among many of the most degraded, is a matter of unfeigned thankfulness ; and, if it had been part of your plan to seek in the historic Church of Christ for that fuller instruction for your converts, of the need of which he has spoken, and for the benefits of those Sacraments which were the Lord's legacy of love to it, he would at all times have been ready to welcome such proofs that you too desired to avoid the evils of fresh separations and divisions among the disciples of the One Lord.

Unfortunately a copy of the General's reply to the Archbishop's letter is not available, but it can be taken for granted that it was not lacking in vigorous enlightenment, for His Grace was certainly in gross darkness regarding many of his points of objection. So far as " the want of teaching " is concerned, there were few interpreters of the Scripture to equal Catherine Booth, who could always be assured of a goodly sprinkling of Church of England clergymen in her congregations, a number of whom became Salvation Army officers. It is not likely that they would have left the Church had the Army lacked "teaching." If "knowledge" meant theological exposition beyond the intellectual capacity of the Army's congregations in those days, then it would have been utterly useless. Crudity had often to be met with crudity. The great truths of Scripture were never disregarded; they were taught in a language that the common people of that day could understand and appreciate. Theology is not taught in kindergarten schools and if, as Christ declared, a man "must be born again," such birth cannot take place without considerable spiritual upheaval or, to use the Archbishop's word, "emotion." The Salvation Army has never lacked reverence, if reverence is meant to be the worship of God "in spirit and in truth." The Army *had* of necessity to be separate from the Church for, in those days at any rate, the Church held strangely aloof from the lower strata of Society; indeed, a man unkempt and ragged would seldom have been allowed to enter the portals of a place of worship, were it Anglican or Nonconformist, as William Booth discovered as a mere boy in Nottingham. The non-observance of the Sacraments by Salvationists has already been thoroughly dealt with,[1] and the immense social work of the Army operating today throughout the whole world has proved the kindly disposed, but nevertheless ecclesiastically prejudiced Edward Benson to have been an unsuccessful prophet and not to be compared in this respect with the far-sighted William Booth.

The Bishops of Manchester (Dr Moorhouse) and Durham (Dr Westcott) were among the several prominent Churchmen who wrote with approval of the Darkest England Scheme, but the Dean of Wells (Dr Plumtre) warned the public against its originator.

One of London's most popular preachers, music critic and author, the Rev. H. R. Haweis, Vicar of St James's,

[1] *The History of The Salvation Army*, vol. ii, p. 133

Marylebone, was a sincere and staunch friend of the Army. A few months before his sudden death on the day following his preaching on Sunday, 27 January 1901, of three brilliant sermons on the passing of Queen Victoria, he had expressed his appreciation of the Army's work. He had, he said, been drawn to the Army by common sense, but he had had prejudices, as a musical man, against its music. Those prejudices had entirely disappeared.

Dean Farrar of Canterbury[1] was another great supporter of the Army, although he did not agree with all the General's views or methods ; he died on 22 March 1903.

* * *

Nonconformist ministers were in the main very friendly to the Army in these days of denominational bias. The Rev. John McNeill, preaching to a fashionable Edinburgh congregation in 1889, said :

> Have you not gone hurrying past the little group of Salvationists at the corner of the Pleasance as you passed to the church ? I have taken off my hat to those ladies who were singing in The Salvation Army.

Dr Asa Mahan, who was associated with C. G. Finney, the revivalist, and who passed away in April 1889 was a true and outspoken friend. More than once he was heard to say that, had he been a younger man, he certainly would have been a Salvationist. The Rev. (later Dr) J. H. Jowett, preached a sermon on the work of the Army in St James's Congregational Church, Newcastle-on-Tyne, on Sunday, 19 June 1890, taking as his text : " And when they found them not, they drew Jason and certain brethren unto the rulers of the city, crying, These that have turned the world upside down are come hither also."

[1] *The History of The Salvation Army*, vol. iii, pp. 85-7

It was [he said] the personal contact of life with life, the laying of heart to heart, the giving away of blood to save another, that constituted the Army's power.

In the course of a masterly sermon dealing with "Saving Truths" at the Spring Assembly of the Congregational Union of England and Wales in the Memorial Hall, London, on one occasion, Mr Jowett said that The Salvation Army "exalted the great truths of the apostles, reformers, puritans and revivalists." The *British Weekly*, reporting the event, added: "His eloquent defence of the Army elicited a burst of applause which could not be restrained."

Writing to the *Baptist* in 1892 the Rev. Charles H. Spurgeon advised: "Imitate The Salvation Army and go in with a smash. Let us take some of their earnestness." Spurgeon died a few days later and the *War Cry* wrote:

Though he followed not us "down here," he will be right down glad to see us up yonder.

More than once he spoke up for The Salvation Army, but his Calvinistic soul did not like its holiness teaching, and he condemned it in his rough and ready fashion. Nevertheless, he wrote prophetically in commenting in *Sword and Trowel*, in July 1888, upon William Booth's *The General's Letters*:

Ages to come will form a higher estimate of William Booth than that which he receives today. . . . We are sorry that we cannot agree with many of his modes of procedure, but that is not the matter now before us—his letters are singularly forceful. . . . Here we have no nonsense, no critical mistrusts; but all is bravely, and even definitely, confident.

Bishop Fowler, addressing the Decennial Council of the Methodist Episcopal Church at Washington, D.C., U.S.A., in 1894, said:

The Salvation Army is rolling up a host of good workers by abandoning pride and respectability to start with, and providing no ambulances, and making no provision for drones.

Other ministerial friends in the United States included Dr Lyman Abbott and Bishop Phillips Brooks. The Rev. Dr Newman Hall, of Christ Church, Westminster, a powerful Congregationalist preacher for sixty years, frequently spoke at open-air meetings conducted by the Hampstead corps ; he passed away in February 1902 at the age of eighty-six. The Rev. Hugh Price Hughes, the most brilliant Wesleyan of his day, in speaking to a colleague a few days before his sudden passing in November of that year, said :

We Free Churchmen are only awakening to the power of the Press. The Roman Catholic Church, with its usual astuteness, has set itself to train journalists—and so has The Salvation Army.

A one-time Chairman of the Congregational Union, Dr Urijah Thomas used to attend the knee-drills (early morning prayer-meetings) at Bristol and took part in Army processions. Dr John Clifford, the famous pastor of Westbourne Park Chapel, London, had this to say in 1894 :

How suggestive are the prophecies of the future of the Army written twenty years ago ! One organ protested, " a little more fame and then a rapid decline." Thank God, the pulse beats as strongly, the step is as firm, and the vision is as clear as ever.

For thirty-four years occupant of the distinguished City Temple pulpit, Dr Joseph Parker more than once raised his voice for the Army in the midst of obloquy and slander. " The more I have looked into that work the more I believed it to be of God," he declared. William Booth was among those who visited him during his last illness. His portrait, in pen and ink, took up the whole front page of the *War Cry* for 6 December 1902, the week following his death. Dr James Stalker, the most influential Presbyterian minister in Glasgow in his time, spoke flatteringly of one of William Booth's addresses to which he had listened, and said that he regarded Catherine Booth " as one of the greatest women of the century."

Chapter Five

GENEROSITY AND GENERALS

Mr Frank W. Crossley, inventor of the internal combustion engine, began to take an interest in The Salvation Army about the year 1886, following a drawing-room meeting addressed by William Booth. The General had thought he had made an excellent impression upon his audience, but to his amazement Mr Crossley jumped up and severely criticized the Army.

Its motives [he said] were doubtless good, and the results here and there among the worst and most ignorant might be gratifying ; but was it wise to organize and encourage a system which, by its extravagances, rhapsodies, and vulgarities was calculated to lower religion in the estimation of those who knew anything at all about it, or to convey a false impression of it to those who were ignorant of its character ?

Two days later, although he reiterated in a letter all that he had said in the drawing-room speech, he sent the General a cheque for £1,000.

Thereafter General and Mrs Booth often stayed at the Crossley home at Bowdon, Cheshire, and Mr Crossley frequently attended the meetings at the little corps at Altrincham. When on holiday at Torquay with Mrs Crossley in the spring of 1889 he knelt at the Salvation Army penitent-form to seek the blessing of holiness. Writing to his sister Emmeline regarding this new experience, he said :

> You should not fail to go to the Salvation Army meetings in Edinburgh tomorrow. I have had a wonderful blessing in my soul the last week and now know in my heart as well or better than in my head (as before) what The Salvation Army is about. You see they have got the testimony *inside* ! . . . Now The Salvation Army has got that inner light, that " revelation," not in all cases in Paul's degree, but of the same kind. They witness to the personal love of Jesus. How few people really have this in the heart ! But this is the secret of The Salvation Army.

At one time he actually bought a full suit of uniform and was to have been enrolled as a Salvationist, but could not bring himself to sign the Articles of War. Eventually he had other leadings—to start mission work on his own account, which resulted in the erection of the Star Hall, at Ancoats, Manchester.[1] Once, when listening to Handel's " Hallelujah " Chorus being sung by a church choir, he walked the length of the pew to say loudly in his daughter's ear : " I'd rather have a good hallelujah in The Salvation Army ! " As a magistrate he was required to take part in the trial at Altrincham of a lone Army lassie for causing an obstruction by holding an open-air meeting on a public thoroughfare, but when the case was called Frank Crossley left the bench and took his stand with her in the dock to fortify her with sympathy and comfort. The case was dismissed.

Writing in 1892 to the *Manchester Guardian* on the Army's Social Scheme Mr Crossley said :

> For several years I was closely associated with the Booths. I have been many times in their company at their home, and have seen their manner of life. From this I am personally convinced that " feathering their nest " is no part of their scheme. Their own personal services and the services of members of other

[1] *The History of The Salvation Army*, vol. iii, p. 208

devoted and self-sacrificing persons in the Army today are given for the public good in return for nothing of a material kind—unless, indeed, you call the uncertain sum, barely sufficient for support, which they receive or collect with great difficulty, "something," and the Booth family takes little even of this.

Frank Crossley died in March 1897. Bramwell Booth said that he was known in the Army as "The Paymaster," he having given the organization more than £100,000 during his lifetime. His financial support enabled the General to open up the Army's missionary work overseas. Alexander McLaren described him as "a nineteenth-century saint, whom Francis of Assisi might have recognized as a brother in faith and spirit."

Samuel Morley, who had been so great a support in Christian Mission days and who later gave £200 for a rescue home for fallen girls, died in September 1886. Another Christian Mission friend, Mr J. E. Billups,[1] died suddenly in Bristol in November 1896. Bramwell Booth represented the General, who was campaigning in the north of Scotland, and spoke at the funeral in Cardiff. The General wrote a two-column tribute in the *War Cry* to the memory of his friend for thirty-three years.

* * *

When William Booth was invited to call upon General Lord Wolseley, Commander-in-Chief of the British Forces, at the War Office in August 1890, he found him especially interested in the Social Scheme. He had, he said, the greatest respect for the Army, had been to its meetings, had listened to the testimonies of magistrates and others concerning its work and had no doubt that it was producing great benefit to the community.

It is interesting to note here that in the Introductory to the

[1] *The History of The Salvation Army*, vol. i, pp. 252-3, 258

first edition of *Orders and Regulations*, published in October 1878, William Booth wrote: "It is a remarkable fact that our system corresponds so closely to that of the army and navy of this country, that we have been able to use even the very words of many of their regulations, and of Sir Garnet Wolseley's Soldiers' Pocket-Book."

When in London three months after the Peace of Vereeniging, and collecting funds for their people whom the South African War had rendered destitute, the Boer Generals, Botha, De Wet and Delarey, called upon The Salvation Army's General at International Headquarters to discuss the possibility of settling men in South Africa, preferably at the Cape. Delarey it was who had captured General Lord Methuen. William Booth prayed with these three at the conclusion of the interview. Before the war the Army had had kindly relations with ex-President Steyn, of the Orange Free State.

* * *

A friend of quite a different complexion was Adolf Beck, who had suffered a long term of imprisonment for murder, a crime of which he was subsequently proved not guilty, and who later received a free pardon from King Edward VII. Writing of his experiences in the *Evening News* in 1904 he said:

> If I could persuade the people of England to give over their prisons to The Salvation Army, I should feel that the years of my misfortune had not been spent in vain . . . somehow The Salvation Army seems to be animated by a spirit that produces conviction in the minds of the most careless.

* * *

A side-line on the ostrich-like attitude of officialdom in some quarters respecting the way of life of the "down and out" population of the period, especially mentioned in *In*

Darkest England and the Way Out, is provided by a letter written on 21 January 1891 by Lieut.-Colonel Henry Smith, Commissioner of Police, to the Lord Mayor of London in reply to a letter written to his lordship by William Booth and published in *The Times*. The General had said that 164 persons had been found by The Salvation Army sheltering under Blackfriars Bridge. There was not a word of truth in these allegations, declared the Commissioner. He had given strict orders, and especially "during the recent inclement weather," that no-one was to be allowed to shelter on or under any of the City bridges! This statement, says Harold Begbie in *William Booth*, was "too humorous for serious consideration," as every observant Londoner knew the tragic facts. William Booth kept his course with a proud silence in the face of such callousness, combined with a crass ignorance of the situation.

X THE YOUNG PEOPLE'S WAR

CHAPTER ONE

JUNIOR SOLDIERS

WRITING in the issue of the *War Cry* for 10 December 1887 the Field-Secretary says:

We intend having 100 little soldiers[1] on the platform at the Exeter Hall meeting on Wednesday, and purpose making little soldiers a regular feature of our Exeter Hall meetings so as to bring the work more prominently before the officers and public.

This announcement disclosed the General's determination to give greater impetus to the Army's work among its own children and those hitherto untouched by other denominations. The number of little soldiers' adjutants had already been more than trebled during the previous twelve months, and in this same month, December, the term "little soldier" was abolished and "junior soldier" took its place in order to embrace an older class of young people. After more than six years of publication the *Little Soldier* became the *Young Soldier*, which title it has retained to this present day.

Headquarters had been forced to acknowledge that the junior soldiers' war had not been a success, the reason being that to a large extent it had rested with individual field-officers, and had not been centralized and controlled from headquarters as was the senior soldiers' war. Field-officers were under the impression that their interest in children was optional. Now things were to be altered and the junior

[1] *The History of The Salvation Army*, vol. ii, pp. 91-4

soldiers' war was to be controlled and directed from headquarters like every other department, Major George Mackenzie being appointed the Chief of the Staff's secretary for that purpose. He was commissioned by the General at Regent Hall on Wednesday, 4 January 1888. On the following day the General held a council with the junior soldiers' adjutants of all England, and that same night met in addition the junior soldiers' sergeants and sergeant-majors of London, of which, so far as the junior soldiers' war was concerned, Mrs Mackenzie was in command. 200 junior soldiers were on the platform at these first councils held in connection with the junior soldiers' war, and the meeting opened with a new song :

> Thousands of children Jesus has saved,
> Making them pure and holy ;
> Teaching them how to fight and be brave
> In The Salvation Army.

The General stated that whereas other Churches were, in the main, fed from their Sunday schools, The Salvation Army had had little or none of this supply.

> We propose to try and set guards and guides and corresponding influences in the contrary direction of the world [said the General]; to supply fun and amusement and merry times for the children, but always in the Lord. . . . The *Young Soldier* had reached a circulation of 101,000 copies per week, the circulation at the beginning of the previous year being only 36,000. . . . At every corps the junior soldiers were to have a barracks of their own. Then indoor meetings and two open-air meetings were to be held on Sundays, and a public and private meeting during the week. Every corps was to be under the direct management of a sergeant-major or field-officer, and was to be divided into companies of twelve children, each to be under the care of a sergeant. Several corps lying near to each other would form a section, under the charge of a sectional sergeant-major or field-officer. So many sections near to each other would form a district under a field-officer with the rank of Ensign. Districts will form

a division under an Adjutant and over all Major Mackenzie and his wife [who was to remain in command of London operations] would be at International Headquarters. Every corps was to have a treasurer and secretary and a roll book.

Two children testified in this council, one aged ten and the other aged five ! The state of the junior soldiers' work statistically was to date : 15,149 junior soldiers ; 1,000 (roughly) junior sergeants ; 739 junior soldiers' corps ; 9 junior soldiers' adjutants ; and 5 junior soldiers' field-captains.

The General again met the junior soldiers' staff and the London junior soldiers' sergeants on the following evening and addressed them on the importance of their work.

You are not to teach Scripture, and fill their minds with ideas about God and Christ, heaven and hell, merely for the sake of their having the knowledge of these things . . . if you don't use all this as a lever to lift them out of the horrible pit of their sins, you had better leave them in ignorance—let them alone—because by so doing you only familiarize their minds with these facts, and so take off the bite and grip when in a future day someone else may try to reach their consciences and their hearts by the recital of these soul-stirring subjects. The Sunday school has largely failed, and failed just in this respect.
The whole of the profits from the sale of the *Young Soldier* [the General continued] would go to help maintain the junior soldiers' work, where there was a field-officer exclusively set aside for such work, but where a field-officer was not kept, only half of the profits should go to the junior soldiers' corps, and half to the Junior Soldiers' Adjutant.

The General also spoke of a monthly penny magazine that he hoped to issue for the instruction of those who were appointed to junior soldiers' work, for parents and the older children. The first field-officers in this connection were appointed to Chalk Farm and Camberwell.

Junior soldiers are also to have every facility for holding an anniversary in every corps, on which occasion they will have the use of the barracks, or may take the town-hall.

A general order for divisional and field-officers regarding the junior soldiers' war was issued in the *War Cry* for 18 February 1888, and among its fifteen clauses was this one :

On and after February 11th all persons under 16 years of age who come to the Senior Corps Penitent-Form must be handed over to the Junior Soldiers' Corps.

No junior soldier could be transferred to the senior corps under the age of fifteen, but could stay in the junior soldiers' corps until the age of eighteen.

The new monthly magazine about which the General had spoken was to be called *The Coming Army* and was announced to be issued on 15 March 1888, price one penny. This was, however, postponed for a month, but actually did not see the light of day until December. In the meantime a column relating to junior work appeared in the *War Cry* commencing with the issue of 7 April. It was explained that in the Sunday afternoon company meeting

the different company sergeants gather round them their children, an opportunity is given for the junior soldiers to quietly speak their experience, and all unsaved boys and girls are now faithfully closed in with as to their sinful condition and how they may obtain salvation. . . . Half an hour soon passes away in this manner and then the prayer bell or whistle sounds . . . the sergeant, assisted by his junior soldiers, now presses the unconverted in the company to seize the opportunity and get saved.

The first book distinctly representative of the junior soldiers war, *Orders and Regulations*, was published in April. By October of the same year 719 junior soldiers' corps were in existence, with 50 field-officers entirely engaged in the work and 33 staff-officers organizing and pushing it forward in every direction—an

enormous development [says Commissioner Railton in the *War Cry*]. We are determined to keep entirely clear of anything approaching "schoolism." Our work is not to train children to repeat the names or words of the great soldiers of God who have lived in the past, but to repeat their lives and acts by becoming the true children of God, and true soldiers of the Army.

Two thousand junior soldiers in uniform were present at the first anniversary of the establishment of the junior work, over which the General presided on Monday evening, 10 December 1888 in the Clapton Congress Hall. This had been preceded by a junior soldiers' staff council on the Friday and Saturday, and by a junior soldiers' demonstration in all parts of London on the Sunday. Two junior bands participated. Captain Harding, of Northampton, stated that so anxious were the children to attend the Sunday evening meetings that they were commenced an hour earlier, and even then hundreds waited in queues to get in and many were unable to do so. In this same city a boy had thrown lime into the eye of a girl junior soldier who was marching in a procession and as a result she had lost her eye. This is the first report of a Salvationist child-martyr. In the course of his address the General said:

So far as I can gather from the condition of the public schools—the genteel schools, boarding schools, Board schools and schools of every description—there is, at the present day, a large measure of impurity and uncleanness floating over the children of the country. . . . Again, I think you will observe a large amount of the spirit of infidelity amongst the children. It is a very common thing to hear quite youths—boys of from twelve to sixteen—announce that they have no belief in God. . . . The remedy is Salvation. It is not education, not night-schools, nor gymnasiums, nor reading and writing classes, nor making them familiar with the stories of Scripture, nor enabling them, like so many parrots, to quote the language of the Bible.

There were 744 junior corps, an increase of 527 since January; 18,000 junior soldiers, an increase of 10,000;

2,528 sergeants, an increase of 1,833; 111 junior soldiers' officers, an increase of 100, supported by the junior soldiers themselves; and 135 junior soldiers' barracks, an increase of 88.

Chapter Two

" A SERIOUS BUSINESS "

An announcement in August 1890 stated that both senior and junior work were to be under the direction of the Divisional Officer, who would in almost every case have a separate secretary for each branch of the work. Junior soldiers' regulations were first published in December 1892, and the band of love—first mentioned in the *War Cry* for 5 November of that year: " The band of love weeknight meeting has in it the elements of success "—at that time was " booming in London and is bound to catch on." It was decided that magic lanterns could be used for the juniors, but that slides must first be approved by the home office.

It was also decided that commencing with the last issue of the 1892 *War Cry* the Orders or Lessons which had hitherto been circulated in pamphlet form should appear week by week in the official organ

so as to ensure the Junior soldiers' sergeants of the poorest corps procuring them and to supply our Salvation families with a Bible reading based on the character, principles and objects of the war.

The junior soldiers' company orders were written by a different officer almost every week. The December 1892 number of *All the World* was largely devoted to children, with articles by the Chief of the Staff and Mrs Bramwell Booth, Railton and Susie F. Swift, the editor, who says:

Let us remember that our work differs and *must* differ very widely from ordinary Sunday-school work—which is usually distinctly divided into effort among the children connected with the church and mission work. Among our childish, as among our grown-up, congregations, we must consider always the "uncared-for." A recent writer in the *Primitive Methodist Quarterly* pronounces the present Sunday-school system a failure, not on the ground which might have been expected—spiritual inefficiency, due to the employment of unconverted and unconsecrated teachers; to the lack of wise, strong superintendence; to the deliberate doing of things likely to foster the love of the world in children with a view to increasing the numbers in attendance, and to an exaltation of mere verbal Scriptural knowledge, which amounts to idolatry and superstition. No! Mr Reynolds' arraignment is on the ground that their teaching tends to supersede that of the family, and tends to relieve parents of their responsibility for religious teaching. Alas, with many of our children we have no such concern. Our junior sergeants' whole effort and aim with half their charges must be to supersede the teaching of the family.

The reward system when first introduced met with objections until the General answered his critics with the apt Scriptural illustration: "Be thou faithful unto death, and I will give thee a crown of life." The Christmas of 1892 saw more than 1,200 Bibles and more than 2,000 text cards distributed as prizes for regular attendance and good conduct in the London division, the junior work of which was under the control of Staff-Captain (later Brigadier) William Lord, then the only Junior Secretary in the country, Mrs Lord being the band of love sergeant-major of the Clapton Congress Hall corps.

The General decided that 1894 was to be the juniors' year.

For the first time in our history [he wrote in the issue of the *War Cry* for 6 January], we will take up the work of saving and blessing the Children as a serious business—a business we have to do—to which we are called, which must be done, and which, by the grace of God, shall be done, and that with all our might. . . . We are in danger of being merely imitators of other workers, and thereby producing little more than an old-fashioned Sunday School, and presenting the Army with nothing more than a Junior Soldier in Sunday Scholar's dress, and hardly that. . . . What do we want? *Nothing less than the salvation of our children for this world and the next.*

He asks for a return to be made, three months from the appearance of his letter, of every corps that has a junior corps connected with it.

I shall call for that Return from all the world. It will be sent direct to me through the Commissioner of each Territory. I want to know exactly how we stand.

He appreciates what is being done by thousands of teachers of the young in other religious organizations, but he fears that

many of them do not go further than simply getting the children together for so many hours a week, to keep them quiet, make them acquainted with Scripture history, teach them hymns and prayers, and good manners, and I know not what else. All excellent so far as it goes, but I want Salvationists to understand that we want our junior work to be a real fight for the salvation of the children.

The inauguration of the young people's legion for those " who are too old for the juniors and too young for the seniors " was announced in the first issue of the *War Cry* for 1896 by the British Commissioner, T. Henry Howard. Its membership was to include young people between the ages of 14 and 18, and the Commissioner described it as " a middle-link completing the chain of life-long soldiership." Members had to " be thorough teetotal, and neither smoke, chew, nor pinch snuff. They are all anti-gamblers, and pledged to maintain the principles of purity." The motto of the legion was to be "For Christ and others. Each day its crowning deed." Salvation education—foreign languages, drawing, shorthand, typewriting; recreation, which included drills and exercises; sociability; outings, demonstrations, and bureaux for finding lodgings for the members; library, instruction in Army principles, government, history and geography were all embraced in the "daring" scheme. A general secretary for the league was attached to the Home Office. It would appear that the first branch was opened in Dover, where the commanding officer was the re-established Adjutant Brindley Boon.[1] An exclusive branch of the young people's legion was launched at International Headquarters by Commissioner Pollard for the young people of the staff in November 1897.

The whole of the front page of the *War Cry* for 25 April 1896 was devoted to an explanation of the junior cadet brigade, which had been recently organized following an appeal by Brigadier Miles in the *War Cry* for 29 February. The brigade was to be composed of junior soldiers who were at least twelve years of age and who purposed to become officers so soon as age, health, experience and ability should render them eligible. They were to study lessons in the Scriptures, Salvation Army work at home and abroad, *Doctrines and Discipline:* and *Orders and Regulations for Field Officers*. They were to have a membership card which would contain a six months' record of their progress, and which would be endorsed each week by the field-officer of the corps.

The first review of more than 100 junior cadets by the General took place in August of the same year in connection with the Army's first exhibition, which was held in the Royal Agricultural Hall, Islington.[2]

[1] p. 175 [2] p. 246

> The junior cadet movement [said the General] was pregnant with great possibilities. The future officer would begin with experience of the war, acquaintance with its methods and organizations and, given a personal realization of the Divine Spirit in their hearts, great things might be expected.

An important notice announced that from 10 February 1898 the junior cadet would be known as the corps cadet. At Whitsuntide 1898 the first training camp for corps cadets was held at the Farm Colony, Hadleigh, the Chief of the Staff leading and some 250 young people—two-thirds of them lasses—availing themselves of the opportunity.

Lieut.-Colonel (later Commissioner) Hugh E. Whatmore was appointed Junior Soldiers' Field-Secretary at the Home Office in November 1896.

Young people's councils as they are conducted today were inaugurated by the Chief of the Staff when he held a day of five meetings with 386 London young men and women in the Congress Hall, Clapton, on Sunday, 14 March 1897. This was described as a "new chapter in Salvation Army history." Some young folk stayed for the Saturday night, the councils beginning at seven o'clock the next morning and not concluding until nearly ten o'clock at night. In June the Chief of the Staff conducted an inspiring Sunday's meetings with representative young men and women of the Army in Sheffield, in a dingy, badly-ventilated underground room. What was described as "the latest series of meetings in the interests of the young blood of The Salvation Army by the Chief of the Staff" was held at Clapton in November. "There has been nothing to equal them in meetings of this kind," said the *War Cry*. Later Portsmouth and then Newcastle-on-Tyne were visited, 250 young people travelling many miles to attend the 7 a.m. knee-drill at the last-named centre.

Chapter Three

"A RISING CONCERN"

The Salvation Army directory, a sort of catechism, " a tiny, but wonderfully comprehensive booklet intended for the use of children under ten years of age—very useful as the basis for many a lesson in infant theology," was introduced in September 1900.

A vast soul-saving campaign to advance the junior soldiers' war was conducted during the following month, the General now being satisfied that the Army was in a position, such as it had not occupied before, for engaging in a big and organized effort. Special meetings for children were to be held at various centres of the United Kingdom by the General himself, the Chief of the Staff and Mrs Bramwell Booth, and Commissioners Carleton, Howard, Coombs, Pollard, Cadman, Nicol and Rees. A manifesto was published in the *War Cry* by the General, who declared that the children had not had their due share of sympathy and attention. The first united young people's campaign was launched in the Congress Hall, Clapton, on a Saturday night, and was conducted by the General. One of the most important gatherings that ever assembled under the roof of this Salvation Army Mecca marked a new thing. No fewer than 299 children knelt at the mercy seat after the General's talk of nearly an hour. The Chief conducted a Sunday morning meeting for young people at Wood Green and then, with Brigadier Kitching, Colonel Whatmore and the provincial staff, cycled to Chalk Farm for the afternoon and to Highgate at night. 222 boys and girls and young men and women claimed salvation that day. Another "right royal day" was spent by the Chief of the Staff with the young people of the London province at Clapton in December. Then there were 305 seekers. Knee-drill was led by the Chief at 7 a.m. as "an appetizer" and the first session commenced at 9 a.m.

General orders for the junior war were issued in the first issue of the 1900 *War Cry* by the Territorial Commissioner, Thomas B. Coombs, to begin with the New Year:

1. Sunday morning junior meetings must be held in connection with each corps in each territory.
2. The *Directory* must be specially taught at this meeting, and at least two Companies must be formed for this purpose—one for children under 10 years of age, and the other for those over 10.
3. Where there is no separate Junior Soldiers' Barracks, the time for the Morning Meeting should be the same as where there is, viz. 10 a.m. to 10.45 a.m.
4. Should any children be absolutely prevented from attending the Morning Meeting, they may repeat their portion of the *Directory* in the Sunday Afternoon Company. Encouragement should be given to the children to attend in the morning, as it will be very largely from the results of that Meeting that the awarding of Prizes for efficiency will be decided.
5. Company lessons will continue for a time to be taken from the *Directory*; but all Juniors must be given to understand that the portion they are under obligation to learn by heart, is that given in the Morning Meeting.
6. Marks will be given for the Morning Attendance, as well as for the Afternoon, and the highest number attainable is 104.

The standard for Prizes for the year 1901 is as follows:

94 Stars . . .	1st Prize
89 Stars . . .	2nd Prize
80 Stars . . .	3rd Prize

Colonel Richard Wilson was National Secretary for the Junior and Young People's War in Great Britain and Ireland at this time.

The *War Cry* for 7 May 1904 stated that

The Chief's Campaigns for the last five years in the interests of the Young People have at last assumed such a proportion as to take the rank of a truly great and distinct movement. We will not disguise the fact that at first and at times he has had an uphill fight to wage. Prejudice and fear stood in the way at the outset. The impetuosity of the first converts, the absence of experience, and lack of rules stamped the effort with those features which some misconstrue as evils, but which a wise, far-seeing Leader classifies as weaknesses inevitable to new departures. Now the whole thing bubbles with the animation of a rising concern. . . . The young are coming out as well-instructed, deeply spiritual, and intense Salvationists.

The Parting of the Ways

1 Ballington Booth 2 Maud Charlesworth Booth 3 Arthur Sidney Booth-Clibborn 4 Catherine Booth-Clibborn 5 Herbert Howard Booth 6 Cornelie Ida Ernestine Booth

Outstanding Officers of the Period

1 Commissioner George A. Kilbey 2 Mrs Dowdle 3 Commissioner James Dowdle 4 Commissioner Thomas B. Coombs 5 Colonel Arnolis Weerasooriya 6 Consul Emma Booth-Tucker 7 Colonel Herman Lägercrantz 8 Staff-Captain (later Colonel) Alfred E. Braine 9 Colonel Harriet Lawrance 10 Captain Charlotte Stirling 11 Captain James Kemp (' Ashbarrel Jimmy '), first Convert of the Railton Party which opened The Army's work in the U.S.A.

XI THE BOOTH FAMILY

BRAMWELL

IN its formative years The Salvation Army was indisputably and understandably largely a Booth affair, for each member of the family, with the exception of the retarded Marian—who was given the stationary rank of Staff-Captain—held a high and responsible position with a distinctive and personal rank. The activities and subsequent influence, progressive in the main, retrogressive in some instances, of these seven exceptionally talented Booth children were therefore inextricably woven into the warp and woof of the organization's history, and necessity demands that they be recorded in a separate chapter of this volume.

Some five years after the passing of Mrs Booth the General formed the habit of writing what he called "a family letter" to "My dear children," which was first read by Bramwell and then passed round to the entire circle. "The *unity* of the Army," he wrote in one of these epistles in 1895, "is an unceasing wonder to me." The unity of the *family*, however, was soon to be broken, as was the father-heart; but William Booth felt it incumbent upon him to let the world know exactly where he stood in a farewell speech prior to his American campaign in 1902:

The Salvation Army does not belong to the Booth family [he said]. It belongs to The Salvation Army. So long as the Booth family are good Salvationists, and worthy of commands, they shall have them, but only if they are. I am not the General of the family. I am the General of The Salvation Army.

And on Bramwell's forty-second birthday in 1898 the father wrote the son :

I am glad you see that it is the making of a new and separate people that is the greatest thing of all. I have been trying to make you all understand it for a good many years and I am in for it more than ever I was, a very great deal.

The personal correspondence between father and son, General and Chief of the Staff, at this period reveals the exceptional beauty of their relationship, but now and again Bramwell has to remind William that he has a will of his own. On 12 September 1892 he writes :

I am better and mean to have my own way more than ever in my life ! If you will only let me. Tender love.

Soon after the tragic death of Emma in 1903 William pays his Chief a moving tribute. Writing in his own hand from his home at Hadley Wood he says :

My very dear Bramwell,

I feel it laid on my heart to write you a line tonight expressive of *my deep gratitude for the love and service and sympathy you have shown me in this hour of sorrow and difficulty*. Your tender concern for me these last days has been nothing new. You have never failed me when battling with the many trials that so often have been my portion during the nearly thirty years that you have fought by my side. You have understood more clearly perhaps than any others who have been with me in the conflict, the object at which I have aimed and the means and agencies by which I have sought to reach it. To that object and those means you have I believe without a question been steadily faithful and I believe you will be to the end. *Living or dying I shall rely upon you.* You have been not only a dutiful son *and a sympathizing Comrade* but *a useful helper*. Your wise counsels and ceaseless toils by night and by day all these years have greatly aided in bringing the Army to the position it now occupies, and will I have no doubt tell beneficially in its future. . . . And now that I have been called to mourn the irreparable loss of dear, precious Emma, you have come nearer to me than ever and I believe that you desire to do all that in you lies to lessen the suffering and make up for the lack of service that loss has entailed upon me. *My dear Bramwell, you will let me miss her, and mourn for her and feel how different the world has all at once become to me. I am sure you will.* Meanwhile I will try and be patient and go forward and for your sake and the precious Army's sake, and the children's sake, that is dear Eva and Lucy and Marie and Flo, and all the grand-children's sake, and the poor sinner's sake, I will strive to live and keep a cheerful countenance and fight the fight appointed me after the fashion God has chosen to the end. This is a very scrappy letter, full of blunders, but it comes from my heart, and I feel that I should like you to have it, if possible, tonight. With love to all at the Homestead,

Your affectionate father, W. B.

BALLINGTON

An announcement under the heading, "The American Sorrow," appeared in the *War Cry* dated 29 February 1896, and was signed by W. Bramwell Booth. His younger brother, Commander Ballington Booth, said the statement, had received early in January instructions to farewell from the United States, preparatory to his taking another command in the following May. Similar instructions had been issued to seven other Commissioners involved in the change of appointments. Upon receipt of their orders both the Commander and his wife had at once written to the Chief of the Staff raising objections and putting forward certain difficulties. Bramwell Booth had replied that the orders were in accordance with the regulations and systems of the Army and that the changes had been long fore-shadowed. To that letter the Commanders had replied, by return mail, enclosing their resignation as officers of The Salvation Army; that was dated 31 January.

According to the Chief's announcement he had communicated immediately with the General, who was campaigning in India, and telegrams from him and the Chief had reminded the Commanders of the impossibility of making exceptions in such changes. Having failed to modify their decision, Bramwell had sent his brother, Commandant Herbert Booth, Colonel Alex M. Nicol, and later Commissioner Eva Booth, to entreat them to reconsider their resignation, or at least to postpone further action until the General returned to London. All these mediatory efforts had failed and a final cablegram from the Commander announced that he and his wife had left their post.

While the resignation of his second son and Mrs Ballington Booth was deeply deplored by the General, and indeed by the whole Salvation Army, William Booth had

only given fresh proof of his conscientious and resolute determination to administer the affairs of The Salvation Army without regard to any family or other personal preferences. I believe [continued Bramwell Booth] that every thoughtful man will rejoice that in the presence of so great a trial The General has had grace and courage to adhere unflinchingly, in a case affecting a loved member of his own family, to the principle which he has laid down for the guidance of others in this matter. Everyone will see that it would be gravely and immediately destructive of all confidence in the whole administration of The Army if it could appear as though to be his son privileged any man on that account to obtain, or retain, more agreeable positions than other men no less devoted could attain. All faith in The General would be gone, and The Army itself would be destroyed by such a violation of the universal sense of justice. I am confident that every lover of goodness will feel deeply for our beloved General when they read this, perhaps the saddest of all tidings which have ever reached him.

Commissioner Eva Booth, who was then in New York, was appointed to take temporary command until the appointment and arrival of the new Territorial Commanders, the General's son-in-law and daughter, Commissioner Booth-Tucker and Consul Emma Booth-Tucker. Then began a vigorous newspaper campaign in the United States in favour of the Ballington Booths, and violent misrepresentation of the British leadership in London. The strong national feeling then evident was fanned into a blazing flame by the Anglo-American controversy on the Venezuelan Question. In a printed letter addressed to the American officers following their withdrawal Ballington and Maud Booth wrote :

Our letter to the International Headquarters of January 31st stated that we were going quietly through with our farewell, but that, for *certain reasons*, we could not feel free to enter upon another command. . . . The letter we wrote has been called a resignation, but it was, in truth, a statement of the situation and our reasons.

But a pamphlet of fifteen pages published by Emma and Frederick Booth-Tucker, and entitled *The Resignation of Commander and Mrs Ballington Booth*, gives copies of their letter of 31 January, in which they say

The only light we have received from God is that upon the path we have now determined to take, viz. : to obey your orders and resign our command, and then as quickly and expeditiously as possible retire—

Bramwell's letter of 15 February, which contained some 8,000 words, including this appealing paragraph :

Ballington, don't do it ! As you value your own soul and the peace of your conscience, and the happiness of Maud and your children, I say again from my deepest heart, don't do it !—

and the General's letter of 13 March, in which he writes movingly, concluding in a cry like that of David for Absalom :

O Ballington, Ballington ! You cannot be in your right reason. The whole thing is like a horrid dream. Again and again I ask myself, " Is this a reality or an imagination ? " For your own sake hesitate ! think ! return ! The worst can yet be averted.

The past may be forgiven. Believe me to be still your affectionate father praying for you all the time.

A large meeting was held in the Carnegie Hall, New York, presided over by the Hon. Dr Chauncey Depew and attended by many important persons, to entreat the General to re-consider his decision and allow America to be an exception to the rule, but the General would not agree ; so at the insistence of many friends, among them Mayor Strong of New York City and the Honourable Chauncey M. Depew, he [Ballington] was led to inaugurate The Volunteers of America assuming the title of General.

Writing from Sheffield some years before, Ballington Booth had penned to his "very dear General" a letter expressing the utmost affection, apparently after having received a complaint from his father :

I also esteem you and I regard you greater than Luther—indeed you are the spiritual Napoleon of the age, and I have never and shall never allow anything in word or deed or office to pass unnoticed and *unrefuted* that is hurtful to you or what I know to be the opposite of the deeply sincere and transparent motive of your heart. I can only ask GOD TO LINK ME CLOSER TO YOU . . . I wish I could become more to you. Somehow I feel I shall do some day !! Your own in loving concern, Ballington Booth.

What was to bring about a refutation of everything so ardently expressed in this letter ? It is obvious that Ballington became increasingly at cross-purposes with the remote control of International Headquarters, and it must be remembered that as a nation the policy of the United States was, as a recent President put it so aptly, " splendid isolation." During the period of crisis the Rev. John L. Scudder, of the Congregational Tabernacle, Jersey City, put the idea of a split from the parent organization into Ballington's mind, if it was not there already, when, in speaking on Salvation Army affairs, he said :

Why, then, we ask, do they not organize a new and distinctly American army? Why should not Commander Ballington Booth become General Booth from this time on? Hundreds of thousands would like to see him occupy that position.

And Ballington himself had declared:

I shall never cease to be an American citizen. My heart is with the American people and I believe in American institutions.

But the General still believed that his son's resignation was but a flash in the pan.

He will come back [he said in a press interview]. All his past assurances and devotion lead me to think it. Under the stress of keen temptation and an avalanche of flattering and persuasion he has yielded. But I cannot think it is for long.

For once the General had underestimated the strength of the opposition. It is surely significant and must be mentioned in fairness to Ballington Booth that his younger sister, Eva, was to remain in command of the United States for thirty years until, indeed, she was elected General in 1934.

It was supposed by many people that Ballington Booth's resignation would mean the collapse of The Salvation Army in the United States of America, but exactly two years later, on 8 March 1898, William Booth was able to write to Bramwell:

So far as I am concerned the bubble has burst, and the delusion has vanished that you cannot make a mighty, overcoming, dashing Salvation Army in the United States.

Ballington Booth was the composer of four well-known Salvation Army songs: "The cross is not greater than His grace," "You've carried your burden," "I'm satisfied with Jesus here" and "Over and over like a mighty sea." He died on 5 October 1940 at the age of eighty-three, and the Maréchale wrote in *The Volunteers' Gazette*:

What a wonderful re-union around the Throne of the Lamb! My father and mother, my sisters Emma and Marian, my brothers, Bramwell and Herbert. What a welcome for my beloved brother Ballington!

Maud Ballington Booth, who succeeded her husband as General of The Volunteer Army, died on 26 August 1948, also aged eighty-three. She was succeeded in turn by her son, Charles Brandon Booth, who is now retired from the leadership.

EMMA

A whole page in the *War Cry*, dated 17 March 1888, was devoted to the announcement of the forthcoming marriage of Miss Emma Moss Booth "so long associated with Training Home work," and Commissioner Frederick St George de Lautour Tucker, "our chief officer in India," which included lengthy letters from the General and Mrs Booth, and Commissioner Tucker himself to his comrades in India. The wedding was made the occasion of an appeal for £5,000 as a wedding present to be used in the training and dispatch of officers and the pushing of Army operations in all parts of the world.[1] Mr T. A. Denny and Mr F. W. Crossley contributed the first donations of £500 each. The £5,000 was gathered in before the day of the wedding had ended. Admission to the marriage ceremony in the Congress Hall, Clapton, on 10 April, the General's fifty-ninth birthday, was by ticket only on payment of five shillings.

The wedding was preceded by a day's meetings in the St James's Hall, and at night "a great Indian Durbar" was held in which the bride and bridegroom participated. Among the speakers was a new convert from Ceylon who, encouraged by the success of The Salvation Army in his

[1] p. 81

native country, had commenced the Buddhist Salvation Army,[1] taking the lead as captain and employing elephants, drums and native music in his gatherings. Eventually he had become a Salvationist.

The new and special title of Consul was conferred by the General upon his daughter Emma, who nevertheless continued to hold the rank of Commissioner in her own right, in June 1895. This was because she and her husband were both Foreign Secretaries at International Headquarters, and it would be more easy to distinguish between them.

While travelling from Kansas City to Chicago, the Consul was severely injured in a collision when the train left the rails and crashed into a huge water tank at Dean Lake, Iowa. Just before a relief train taking her and Colonel Holland—the officer in charge of the Land Colony at Fort Amity in Colorado and who was also injured—reached Marceline station, in Missouri, the Consul passed away. This was on the morning of Wednesday, 28 October 1903. The Salvation Army world was stunned by the announcement that one of the foremost women-Salvationists in the world, in the prime of life—she was only forty-three years of age and the mother of seven children—had met so untimely a death, and thousands of telegrams, letters and messages poured into International Headquarters. The entire continent of North America was deeply stirred.

The General bravely struggled with the waves of sorrow.

> It was a rough entering to the Gates of Paradise [he said]. She was the least, more inadequately-estimated girl of the family. Comparatively few knew her. But I knew her. It seems a sort of treason to talk of anything or think of anything but her, and yet the war must go on. . . . My loss is great—irreparable. . . . Thy will be done ! '

A memorial service held in the Princess Rink, Chicago, was

[1] p. 122

attended by 3,000 persons, and another in the Carnegie Music Hall, New York, where 10,000 were unable to obtain admission. At the Memorial service in the Congress Hall, Clapton, the General paid a father's tribute :

Her death is an unutterable loss ! She was a Salvation Soldier of incomparable worth. . . . She had powerful intellect, a clear judgment, a brilliant wit, an exuberant flow of spirits, and an inflexible will ; and all her powers were sanctified to the noblest end. She was a godly woman, with a living faith in the living God. She lived in Him, communed with Him. He was a reality to her. . . . I prized her beyond rubies. . . . As a speaker she was eloquent and persuasive to a high degree. . . . She was perhaps accurately described by those who knew her best as a "superb manager of men."

Yet another memorial service, described as a Meeting of Sympathy, was led by the General in the Metropolitan (Spurgeon's) Tabernacle, London ; Commissioner Booth-Tucker and his eldest daughter Motee (now Mrs Commissioner Hugh Sladen) journeyed from America to participate. 3,000 people were present.

HERBERT

Principal of the men's training home at Clapton at the age of twenty-two, in command of the Army throughout the British Isles at twenty-seven, and of Australia at thirty-four, Herbert Howard (officially registered as Henry) Booth was obviously exceptionally capable, but the private letters of William Booth give ample proof that his third and youngest son frequently rebelled against the authority of Bramwell, much to the disappointment of his father, with whom he also occasionally came into conflict. "Should he have *power*, which he will have, what will become of me ?" pathetically asked the father of the mother, who was his " adviser and comforter." This was in 1889 and Herbert had just returned from a journey around the world. Nevertheless, it was soon after that he was given command of the work in the British Isles, which position he held for four years. That the General had no qualms regarding Herbert's ability to hold even greater commands is revealed in a letter he wrote to Bramwell in connection with the succession to the Army's leadership :

You will follow the general directions just given as to the selection of your successor. So far as I at present know the Army I think in the first instance your choice should fall upon Herbert.

The first page of the *War Cry* for 27 September 1890, and the three following pages were devoted to a report of the wedding in the crowded-out Clapton Congress Hall of Commandant Booth to Captain Cornelie Ida Ernestine Schoch, daughter of Staff-Captain and Mrs Schoch, of Amsterdam,[1] on 18 September, at 11 a.m. Reserved seats were one shilling each, but admission to the other seats was only one penny. The ceremony was conducted by the General, the bride wore a sash of red, white and blue on which was worked the words " Evermore God's," her three sisters wore white sashes bearing the word " Consecrated," and the wedding-ring was made from gold that Herbert had himself " fossicked " in Australia from a worked-out gulley. Mrs Booth was dying at Clacton,[2] but her portrait stood on a chair near to that of the General.

Following the wedding the General led a great " wind-up " meeting in the Exeter Hall, where he inaugurated his scheme for raising 4,000 cadets. It was, he declared, a red-letter day in the history of the Army throughout the world, for in addition to the wedding, a new headquarters was being opened in Kimberley, South Africa ; a Day

[1] p. 15 [2] p. 302

with God was being held in Rotterdam in celebration of the wedding, the bride being the daughter of the Dutch pioneer ; a great council was being conducted in Toronto by International Commissioner Cadman ; and a party of seventeen officers from England were being welcomed in Melbourne, Australia. That night Colonel (later Commissioner) McKie farewelled for a voyage round the world " of encouragement and consolation."

While in command of Australia Herbert was obsessed by the thought that the Army's government needed a radical change and sent to Bramwell a detailed criticism of its methods, making a powerful plea for decentralization. On 3 February 1902 Herbert and Corrie Booth wrote their letter of resignation to " Our dear Father and General " and signed it " Your broken-hearted son and daughter."

> The system which subjugates all the chief officers of the Army to the vote of their subordinates and yet leaves the supreme heads in *absolute control* seems to us *unjust, unreasonable and oppressive* [they said]. . . . We go with our three little children to face the wall and to start life afresh supported only by God and a good conscience.

> He knew very well that some of the motives prompting him to leave the Army were base [says Brian Lunn in *Salvation Dynasty*]. If he remained, it would be impossible for him to make any provision for the future of himself or of his family. Thus he would always be at the mercy of " the General for the time being," to whom he had vowed life-long obedience. He might never again have a position which he could fill with so much credit as the Australian Command. If he went out now with these laurels fresh upon him and his neatly-packed lecture case, there might be a competence and more for him in the evangelistic field ; and he would have the new sensation of being free to pocket his earnings.

Herbert had no ambition to work *under* the Chief ; he wished to work *with* him on an equal basis ; but Bramwell had no intention of yielding any of the authority he was already exercising. William Booth pleaded with Herbert to work more harmoniously with Bramwell, but to no avail. Herbert's mind was made up, and at the back of it was the thought that one or other of the Governors of the Australian states, who were friendly toward him, would find him a high position. What he forgot to take into account was that their friendliness was due entirely to the admiration and respect they had for The Salvation Army as a whole and not to its temporary leader. So on 22 March 1902 the *War Cry* announced that "Mr Herbert Booth has resigned his command in the Army."

Herbert took with him the lecture-film which he asked he might have for £300, and later wrote a 20,000-word answer to his father's reply to his letter of resignation. Corrie died in 1916 in England while Herbert was in Australia. Four years later he married Miss Annie Lane, who had been Corrie's assistant. He died at the age of sixty-four at Yonkers, New York, on 25 September 1926. Ballington and Evangeline saluted his memory with eulogies at the funeral service.

EVA

Captain Eva Booth took charge of Marylebone corps, then known as the Great Western Hall, in November 1886, and also had charge of the cadets being trained there; Captain Nicholls served under her with the temporary rank of Lieutenant. A few weeks later the Captain gave the main address on a Sunday night shawl-clad and "all tattered and torn, as she visits in the slums and alleys." During her six months' command Captain Eva had Sergeant-Major (later Lieut.-Commissioner) Edgar Hoe and Corps Secretary (later Commissioner) Albert E. Powley among her local officers; Bertram Mills, who was to become the world-famous circus proprietor, as a bandsman; and the Hon. Emma Sugden, daughter of Lord St Leonards, as one of her soldiers. More than once the silver-tongued Liberal statesman, the Rt Hon. John Bright, was to be seen sitting on a back seat of the hall fascinated by the young Captain's eloquence. "You must pack her in cotton-wool and keep her in a glass case," he wrote to the General. "She belongs to the public platform."

William Booth had an especially warm place for Eva in his affections. Writing to Bramwell from New York on 19 March 1898, he said:

I am leaving Eva. Her Command is immensely improved, and my impressions of the soundness of her judgment and of her prudence and enterprise are a long way beyond what they ever were before. She has revolutionized this concern. It is a long way on for being thoroughly Salvation Army, and its loyalty is beyond question.

LUCY

The General's youngest child, Commissioner Lucy Milward (Ruhani) was married in the Clapton Congress Hall to Colonel Emanuel Daniel Hellberg (Raj Singh), a Swedish officer, by her brother, the Chief of the Staff, in the absence of the General, who was campaigning in Canada. This was on 18 October 1894, the Colonel then being Under-Secretary for Foreign Affairs at International Headquarters. After the wedding Commissioner Mrs Booth-Hellberg—as usual, the bridegroom changed his name to include the "Booth"—and Colonel Booth-Hellberg sailed for service in India, where the wife was in command and the husband was her Chief Secretary, with Ceylon included in their jurisdiction.

CATHERINE

William Booth's eldest daughter, Catherine, the Maréchale,[1] was married to Arthur S. Booth-Clibborn in 1887. Fourteen years later, in 1901, Booth-Clibborn became obsessed by a fanatical conviction that John Alexander Dowie, of 'Zion City', in the United States of America, was another Elijah, the fore-runner of the Second Coming of Christ. On 30 November Booth-Clibborn addressed to this impostor a letter which began: 'I have decided to offer myself to you, dear Doctor, and do so, firmly believing it to be the will of God'. This letter was published by Dowie in his weekly organ. Although Catherine did not share her husband's views, she felt duty-bound to stand by him and so, on 10 January 1902, despite Bramwell Booth's strenuous efforts to persuade them to remain in the Army, the Booth-Clibborns resigned. Arthur joined the community at 'Zion City', but Catherine was not only able to withstand acceptance of the pretender's claims, she exploded them.

MRS MARY NEWELL

In March 1902 the General suffered bereavement in the passing of his younger and only surviving sister, Mrs Mary Newell, a soldier of the No 1 corps in Nottingham, to which city he proceeded direct from officers' councils in Paris in time to see her breathe her last. Her funeral—1,000 persons gathered at the graveside—was conducted by the British Commissioner, Thomas B. Coombs.

[1] *The History of The Salvation Army*, vol. ii, p. 263

XII OUTSTANDING SALVATIONISTS

CHAPTER ONE

OFFICERS

COLONEL JAMES BARKER[1] passed away in his fiftieth year at Hadleigh Farm Colony, Essex, on Sunday, 12 May 1901. It was said that he did more to enlist the practical sympathy of statemen, public bodies, and philanthropists for the Army than any other Salvationist outside the General's family. The front page of the *War Cry* for 25 May, and the whole of three inside pages, were given to an account of his career. His life can best be summed up by the sentence: "He was the prisoners' friend."

MAJOR (later COMMISSIONER) HENRY BULLARD (JAI SINGH), was brought in 1888 to International Headquarters from India, in which country he had been a pioneer, and appointed the first Indian Secretary, to deal with all matters affecting the Army's work in that country. Born in Leamington, he had been a member of the Bible class taught by Frances Ridley Havergal, the hymn-writer.

BRIGADIER HEDWIG VON TAVEL-HAARTMAN, the Finnish pioneer,[2] died in Hamburg, Germany, on 15 October 1902, after only thirteen years' service. Appointed to German-

[1] *The History of The Salvation Army*, vols. ii and iii
[2] p. 46

The Maréchale

Captain Catherine Booth singing in a Parisian café (from the painting by the Swedish artist, M. Cederstrom)

The Wreck of the SS *Wairapa* off the Coast of New Zealand on 1 November, 1891

Staff-Captain Annette Paul, Captain Flavell and another Salvationist helping to point a soul to Christ amid the storm

Switzerland following nine years in her native country, she married in 1899 the then Staff-Captain (later Colonel, D.Sc.) von Tavel, but she kept her rank of Brigadier and was not known officially as Mrs Staff-Captain von Tavel as was customary.

MRS CAPTAIN ("MOTHER") WEBB was the first officer,[1] "one of the grandest of women, the truest of saints, and the bravest of Christ's soldiers," died at the age of fifty-six from cancer in the throat on 18 November 1890, four years after she had commenced the work in the Walworth Road.

COMMISSIONER JAMES J. DOWDLE, for thirty-three years an officer, was born in 1840 in a Wiltshire village and died nearly sixty years later, on 21 July 1900. The General conducted the funeral service at Abney Park Cemetery and also a memorial service in the Clapton Congress Hall when, on both occasions, "vast audiences" were present. The Commissioner had travelled with his inseparable "fiddle" in America and Australia and on the Continent, and led many soul-saving campaigns. Colonel (later Commissioner) John Lawley had been a convert of Dowdle's in Bradford. Colonel and Mrs Dowdle, of the Tees and Tyne division, were appointed in October 1886 to headquarters "for special evangelistic work in any part of the Army." The Colonel's first assignment was to accompany the General on his first overseas visit—to Canada and the United States.

CAPTAIN HANNAH FRANKS (JIVE) was the first English officer to die on the Indian missionary field, in the November of 1888. She was born at Dishforth, near Thirsk, Yorkshire, but entered the work from Bradford where, while a factory lass, she had been first a Christian Missioner, and later became the first colour sergeant at the No 1 corps. In 1882 she entered the training home and after eleven weeks

[1] *The History of The Salvation Army*, vol. iii, p. 20

was appointed to New Basford. She landed in Bombay in November 1883.

MRS CAPTAIN WILLIAM (CAROLINE) FROST, along with her husband, came from Guernsey, Channel Islands and was appointed an officer. She became the first regular midnight officer[1] and she and her husband were made directly responsible for the women's rescue work in Chelsea. A trained midwife, Mrs Frost had put two beds in the attic of her own home, where she cared for lost young women, and this became a miniature receiving home. It was at Mrs Bramwell Booth's personal request that she and her husband went to London.

STAFF-CAPTAIN SUSAN ("HAWKER") JONES had remarkable success in rescue work at her various corps.[2] She was born at Banghurst, near Basingstoke, where she died on 25 April 1892.

COLONEL WILLIAM J. PEARSON[3] passed away on 17 October 1892, at sixty years of age and after eighteen years of service. A great funeral demonstration was led by the General in the east end of London. Born in Derby in 1832, Pearson joined the Christian Mission in 1874 at William Booth's written request. Holiness and faith-healing meetings were his particular business and delight. He was, at the time of his passing, the Army's outstanding and most prolific song-writer.

MRS FRED W. FRY (AGNES CAROLINE PECK) became a Christian Missioner at Salisbury and entered the Gore Road training home in 1880. She was a pioneer in Ireland. At Newtownards the Roman Catholic priest said in a public meeting he

[1] *The History of The Salvation Army*, vol. iii, p. 50
[2] *The History of The Salvation Army*, vol. iii, pp. 27 and 56
[3] *The History of The Salvation Army*, vol. I, p. 109

had called to form a Catholic temperance society: "Since the Hallelujah lasses have been to the town all the Protestant drunkards have been saved, and all the drunkards who are left are Catholics." During her eight months' stay at Manchester IV no fewer than 1,838 persons knelt at the penitent-form. After serving in Wales she married Staff-Captain Fred W. Fry, the first Salvation Army bandsman, who was then on the staff of the "musical department." Theirs was the first wedding to be held in the Congress Hall, Clapton, and was conducted by the General. Mrs Fry died on 27 February 1887.

COLONEL PEPPER,[1] of Salisbury, passed away in November 1901.

MRS COLONEL WILLIAM RIDSDEL, "the first wearer of a hallelujah bonnet"—according to the sub-heading in large type across the front page of the *War Cry*—was promoted to Glory from Bristol on 28 March 1890.[2] "The Army's biggest funeral," as the *War Cry* described it—giving most of the front page of the issue for 19 April to a pen-and-ink drawing of it—was conducted by the General on Good Friday. Tens of thousands of spectators turned out to watch the procession of some 1,500 officers and soldiers pass through the streets.

MAJOR ALEXANDER T. SMITH was a pioneer British officer in the United States, and it was with him that Commissioner Railton placed the keeping of the first flag presented by Mrs Booth to be carried to America. He served for many years behind the scenes on the New York headquarters, and was the composer of the chorus, "Oh, yes, there's salvation for you." He was given a funeral of such magnitude that it startled New York. America had seen nothing like

[1] *The History of The Salvation Army*, vol. ii, p. 321
[2] *The History of The Salvation Army*, vol. i, p. 177; vol. ii, p. 47

it before, and Commander Ballington Booth said that perhaps it had been exceeded only when the Army Mother was borne to the grave.

EX-COMMISSIONER FRANK SMITH, who resigned in 1890,[1] was re-accepted in November 1901 and appointed with the rank of Brigadier to the command of the Bolton division. He left again a few years later to become a politician, and was eventually elected Member of Parliament for Nuneaton.

STAFF-CAPTAIN (" HAPPY-GEORGE ") TABERER[2] passed away on the anniversary of the Army Mother's promotion to Glory, 4 October 1902. For many years he had been prevented by failing health from taking part actively in Salvation Army service. He commenced the work in Hull and Bristol ; the opening in Bristol was one of the great events in the Army's history, when 3,007 conversions took place during the first six months.

COLONEL ARNOLIS WEERASOORIYA was born of Buddhist parents in Ceylon, and being the eldest son, was set apart for the priesthood. College life brought him first into touch with The Salvation Army. News of the Sheffield riots impressed him deeply and the reading of Haslam's *From death unto life* made him totally unsatisfied with Buddhism, so that he sought Christ in his own room. He later attended a Salvation Army holiness meeting, sought this blessing, and became one of the first of India's cadets. Becoming Commissioner Booth-Tucker's right-hand man, he was speedily promoted to Captain and later to Major. In May 1886 he visited England, and in the following year became the first national officer to be given the rank of Colonel, having control of more than 100 English officers and some 100 national officers. Booth-Tucker said of him:

[1] *The History of The Salvation Army*, vol. iii, p. 102
[3] *The History of The Salvation Army*, vol. ii, p. 202

For five years he had fought by my side, and our love for one another was like that of David and Jonathan. In times of sorrow he was an unfailing and sympathetic comforter—in times of doubt and difficulty he was a sagacious and far-sighted counsellor, seeming to foresee dangers with an instinctiveness which almost amounted to prophecy—in times of danger he was an intrepid, dauntless hero.

Chapter Two

SOLDIERS

Outstanding Salvation Army personalities are by no means confined to the officer-ranks ; and some of the greatest of its saints were before conversion the greatest of sinners. Among those soldiers whose names must be recorded are :

" MOTHER " CLAPP who had worked for a considerable period with John Eason[1] in a tent on the London Fields, and was one of the first to assist in the transfer of that work to the Christian Mission, which was then started in the Loddiges Hall. She attended the open-air meetings carrying a large, bulky old umbrella which she used against anyone who attempted to interfere with the missioners. When Miss Catherine Booth (La Maréchale) spoke for the first time in the open-air opposite the " Cat and Mutton " public-house in Broadway, Hackney, it was the warm, motherly hand of Mrs Clapp that encouraged her. For a number of years Mrs Clapp was the treasurer of Hackney corps, which she often represented at the conferences in the days of the Christian Mission. She died on 9 November 1891.

[1] *The History of The Salvation Army*, vol. i, p, 170

"ORANGE HARRIET" JACQUES, who died on 9 January 1892, at Barnsley, Yorkshire, where the funeral service was conducted by Mrs Commissioner Cadman. The mile route to the cemetery was lined on either side with thousands of spectators. For many years a heavy drinker and a most violent woman when "under the influence," "Orange Harriet," so-called because she was a hawker of oranges, was converted in the days of The Christian Mission.

BILLY MCLEOD, a famous and highly-esteemed Manchester prize-fighter, but nevertheless a wife-beater and a drunkard of the deepest dye, became a Salvationist and remained so for fifty years until his passing in 1935 at the age of eighty-one. He thrilled thousands of people in many parts of Britain with his remarkable story.

"DAD" (ARCHIBALD) SLOSS was one of the most notorious burglars of Queen Victoria's reign, and had spent more than forty years in various prisons and convict settlements in Great Britain and Australia. A real terror to both detectives and prison governors, he had received no fewer than 300 cuts with the lash for various acts of insubordination—as his back too terribly evidenced. In 1890, while prowling in the vicinity of the City of London, meditating on his next "job," he strolled into the Clerkenwell shelter and was for the first time "knocked over" by the kindness of an officer. The next night saw him back again and wonderfully transformed by the grace of God. He had not a lazy bone in his body. His thick, white whiskers and muscular, but stooping, form was for years a familiar sight between the prison-gate home at King's Cross and the prison gates of London. He became both respected and loved by hundreds of neighbours around the home. His conversion upset all the fiddle-faddle theories of heredity, for he was born, bred and trained to be a criminal. He died in January

1900 and was laid to rest with full military honours. His body was borne on a gun-carriage drawn by four greys, two others being mounted by officers; perhaps the most unique funeral of its character ever seen in London. Commissioner Cadman, who understood the old lag better than most, conducted the funeral service in the Clapton Congress Hall and at the graveside in Abney Park cemetery.

COLONEL W. FRYER, of the Auditor-General's Department, Madras, India, was led into a vital experience of Christ by contact in his office with Mrs Lieut.-Commissioner Hoe, who was collecting for Army funds. He became a Salvationist and marched proudly at the head of a Salvation Army procession carrying the flag. Later he was commissioned as the corps sergeant-major, and was a most enthusiastic open-air leader. At the conclusion of an open-air meeting this influential yet humble military officer would distribute his wealth to the poorest of his listeners.

MISS ADA WARD who "on Saturday [27 February 1897] concluded an engagement at the Prince's Theatre, Portsmouth, created some sensation last night by preaching at the local branch of The Salvation Army," reported the *Evening News*.

After the performance on Saturday she called her company together and announced her intention of quitting the stage and divided her jewels and wardrobe amongst them.

Ada Ward was a world-travelled and popular tragedienne and was playing Lady Isabel in *East Lynne* at the time of her conversion at the Lake Road citadel, to which she was invited by her Salvationist-landlady. Another actress converted about this time was FLORENCE WORTH, who became an envoy.

BOB DYSERT was elected a member of the Stockton-on-Tees corporation in 1897 and was returned unopposed in 1900.

A Salvationist for seventeen years and a plater, he was unable to read or write when he was converted.

BANDSMAN JOHN MALLABY, also of Stockton-on-Tees, was likewise unable to read or write at the time of his conversion, but he became the proprietor of three refreshment houses in Stockton, Middlesbrough and West Hartlepool respectively.

DAVID WILLIAM ROBERTS, of Cefn, a Salvationist for twenty-two years, became a county councillor in 1904, being the first nonconformist to be elected. He was also top of the poll at the parish council election.

XIII VILIFICATION AND VICTORY

IN the Army's early days scarcely a week went by during which William Booth was not the subject of libel or slander by those who were his avowed enemies, by those who were professing Christians, or by those who had once fought under his flag, and these last caused him the deepest grief.

After attacking the Army for several months in specially-organized public meetings in Chipping Norton and elsewhere, an ex-officer by the name of George Brick[1] who had resigned his commission, was eventually brought to book by Mr Lampard, the father of a missionary officer, who took legal action against Brick for the return of £50. The case came before Mr Justice Wills and a common jury in May 1890, and a full report of the proceedings by Commissioner Booth-Tucker took up no fewer than eleven columns of the *War Cry*. The result was described as

> another great legal victory which has truly exceeded our most sanguine expectations, and which could scarcely have been greater had judge, jury and lawyers been one and all Salvationists! . . . The time we spent in Court No. V of the Queen's Bench Division . . . has been to us in a true sense a " Two Days with God."

The gist of the action was that Brick, having professed the utmost remorse for his conduct and a sincere desire to be reconciled to the Army, had written out and signed a retraction, and in addition he had handed over to Lampard

[1] p. 233

the manuscript of a book he had threatened to publish vilifying the Army. Lampard, who was impressed by his seeming sincerity, had agreed to lend Brick £200 to enable him to rid himself of his legal entanglements—he had brought an action for libel against the General, and Dr (later Sir) Washington Ranger, the Army's solicitor, had brought an action against Brick for libel. But, following the advance of £50 Brick, who in the meantime had written for more money, issued a poster announcing that he had been offered a large sum of " hush money " by the Army and had received £50 on account. Lampard demanded an explanation, but Brick reiterated his assertion and refused to return the money, whereupon Lampard had taken the matter to court. Brick alleged that the Army had offered to pay him £750 for his book or to induce him to withdraw the charges. The actual position was that Brick had approached the Army's solicitor and had offered, upon payment of £750, to withdraw both his book and his charges. The Chief of the Staff and Commissioner Railton both gave evidence. Among other things Brick stated in the witness-box, and for the first time, that headquarters was a house of ill-fame ! After only fifteen minutes of consideration the jury returned a verdict for the plaintiff.

Brick had been associated with ex-Commissioner Sherwood who had entered a legal claim for £1,000 damages against the General for wrongful dismissal. The case was to have been argued before Mr Justice Matthew at the Manchester Assize Court on 6 March, but when it was called, Sherwood's chief legal adviser informed the judge that he had suggested to his client that he ought not to continue the action seeing that the matter had been already dealt with by an informed tribunal, a Salvation Army court-martial, and that terms had been arranged with the defendant's counsel. These terms were : judgment for the defendant, both upon the claim and the counter-claim, there being no costs to either side, the defendant undertaking that there should be no execution upon the counter-claim. Mr Gully, Q.C., M.P., explained to the judge that the General had felt bound to contest the action on a ground of principle which was extremely important to the Army. Judgment was thereupon entered for the General. This case revealed the important element that a Salvation Army court-martial's decision cannot well be disputed in law by a person who has submitted to appear before such a tribunal.

Five staff-officers had given consideration to Sherwood's case, at his own request, and had unanimously decided against him. They found that he had, while a salaried servant for the Army, made an agreement to obtain for himself £134 commission by superintending the alteration of the Star Hall Music Hall, Ancoats, into a mission hall for Mr Frank Crossley, and this work was largely done in the offices of the Army. Sherwood had been asked to pay the money into the Army's funds, which he had refused to do.

Writing to his father on 20 June 1892 Bramwell Booth said:

Let us have patience. We are learning. The floods of slander we have passed through in Manchester would have drowned anything but a Noah's ark, yet we *are* afloat.

And writing to Bramwell on 10 February 1893 William Booth says:

What have we need to care about anything if we can save souls? God will take care of us. Let them revile and slander to their heart's content.

In the latter part of 1896 Samuel Horatio Hodges, a one-time Major, wrote to the General deeply regretting having written and published some five years before a pamphlet entitled *General Booth, the Family, and The Salvation Army*, which reflected upon the honour of all three. His whole-hearted retraction and wish for reconciliation, together with William Booth's magnanimous reply, were published in the *War Cry* for 2 January 1897. John Hollins, a former Salvationist, wrote in 1903 a book which he entitled *The Salvation Army—a short study of its defects and possibilities.* Three assumptions constituted his *raison d'être* for the volume, the second of which was " That its [the Army's] present organization is unfitted to be the permanent vehicle of a Christian Movement." He was but one of many prophets who foretold the Army's eventual eclipse and collapse.

The Rev. J. Llewellyn Davies, in a Christmas Day letter to *The Times* in 1888, arraigned the work of the Army in Marylebone as a " unique failure," principally on the ground that it was, apparently, unable to give him the names of any persons residing within a certain area fixed by him, who had been reclaimed, but suggesting that its members had been gained from the Churches. On the following day Mr Davies was furnished with the names and addresses of six Marylebone soldiers who had been saved at the Great Western Hall and who were living in the district. Mr Davies, however, declined to investigate and the testimonies of the six comrades in question were published in the *War Cry* dated 19 January 1889, together with a synopsis of the careers of fourteen other cases of conversion in Marylebone, including the daughter of a minister, who had been ruined by a military bandmaster.

The vicar of Newport, Essex, expelled fifty of his Sunday school children for attending a little soldiers' tea meeting, and solemnly expostulated with their parents on the danger of their offspring becoming infected with heresy. This was in 1891. In the following year the *Standard*, the *St James's Gazette* and other periodicals attacked the General because of his " iron-rule tyranny."

William Booth must have been mightily encouraged,

following the smearing campaign of many years, to read one of the most remarkable tributes ever paid to his organization in an article written by the Rev. Arthur Mursell and published in the *Christian Commonwealth* in March 1903 :

My brethren of The Salvation Army have beaten me in the competition of sympathy and courage where I had deemed myself most strong. I had set up as the friend of the poor, the driven, and the erring, and I had put on my Sunday clothes and asked them to come and hear me say, " Firstly, secondly, thirdly, and finally," and because they would not come, and could not stand it, I had bewailed their indifference and stolidity, and denounced their habits, banned their pleasures, and tried to shut up their haunts. But the tender and quick instinct of comradeship elicited from the Salvationist a more excellent way. He puts on a uniform of equality, not of assumption. He says, " Come and stand beside me " ; not " Come and *sit* under me." He does not need my blessing, having assured that of the Great Master whom he serves. . . . But I *do* say, God bless him, for the fists he has unclenched, for the bruises he has saved, for the homes which he has cleansed, the families he has reconciled, the loves he has restored. God bless him for a million softened hearts, and for the sweet *piano* he has commanded in the once harsh tones of the gamut of domestic life ; for the oaths he has suppressed, for the staggering steps which he has steadied, for the brows which he has lifted, the feet he has strengthened to stand up, and the knees that he has taught to kneel. It is a blessing that is rising from widow and orphan hearts the wide world over, and one which mothers make their little ones repeat from cradle, cot and *crèche*, when a sober husband brings a father's smile where once he brought a sot's disgrace. These people are doing a work in coping with the great tragedy of poverty which is an example to the whole Church Catholic. They are throwing lifebuoys to the drownlings, while many of us are forming committees, allocating honours, and passing votes of thanks ; they are buffeting the waters while we are bawling from the shore ; they are scaling the fire-ladder while we are tinkering with the telephone ; *they are rescuing and restoring while we are wringing our hands.*

Appendix A

THE GENERAL'S SUMMARY OF HIS VIEWS ON FAITH-HEALING

What, then, is our attitude to Faith-Healing? Do we leave God out of the question? *God forbid!* Surely, there is nothing in what I have written that could by any process of reasoning justify such a question. But, lest there should be any misunderstanding, let me conclude this Memorandum with a brief summary of our views.

We believe:

1 That God hears and answers His people's believing prayer.
2 That in answer to prayer He does for them what is beyond the power of human skill. He pardons sins, changes hearts, delivers from trouble and temptation, and heals disease.
3 That at times, specially when help is beyond all human skill or means, He works these wonders for His people by no other means save prayer and faith.
4 That where He has promised, in His Word, to bestow the blessing we desire, we must believe without further evidence than that Word affords us.
5 That, though by His death Christ did not procure for man healing of the body in the same way that He obtained Salvation for the soul, yet He did die to bring him into such relations with the Father that all the true needs of obedient and believing Saints will be supplied.
6 That we ought to take all our sicknesses to God, and pray in faith for their removal, but always with perfect submission to the Divine Will.
7 That, when the sick have the conviction wrought in their hearts by the Spirit that God is willing to heal them, they are justified in believing that the work will be done for them. And when that conviction is wrought in God's

people on behalf of others who are sick, faith in Him for their healing is both justified and commanded.

8 That this conviction may, when it is not opposed to the will of God, be attained by fasting and prayer. He will teach us what to ask for. As the Apostle says : " We know not what we should pray for as we ought : but . . . He that searcheth the hearts knoweth what is the mind of the Spirit, because He maketh intercession for the saints according to the will of God."

9 That, where the Gift of Healing the Sick may have been imparted, it should be exercised to the glory of God, and not to the exalting of man, and in entire subordination to the more important work of healing and sanctifying the soul.

10 That we ought always to sympathise with the sick, pray in faith for their recovery, and, at the same time, use all available and lawful means to check disease, relieve suffering, and prolong life.

11 That, in cases where God is not pleased to answer the Prayer of Faith, and to restore the sick person for whom intercession has been made, without the use of means, there ought to be a return to the use of means that, in the providence of God, are usual and convenient in such sickness.

12 That we ought to strive to look through the means thus used to God, recognising that if there be any virtue in a medicine, it is by the power of God ; and if there be any skill in a surgeon, it is given him by God, to be employed for others. " For of Him, and through Him, and to Him are all things, to Whom be glory for ever."

13 That when sickness, suffering, affliction, or death seems to be in the order of God's Providence for us, or for those we love, and when, having besought the Lord in submission and faith that these visitations may pass away, and He is not pleased to remove them or spare us from them, we ought to be resigned to His will, prove that His grace is sufficient for us, and thus, whether we live or die, glorify God in our bodies, which are His.

14 That " none of us liveth to himself, and no man dieth to himself. For whether we live, we live unto the Lord ; and

whether we die, we die unto the Lord: whether we live therefore, or die, we are the Lord's."

Appendix B

THE AIM OF THE TRAINING OF SALVATION ARMY OFFICERS

By Mrs General Booth, written in 1884

The great aim of all our training is to fit our officers for the *work they have to do*. We imagine all mere learning, for its own sake, quite aside from the object we have in view, is calculated to unfit its recipients for actual warfare. Just as in temporal things the apprenticeship is intended to teach the apprentice the particular trade to which he is destined, so we think training for the work of God should be adapted to qualify its recipients for that work, and that it would be just as sensible to spend the time and exhaust the energies of the apprentices intended to build houses or ships, in studying the problems of astronomy as to teach men and women destined for the spiritual warfare dead languages and a great many other subjects usually imposed upon students for the ministry. We say, teach the builder how to build houses, and the shoemaker how to make shoes, and a soul-winner *how to win souls*.

First we begin with the heart. We receive no candidates but such as we have good reason, after careful enquiry, to believe are truly converted, and are actuated by pure motives in seeking to enter the work. Yet we find many of them not sanctified, that is, not having fully renounced the flesh or the world, and thoroughly given up to God. There are linking evils to be discovered and renounced, mistaken notions to be corrected, the remains of self-seeking to be crucified, and the soul led up to the thorough abandonment of selfish interests, which we regard as indispensable to an experience of the fullness of the Holy Spirit; and to success in winning souls. Consequently the most time and the greatest strength of the principals and of the Staff are devoted to this department of labour; not only is the daily lecture devoted to the most heart-searching spiritual truths, founded, of course, on the Scriptures, but every candidate is seen privately, talked and prayed with and counselled according to his or her individual necessities by the principals.

We take it to be a fundamental that if the soul is not right, the service cannot be right, and therefore make *the soul the first and chief care.*

Secondly, we try to train the head, so as to put our officers a little in advance in intelligence and information of the people to whom they are to minister. To this end we teach such general information as we find most necessary for their future position.

Thirdly, the next point is to instruct the candidates in the principles, discipline, and methods of the Army, through which they are to act upon the people. Not only is this done in theory in the drill room, but they are led out into actual combat with the ignorance, sins, and woes of the people ; in open-air marches and meetings, house to house visitation, *War Cry* selling, slum visiting, the hunting up of drunkards and harlots, the children's work, and in any kind of guerilla warfare which may at the moment present itself.

We try in this way to teach them, first, how to bear the cross, not an ornament called by that name, but the veritable cross of Jesus Christ, who was followed by a howling mob on His way to Calvary. They learn by experience as well as in sentiment how, when smitten on the one cheek, to turn the other, and how to respond to blasphemy, spitting, and often cruel buffetings, by blessing, to bless those who curse them, and pray for those who despitefully use them. We teach them how to approach the worst of the people who, alas, hate what they have seen of religion and all connected with it, and how to attract their attention and get an entrance for the truth into their outward ear, so that it may have a chance of reaching their hearts.

Thirdly, we teach them how to appeal to the *consciences* of the people, not by preaching smooth things and exhibiting a God of all love, minus justice and judgment, but by attacking their sins and arousing that sense of condemnation and apprehension which lies dormant in every sinner's heart. In short, opening their eyes and turning them from darkness to light.

Fourthly, we teach them how to inspire hope in the most

hopeless, appealing to the soul irrespective of the particular form of outward sin into which each individual has fallen, showing them how frequently God's most precious jewels have been hewn out of the hardest of Nature's granite, and how the vilest persecutors have often been transformed into the most illustrious saints and soldiers.

Fifthly, we try to show them how to exhibit the Saviour as a full and sufficient sacrifice for sin ; as an Almighty Deliverer from the power of evil habit outside, and from the strength of evil passions and propensities inside ; in short, how He is able to save them to the uttermost that come unto God by Him and is their sufficient strength and deliverer and guide for every future temptation and emergency.

Sixthly, we teach them how to utilize the trophies they may be permitted to win, showing them how best to spend their strength for the salvation of those around them.

The foregoing is the unceasing aim of our training, in all its ramifications. We are conscious of having yet much to learn, but how far we have succeeded in giving this kind of training, the tens of thousands of the roughest classes of the world's population saved through the instrumentality of our officers is the best evidence. Whether our officers can claim apostleship in the estimation of the Church or not, they can certainly say with Paul : "If I be not an apostle unto others, yet doubtless I am to you : for the seal of mine apostleship are ye in the Lord."

The results of our work have justified the conviction with which we began, that, to make apostolic people would ensure apostolic results. We have never had a question in our minds but that the Gospel would prove the same mighty power of God when truly lived out by those who preach it and energised by the Holy Spirit as in its earliest dispensation. The results have confirmed us ten-fold in this conviction.

Appendix C

WHITCHURCH—SUMMING-UP OF THE LORD CHIEF JUSTICE

. . . I cannot help knowing of the hostile manner in which many of the lesser constituted authorities of the country have behaved, and that here and there the arm of this court has been obliged to be extended over them to tell the magistrates that they must not make their fancies—or their honest opinions, if you please—upon this or that subject, a measure of the administration of justice. Everybody has a right to his opinion, and to maintain his opinion, unless he breaks the law, or in some manner disturbs the peace of the subjects over whom the Queen rules. That, gentleman, is the plain law. . . .

It seems that Mr Herbert Booth is Commandant, and that Mr Barritt also bears some title in The Salvation Army. It is said that these two persons have by themselves and by the assistance of others whom they animated and led to do so, obstructed the Queen's highway. . . . But it is not every trivial obstruction which is looked upon as an obstruction, as had been laid down by great judges in former days—judges, as we know from history, by no means inclined, in their own individual opinions, to favour popular rights or noisy and riotous assemblies.

Over and over again such judges as Lord Ellenborough, who, although he was a very great lawyer, and was the very last man who would have been likely to have expressed himself, unnecessarily, favourable to popular rights, have said that there must be good sense in the exercise of these things, and that it is not every small obstruction—though it be an obstruction, and though it is very difficult to lay down the law so as to say within the strict definition of the law it is not an obstruction—which is the subject-matter of criminal proceedings. . . . There are other pieces of evidence in the case which seem to show, not very clearly . . . that there was for a short time a filling of this square by these people, and a determination as they were there that no one else should be there, and if that were so, and is the true view of the evidence, whatever the moral guilt is, and whatever the punishment shall be, I cannot say the law has not been broken. In my judgment, if that is the view you take of it as men of good sense, I should say you ought to find the defendants guilty, and leave to me to pass such reasonable sentence upon them as I should think right to vindicate the law.

But there is another view of it altogether. . . . The view that Mr Willis presents, very ably and very temperately, to you is this: He says there was no intention whatever to obstruct, although possibly in a little town like Whitchurch the presence of two thousand five hundred people, if that were the number, might lead to some inconvenience. No doubt a very considerable number did assemble, because there were special trains run from Salisbury and Southampton and Bristol, and they were all concentrated at Whitchurch, near where these magistrates resided who had made all these convictions, and therefore it was desirable, and The Salvation Army were anxious, to make a demonstration. As I say, if they did it within the law, they had a perfect right to make a demonstration, but it is very likely that in a little town (some people call it a village), or, at any rate, in a small place like Whitchurch, the mere advent, the mere appearing into it of two or three thousand people, would of itself crowd the streets, and, although it might bring business, would interfere with traffic, and if they collected together in any particular spot or in any of the narrow streets of the town—still more, if marching, two detachments met one another in a narrow gorge—of course there is an obstruction, and people cannot for the time move so freely about a little place like Whitchurch as they can when these two thousand five hundred people are not there. But to begin with, and I think you will agree with him there, in the first place these two thousand five hundred people, or that large number of people, had a perfect right to be there. So they had. Being there, they had a right to walk and up down the streets of Whitchurch, provided they did not do anything to break the law, that is to say in this case, provided they did not really seriously and for any length of time obstruct the traffic of the streets. I use the word "traffic," because that is what it comes to. I do not mean merely carriages and horses, but the traffic and the going and coming of Her Majesty's subjects. But if they were there lawfully, and if they did nothing there but stand and listen to a speech for a certain time, not in the least intending to stop the people of Her Majesty's subjects in that neighbourhood from going up and down the streets of Whitchurch as they thought fit, but simply to make a demonstration, then if they did for a time, say for twenty minutes or three-quarters of an hour, or whatever the time may be—in fact, make the passage of the streets of Whitchurch, or of this square in Whitchurch, less convenient than it was at times—I should say the prosecution had failed to make out that there had been real and substantial obstruction for a reasonable and adequate time before the defendants can be found guilty. . . .

If a person comes outside a man's house knowing he has someone whom he values ill, and intends to annoy by playing horns and beating drums and knocking things one against the other, it is a breach of law undoubtedly. But all that is proved here is that which I am bound to tell you is no breach of the law, and that is that these people went down the street blowing trumpets or horns and beating drums. They have a right to do that if they do not do it to an extravagant degree, and do not do it for the purpose of annoying. We must not be too sensitive about these things. Lord Justice Knight Bruce, I remember, said excellently well, in a case before him, the law does not lend itself to the wishes of delicate people. The plain, simple, ordinary habits of life are the habits that are supposed to be interfered with, and if all they did was to walk down the street with a band, not stopping before the houses or doing anything to annoy, but walking along, and as it went by the band annoying or distressing a sensitive person inside. I tell you that is a kind of thing that in a free country men and women must submit to. You know that the famous Mr Babbage did not like barrel-organs, they disturbed his mind ; but the law said he must get on with his calculations how he could, and the barrel-organs must not be interrupted ; it was a thing they had a right to do. Of course, it is a totally different thing if five or six barrel-organs sat down in front of a house all day long for the purpose of annoying, but that I have not to decide. As I said in the course of the trial, I do not see how you are to distinguish The Salvation Army band from the Guard's band playing down the street. It may distress and disturb exceedingly anyone in a house ; but the Guard's band has a perfect right to play its music in the street, and if it annoys them, people must submit to it until it has gone by. . . .

Therefore, gentleman, I leave the case to you with this observation,—do not find the defendants guilty unless the prosecution have made out the case to your complete satisfaction, and they will not have made out the case to your complete satisfaction unless you think there has been a substantial physical obstruction of the highway in Whitchurch so as to be a real annoyance and a real interruption of the rights of the Queen's subjects to pass and re-pass along the Queen's roads.

POSTSCRIPT

Mr Lea, a friend of the Army, having left in his will £4,000 to the General "for the spread of the Gospel," and another £4,000 for the same object, to be paid after the death of his niece, a dispute was raised as to whether it would be safe to pay the money to the General without what was called a "scheme" —i.e. a plan arranged by the Attorney-General as to how the money was to be spent. After long delays and "an enormous expenditure" of money on legal expenses Mr Justice North gave it as his judgment in February 1887 that The Salvation Army was doing a great work under General William Booth and after having carefully examined the accounts regularly published in 1886 he considered him competent to receive the legacies.

* * *

The British Weekly offered a prize for the best essay on The Salvation Army, and in its issue for 4 March 1887 remarked:

It is a significant circumstance that the essays giving an affirmative answer to the question, "Has the influence of The Salvation Army been on the whole beneficial?" were *ten times as numerous* as those which gave the negative.

* * *

In the latter part of 1889 a distraint warrant was executed upon the Stockport corps for non-payment of the poor rate, amounting to £15. The warrant was formally issued against the General as head of the Army. The amount demanded not being paid, some of the effects at the barracks at Waterloo were offered for sale and purchased by a friend who returned them to the corps. When the new rate was made the Army decided, as a test case, to appeal through its solicitors, who said that the grounds for the appeal against the assessment were that the premises of The Salvation Army were "exclusively appropriated to public religious worship," and were "duly certified" within the meaning of section I of 3 & 4 William IV, c. 30. The chairman declared that there was not the slightest wish on the part of the assessment committee to oppress or harass the Army and the appeal would be allowed. The case aroused considerable interest throughout the country.

* * *

In May 1891 the *Baptist* reported that

> The students of Cambridge University on Monday debated the methods of The Salvation Army. The discussion was, on the whole, serious and sensible. The vote showed well for the Army, which it supported by a majority of 84 to 50.

* * *

A steam laundry was in operation in Maury Road, Stoke Newington, London, in connection with the Women's Social Work, apparently from the spring of 1893. All family and other work was " well and efficiently done," and " facilities and special terms were granted to schools, boarding houses, &c."

* * *

The coal strike of 1893 having entered upon its sixteenth week during November, without any definite hope of an immediate settlement, the General instituted a " Sufferers' Saturday " on the 18th to help alleviate the hunger horrors, and in connection with what became the General Food Fund.

* * *

Speaking in 1894 the General said :

> The Salvation Army is not inferior in spiritual character to any Christian organization in existence. We are in no wise dependent on the Church. . . . If it perished off the face of the earth tomorrow we should be just as efficient for the discharge of the duties we owe to men as we are today. . . . We are, I consider, equal every way and everywhere to any other Christian organization on the face of the earth (1) in spiritual authority, (2) in spiritual intelligence, (3) in spiritual function. We hold " the keys " as truly as any Church in existence.

* * *

The fore-runner of the gramophone, the phonograph, was being used by Brigadier Noyce in his meetings in the English villages four or five years prior to the opening of the twentieth century. He made his own records of Salvationist vocal soloists and bands, including that of International Headquarters, and a speech by the General. The Brigadier would invite a good singer to the platform during his children's meetings, make a record of a song on the spot, and play it back to the audience. But phonographs were first used in the Army in America. The Brigadier's machine weighed a hundredweight and a half.

* * *

The massacre of hundreds of Armenian Christians raided by the Turkish Government, both in Constantinople and the provinces, in the fall of 1896 caused a wave of indignation throughout the world, and it was actually suggested that England, single-handed and heedless of the consequences, should mobilize her fleet, force the Dardanelles, storm and shell Stamboul, depose the Sultan, and undertake to restore order there, and adopt measures to ensure the protection and liberty of the Christians in Turkey. Large numbers of Armenians were either deported or succeeded in making their escape, mainly to France, from a country where the prospects of further disorder and outrage seemed sadly certain. Mr Gladstone was incensed and advocated the withdrawal of the British Ambassador from Constantinople, and the dismissal of the Turkish Minister from London. On hearing of the plight of the refugees in Marseilles the General dispatched Staff-Captain Holder to that city with the object of ascertaining whether the Army could do anything to mitigate the distress, and later Colonel Stitt, the Secretary for International Social Affairs, was sent out to organize operations for housing, feeding and transferring the refugees to hospitable countries, with the substantial help of Lady Henry Somerset and Miss Frances Willard, who had commenced the relief work. A French Salvationist-farmer located a party on his estate. These Armenians were described as "the cream of the Turkish working-classes." Temporary help was also given by Commissioner Lucy Booth-Hellberg and her officers to those who passed through Paris and Boulogne on their way to London, thence to Hadleigh Farm Colony, where many were accommodated prior to emigrating to America.

* * *

To Major (later Colonel) Joshua Spooner belongs the credit

of adapting the motor-car to an Army procession, which it headed at Luton and, with a big cycle brigade behind it, caused an immense sensation. This was in July 1897.

* * *

The first secular elementary school opened by the Army in England was on the Land Colony at Hadleigh at the beginning of January 1903 for the children of the colonists and the villagers. 108 names were registered, the headmaster being Staff-Captain Collins, whose appointment H.M. inspectors endorsed in superlatives.

* * *

The cinematograph was introduced as " a novel method of influencing the unsaved " in 1903, under the management of Major (later Brigadier) Fred Cox and Adjutant Howse, who on five occasions carried their heavy apparatus to the very top of St Paul's Cathedral, plunged into the dirty waters of the River Lea in order to obtain a life-like photograph of a supposed rescue from drowning, and even entered the den of the hippopotamus at the Zoological Gardens, to be chased out for their pains by that cumbrous but swift-moving beast. The cinematograph was able to provide a two hours' programme. The films were

> ribbon-like in appearance, being about an inch in width and 150 feet in length. Each film contains upward of 2,000 photographs taken at the rate of about fifteen a second. All have been taken, printed and developed by our own Officers [says the *War Cry*], and are projected on the screen by means of a light which represents about 2,500 candle-power. . . . The first animated picture thrown on the screen was at a Salvation open-air meeting held in Whitechapel Road.

The machine was then taken to Southend-on-Sea for a weekend and fifteen people professed conversion. A lady who drove up to one of the meetings in a carriage and pair said it was " the most beautiful and interesting entertainment she had ever seen."

BIBLIOGRAPHY

The works listed below are additional to those listed in the bibliographies of previous volumes and, unless otherwise stated, are published by Salvationist Publishing and Supplies, Limited, Judd Street, King's Cross, London, W.C.1. Some are out of print, but may be seen at the National Reference Libraries. If information in the *History* should differ from that to be found in the books and papers listed below, it is because further research has proved earlier publications incorrect.

Official Publications

The War Cry, from 3 July, 1886 to 23 July 1904
All the World, from 1886 to 1904
The Salvation Army Year Book, 1919, 1939, 1958, 1962
The Officer's Review (For private circulation only), April-June 1943, and June-September 1944
The Staff Review (For private circulation only), October 1930
The Musical Salvationist (Words and music), from 1886 to 1904
Assurance (Magazine of The Salvation Army Assurance Society Ltd. For private circulation only), May 1948, December 1958 and June 1963
The Song Book of The Salvation Army, 1953
The Victory (Australian youth magazine), April 1948
Orders and Regulations for Soldiers, 1890
The Bandsman and Songster, first published in April 1907
The Musician, first published in January 1938

Biographies

Hedwig von Haartman, by Commissioner Mildred Duff, 1904
Women of the Flag, by Minnie Lindsay Carpenter, 1945
Soldier of Peace—Gunpei Yamamuro, by Cyril J. Barnes, 1956
Indian Pilgrim,—Narayana Muthiah, by Rosalie M. Wheaton, 1960

Always Ready to Sail—Alfred J. Benwell, by Flora Larsson, 1958
Slow of Speech ?—Henry F. Burfoot, by H. Pimm Smith, 1953
Son of Sri Lanka—Arnolis Weerasooriya, by Victor Thompson, 1953
Lyons in the Jungle—John Lyons, by Arch R. Wiggins, 1945
Wise Man of the East—Solomon Perera, by Victor Thompson, 1956
He Heard from God—Frank Crossley, by E. K. Crossley, 1959
The General—Evangeline Booth, by P. W. Wilson (Hodder & Stoughton, 1935)
"The Life-Story of General Booth," by Sarah A. Tooley (Article in the *Temple Magazine*, November 1897)
Herbert Booth, by Ford C. Ottman (Doubleday, Doran & Co., Inc., New York 1928)
God's Soldier—General William Booth, by St John Ervine (Heinemann, 1934)
Bramwell Booth, by Catherine Bramwell-Booth (Rich & Cowan, 1933)
Down in Demerara—Alexander Alexander, O.F., by Frederick L. Coutts, 1944
The Curate of Onslow Square—W. Elwin Oliphant, by William Burrows, 1960
The Prophet of the Poor—William Booth, by T. F. G. Coates (Hodder & Stoughton 1905)
The Maréchale—Catherine Booth-Clibborn, by James Strahan (Geo. H. Doran Co. of New York, 1914)
The Life of Mrs Booth, by F. de L. Booth-Tucker, 1892
T. H. K.—Theodore Hopkins Kitching, by Arch R. Wiggins, 1956
Lucy in Lion Land, by Noel Hope, 1928
Samuel Logan Brengle, by Clarence W. Hall (National Headquarters, New York, 1933)
John Roberts, Evangelist, by Ethel B. Rohu, 1952

History

Zulu Crusade, by J. Allister Smith, O.F., 1945
What hath God Wrought ?—The History of The Salvation Army in Canada, by Arnold Brown (The Salvation Army Printing and Publishing House, Toronto, 1952)

Beneath Two Flags, by Maud B. Booth (Funk & Wagnalls, 1889)
The Undauntables, by Matilda Hatcher (Hodder & Stoughton, 1933)
Salvation Dynasty, by Brian Lunn (William Hodge & Co., Ltd., 1936)
Our War in South Africa, by Commissioner G. S. Railton, 1901
Salvation Chariot—A Review of the First Seventy-one Years of The Salvation Army in Australia, by Percival Dale (The Salvation Army Press, Melbourne, 1952)
An Outline History of The Salvation Army in New Zealand, by Cyril R. Bradwell. (Thesis submitted for the Degree of Master of Arts and Honours in History, 1950)
Soldiers without Swords—A History of The Salvation Army in the United States of America, by Herbert A. Wisbey, Jr. (The Macmillan Company, New York, 1956)
The Story of The Salvation Army Assurance Society, Ltd., in Brief, by Lieut.-Colonel John Rivers (Chief Officer, 1935)
The Resignation of Commander and Mrs Ballington Booth, by Emma and Frederick Booth-Tucker (Headquarters, New York, 1896)
The Betrayal of Bramwell Booth, by Frank Smith (Jarrolds, 1929)
Delayed Harvest—The Salvation Army in Rhodesia, by Victor Thompson (Unpublished), 1957
Femti Års Korstog for Gud og Norge—Fifty Years' Crusade for God and Norway, by H. A. Tandberg, 1937. (Published in Norway)
Frelsens Hær i Danmark Gennem 50 Aar—Through Fifty Years, The Salvation Army in Denmark, by Neils Edelbo, 1937. (Published in Denmark)
Revolutionäres Christentum—The Salvation Army in Germany, by Colonel Max Gruner ; volume I, 1953 ; volume II, 1954
The History of Salvation Music, vocal and instrumental, by Richard Slater (Unpublished, 1925)

Doctrine

The Sacraments, the Salvationists' Viewpoint, 1960
Faith-Healing—A memorandum, by William Booth

Other Books

The Salvation Army—A Short Study of its Defects and Possibilities, by John Hollins (Modern Language Press, Ltd., 1903)

The Salvation Army and the Public, by John Manson (Routledge, 1906)
Social Diseases and Worse Remedies, by T. H. Huxley, F.R.S., 1891
General Booth and The Salvation Army, by A. M. Nicol (Herbert & Daniel, 1910)
On the Banks of the River, by Bramwell Booth, 1894
Municipal Eastbourne, 1883-1933, by H. W. Fovargue, 1933
Salvation Army Songwriters, by Lieut.-Colonel Richard Slater, 1930

Periodicals

The Volunteer Gazette, Official Organ of the Volunteers of America, 15 November 1940 and October 1948
The Weekly Dispatch, 7 June 1891
The Eastbourne Courier, 19 August 1949
The Daily News, 27 October 1891
The Eastbourne Express, 9 June 1891
The Sussex Daily News, 4 June 1891
The Argus, 12 and 13 June 1891
The Eastbourne Chronicle, 1891-2
The Sussex Express, 1891-2
The Penny Illustrated Paper
Great Thoughts, 1890

Reports

"The Salvation Army as a Social Force," by Fred A. McKenzie, in the *Windsor Magazine*, 1900
Minutes of Evidence and Proceedings taken before the Lords Committee, Eastbourne Improvement Act 1885 *Amendment Bill*, 1892
Letter from Commander and Mrs Booth, 1896

Emendations (1st editions)

Volume Two (additional) :

page 138, para. 3 : Delete : " whose vicar was the father of Commissioner Adelaide Cox.

page 292, l. 13 : for " Woodward " *read* " Woodman "

Volume Three (additional) :

page 119, l. 20 : should read : "Men's shelters in Montevideo in 1891, in Argentina in the same year at La Plata, and in Chile . . .

page 288, l. 28 : for " Connaught " *read* " Cambridge "

INDEX

INDEX